Skills and Strategies for Coaching Soccer

SECOND EDITION

Alan Hargreaves
Richard Bate

Human Kinetics

Library of Congress Cataloging-in-Publication Data

Hargreaves, Alan, 1933-
  Skills and strategies for coaching soccer / Alan Hargreaves and Richard Bate. -- 2nd ed.
    p. cm.
  ISBN-13: 978-0-7360-8022-4 (soft cover)
  ISBN-10: 0-7360-8022-8 (soft cover)
  ISBN-13: 978-0-7360-8620-2 (Adobe PDF)
  ISBN-10: 0-7360-8620-X (Adobe PDF)
  1. Soccer--Coaching. I. Bate, Richard, 1946- II. Title.
  GV943.8.H37 2009
  796.334--dc22

                              2009018077

ISBN-10: 0-7360-8022-8 (print)   ISBN-10: 0-7360-8620-X (Adobe PDF)
ISBN-13: 978-0-7360-8022-4 (print)   ISBN-13: 978-0-7360-8620-2 (Adobe PDF)

Acquisitions Editor: John Dickinson; **Developmental Editor:** Laura Floch; **Assistant Editors:** Carla Zych, Cory Weber; **Copyeditor:** Patsy Fortney; **Graphic Designer:** Nancy Rasmus; **Graphic Artist:** Julie L. Denzer; **Cover Designer:** Keith Blomberg; **Photographer (cover and interior):** Nigel Farrow; **Visual Production Assistant:** Joyce Brumfield; **Photo Production Manager:** Jason Allen; **Art Manager:** Kelly Hendren; **Associate Art Manager:** Alan L. Wilborn; **Illustrator:** Tim Brummett; **Printer:** United Graphics

We thank Dene Magna School in Mitcheldean, Gloucestershire, UK, for assistance in providing the location for the photo shoot for this book.

Human Kinetics books are available at special discounts for bulk purchase. Special editions or book excerpts can also be created to specification. For details, contact the Special Sales Manager at Human Kinetics.

Printed in the United States of America   10 9 8 7 6 5 4 3 2 1

The paper in this book is certified under a sustainable forestry program.

Human Kinetics
Web site: www.HumanKinetics.com

United States: Human Kinetics
P.O. Box 5076
Champaign, IL 61825-5076
800-747-4457
e-mail: humank@hkusa.com

Canada: Human Kinetics
475 Devonshire Road Unit 100
Windsor, ON N8Y 2L5
800-465-7301 (in Canada only)
e-mail: info@hkcanada.com

Europe: Human Kinetics
107 Bradford Road
Stanningley
Leeds LS28 6AT, United Kingdom
+44 (0) 113 255 5665
e-mail: hk@hkeurope.com

Australia: Human Kinetics
57A Price Avenue
Lower Mitcham, South Australia 5062
08 8372 0999
e-mail: info@hkaustralia.com

New Zealand: Human Kinetics
Division of Sports Distributors NZ Ltd.
P.O. Box 300 226 Albany
North Shore City
Auckland
0064 9 448 1207
e-mail: info@humankinetics.co.nz

To our wives, Janet and Maggie.

CONTENTS

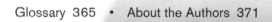

DRILL FINDER

PREFACE

THE FIRST EDITION of this book was published in 1990 and was immediately popular throughout English-speaking nations such as the United States, Canada, and Great Britain. It is also distributed by the Australian FA as one of their recommended coaching books. This second edition, with the help of Dick Bate, currently the director of elite coaching courses for the English Football Association, has been completely revised. We have added several new sections, in particular a chapter on tactics and teamwork, and all the skills chapters now include a section devoted to developing the talents of your all-star players. Other chapters incorporate developments in modern thinking regarding fitness and conditioning as well as nutrition and diet.

The main focus of the book has not altered. It was meant to be a coach-friendly book, and it still is. We share the ideas and methods we have found to be successful with players of all levels of ability. It is designed specifically to help parents, especially those who coach youth soccer teams, perhaps including their own children; students and specialist teachers; and all who wish to gain qualifications awarded by their national coaching organizations.

We have retained the original four parts because each one is significant in its own right. Collectively, they cover all aspects of coaching. Part I addresses the development of a personal coaching philosophy and describes how to work with both individuals and groups. Part II offers a complete understanding of how to introduce and develop the basic skills of the game to players of all levels of ability, from beginners to all-stars. Part III addresses tactics, team formations, and the principles of play and explains how to judge whether your team is playing well. Finally, in part IV, we offer advice on team management skills, physical and mental preparation, working with problem players, fitness and conditioning, and diet and nutrition.

Part I Preparing to Coach

In the first three chapters we invite you to consider developing a personal coaching style that recognizes a concern for the dignity of the individual and encourages in all players a love for the way the game is played. All players, especially young players, who are encouraged to make decisions in an atmosphere of positive reinforcement are more likely to develop into valued team members, enjoy playing the game, and contribute to team unity and spirit.

In our experience, which includes working with professional and international teams, where winning can be a matter of job security or fierce national pride, players must be encouraged to believe that winning comes mainly as a result of good play, by which we mean play that is both fair and skillful. A coach who shares this belief will enjoy coaching and, in our view, is more likely to become a winning coach. Remember, the best team doesn't always win, but it usually does.

Part II Skills and Techniques

The seven major skills, as well as goalkeeping, are presented in chapters 4 through 11, each of which contains a unique sequence of progressive practices. For each skill, we present the basics of execution and quickly progress to its successful execution in match situations.

In this part we present progressively more challenging practices in accordance with the developing skills of the players. No drill is an end in itself; rather, it is a platform for development. For this reason, we include many examples of small-team games and practices to reinforce the skills learned in the practice session.

Part III Tactics and Teamwork

Chapter 12 addresses the principles of play, which you can use to analyze how well or how badly your team is playing. Chapter 13 then goes on to explain the strengths and weaknesses of the various team formations and systems of play so that you can select, or modify, your own tactics in accordance with the state of the game or the quality of the opposition.

Chapter 14 builds upon chapters 2 and 3 and deals with the planning and implementation of methods and drills designed to coach in full-game situations. Chapter 15 is new and addresses the advanced tactics of team play. We appreciate that not all coaches have players of sufficient maturity to absorb and execute these tactics. Regardless of the level of your players, however, if you want to confirm or extend your knowledge of team tactics, we believe you will find this a fascinating chapter. Finally, in chapter 16 we deal with set pieces—the tactics you can use when attacking or defending at throw-ins, corner kicks, free kicks, and penalty kicks. Coaches of teams of all levels will find the drills and tactics in this chapter to be of immediate value.

The combined aim of parts II and III is to produce players who are both technically skilled and tactically aware—an objective that holds true for players of all levels.

Part IV Team Management

In chapter 17 we offer advice on preparing your players on game days, both physically and mentally. We deal with pregame talks, warming up, what to say at halftime, and how to say it. We spend some time on postgame talks particularly because we want our players to appreciate that the result of the game, important though that is, is not the only way to evaluate the team's performance during the game.

Chapter 18 contains advice on how to identify and work with problem players. We also include a section on how to approach parents who might be causing difficulties—parents can cause problems too! Chapter 19 deals with fitness and conditioning. Our fitness tests and drills are all designed to take place outside on the playing field, wearing soccer boots (cleats). In this way, every coach can make use of them—all he or she needs is a soccer field or grassy area. Of course, those lucky enough to have indoor training facilities will be able to adapt some, if not all, of them. We also show how to adapt these activities to condition players of differing levels of fitness at the same time. We include drills for stamina, acceleration, speed, and footwork. Finally, we offer advice on nutrition and diet. A careful analysis of the various types of food, and their benefits, leads to suggestions about what and when to eat on game days, and the day before.

We believe that this new edition of *Skills and Strategies for Coaching Soccer* is an indispensable guide for coaches in any setting. It retains much of the material from the original book but also provides a complete review of the principles, methods, and tactics that have developed over the years. In addition, the text and diagrams are easy to understand so that any coach, beginner or advanced, will find this book helpful. Also, the inclusion of a drill finder will allow you to quickly locate the drills and skills that you are looking for. Of course, we hope that you will be sufficiently interested to read all of the chapters and share with us a genuine love for the game.

ACKNOWLEDGMENTS

THE ACKNOWLEDGMENTS FOR this new edition naturally include mention of those who were especially helpful with the production of the first edition, specifically Allen Wade, former director of coaching for the Football Association, for permission to reproduce his original work on the principles of play; his assistant director, Charles Hughes; Kevin Verity, coauthor of an earlier Madeley College publication; Bill Harvey, for help with the development of systems of play; and Eric Hassall and colleagues at Wardell Armstrong. In the United States, mention must be made of John Curtis; Roger Thomas; Martha and Peter Schraml, who codirected our Professional Soccer Academy in Simi, California; in particular, Dan and Marty Campbell, without whose friendship the opportunity to write the original book would never have arisen; and to the artists who created the original artwork, Tim Birkin, John Hartshorn, David Hassall, and Elizabeth Salt.

For the new edition, Dick Bate also wishes to acknowledge the influence of Allen Wade, who was his inspiration as a coach, and always has been, and that of Jack Detchon, who was the first coach who taught him anything about playing the game—at the age of 22!—and has remained a coaching confidant ever since. He gratefully acknowledges their contribution to his love of the game and of coaching in particular. Finally, thanks to Howard Wilkinson, who has also been a major influence on his thinking.

Both authors wish to thank and acknowledge the artist, Tim Brummett, who recreated the illustrations for this edition. Thanks also go to the help of Dene Magna School, Gloucestershire; the head teacher, Rob Broadbridge; the head of physical education, Scott Albon; and Matt Barnard, Tom Liddington, Giorgi Hlad and Jordan Warren who modeled the action photographs. Also, thanks go to the photographer, Nigel Farrow, for his professional expertise and unfailing patience.

Finally, we wish to thank both John Dickinson and Laura Floch of Human Kinetics for their continued support throughout the writing of this book and their guidance in structuring both the written and graphic material.

KEY

Color Key for Drill Skill Levels

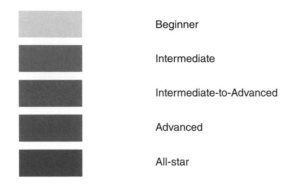

	Beginner
	Intermediate
	Intermediate-to-Advanced
	Advanced
	All-star

Diagram Elements

───────▶	Player movement
─ ─ ─ ─ ─▶	Ball movement
∿∿∿∿▶	Dribble
━━━━━▶	Direction of play
Co	Coach
FB	Fullback
GK	Goalkeeper
S	Server
SW	Sweeper
W	Winger
○	Ball
Ⓐ Ⓑ Ⓧ Ⓨ	Players

Screened-back players, symbols, and lines indicate
future or past movement in select diagrams

Preparing to Coach

PART I HAS three chapters. In chapter 1 we invite you to consider three ethical issues that you will have to consider at some time in your coaching career: what exactly you, personally, hope to achieve from coaching; the meaning and importance of "good play"; and the importance of winning.

In chapter 2, we describe a number of personal coaching strategies that have been helpful to us when dealing with individual players. We believe that some, if not all, of the strategies will help you relate to the members of your team individually. In chapter 3 we describe another series of fundamental coaching strategies, but this time in relation to the way you coach larger groups of players and organize team practices.

Collectively, the ideas introduced in part I will give you a better appreciation of the content in the following parts on the coaching of skills, tactics, and team management. Even if you are entirely familiar with everything in part I, we hope you will read it. We have found that having one's own ideas confirmed by someone else can be an encouraging experience.

Ethics and Your Coaching Philosophy

DURING THEIR SOCCER careers, players work with many coaches who have their own ideas and personal coaching styles. Although coaches differ in their approaches to tactics and teamwork, we hope they share a common view about good sporting behavior and the way the game should be played.

This chapter discusses three issues that constitute, in our opinion, the basis of a code of soccer ethics. The first deals with why so many people throughout the world are attracted to soccer as a lifetime experience—first as players and then as coaches, administrators, or spectators. The second issue concerns the characteristics of what we call good play, by which we mean skillful and fair play. The third involves your own personal coaching philosophy. You may not agree with all of our views, but the following material should help you clarify your own ideas about the satisfaction and long-term achievements you personally expect to gain from coaching soccer.

Soccer as a Lifetime Experience

Those who are attracted to soccer as a lifetime experience are not usually motivated simply by the prospect of keeping fit or meeting people, important as these objectives may be. People of all ages play, coach, and watch soccer because they love the game itself and because they experience inner feelings of enjoyment, satisfaction, and achievement from their involvement with the sport. They find that being involved in soccer is worthwhile for its own sake.

Every coach is responsible for creating an enthusiastic atmosphere that safeguards this enjoyment factor, especially for younger players. But coaches cannot force players to enjoy the game, which is why personal coaching ethics are so important. The art of coaching involves getting players to enjoy soccer for its own sake, not because a coach tells them they should. A love and enthusiasm for soccer has to be nurtured and encouraged. Achieving this leads directly to the second major consideration of soccer ethics. The link among all who love soccer is the ability to recognize and appreciate the meaning and importance of good play.

Meaning and Importance
of Good Play

Good play means play that is skillful. People enjoy soccer as a lifetime sport either because they are or were skillful players, or because they are intelligent coaches or spectators who can appreciate skillful play by others, including team tactics.

The development and appreciation of skill are of paramount importance in coaching. Of course, the level of skill your players can achieve will vary according to their age and experience. With all players, but especially younger ones, you must work hard to promote the desire, or intention, to play skillfully.

A useful example, which also demonstrates the importance of intelligent observation of the game, is the ill-informed spectator who shouts at players to "kick it" whenever the ball comes to them. The informed coach, in the same situation, may urge players to control the ball rather than kick it. The informed coach appreciates the more advantageous moves that result from a controlled, composed mastery of the ball. We believe that the player who continually tries to exercise control is more likely to develop into a skillful player. Similarly, as a coach, if you appreciate and reward the intention to play skillfully, you will be more likely to be successful in the long run. You will certainly gain immense satisfaction, and respect, when players improve as a direct result of your good coaching.

The second criterion of good play is that it must be fair play. Soccer is played according to a set of rules. More important, players should respect not only the letter of the law, but also the spirit of the law. For example, tackling a player hard and tackling a player so hard and in such a way that he cannot take any further part in the game are fundamentally different actions. The difference between a hard but fair tackle and a dangerous or vicious one lies in the intention of the player executing the tackle and not in the referee's judgment, which is always retrospective. Soccer is a game of skill, not of brute force, and it will only thrive in an atmosphere in which skillful, intelligent sporting play is appreciated by all who play, watch, and coach. To a person who really loves soccer, what matters most is not who wins the game but the way the game is played. Wanting to win is important, crucially important, but if players have to commit fouls, argue, or make obscene gestures to win, then although they might have won the match, to a much greater extent the game itself has lost. A typical example of such undesirable play is the so-called professional foul, as discussed in the sidebar.

Professional Foul

A new kind of foul, called the *professional foul*, has recently crept into the game of soccer. It occurs mainly when a defender deliberately catches a ball or body checks an opponent. In most cases the foul is committed to prevent the opposition from scoring; it is called a professional foul because, although the individual is penalized, the team benefits.

If nobody gets hurt, why is the professional foul considered such a negative influence in the game? The professional foul is wrong because it spoils the game. Soccer was designed to be played according to certain rules and in a spirit of fair play. If players deliberately violate these rules, then the game as it was meant to be played no longer exists. Coaches and players must accept their responsibility to the game itself and work together to eliminate any form of behavior that undermines or weakens the game. Such a stance is clearly an ethical one and, as such, should be part of the personal philosophy of each coach, and thereby, of each team.

Importance of Winning

Consider to what extent you agree with our philosophy—that the primary responsibility of every coach is to develop a love for the game by encouraging play that is skillful and fair and that takes place in an enjoyable sporting environment. In considering this, you must also examine the importance of winning.

There is nothing wrong with wanting to win. The purpose of coaching is to improve performance and, ultimately, to improve the chances of winning. Our experience includes coaching professional clubs at the highest level, in which winning and job security go hand in hand. It also includes competing in the Olympic Games, in which winning is a matter of fierce national pride. All these experiences have shown us that a coach who continually encourages and emphasizes good play is actually more likely to be a winning coach. That coach's team will be better coached, better organized, more skillful and, most of all, more resilient in times of stress than other teams because the players experience a strong sense of team spirit.

Of course, everyone engaged in competition must try to win until the last possible moment. The game is not lost until the final whistle. Not to try one's best is also insulting to one's opponent and diminishes or even destroys the game as a spectacle. Our philosophy, therefore, certainly embraces the desire to win. Indeed, it emphasizes that players should be fit enough and, as mentioned, should strive to win until the very last moment of the game. However, this philosophy does draw a very clear line between wanting to win and wanting to win at all costs. We reject the behavior of a coach who, in seeking to win, advocates dangerous tackling, verbally abuses players or officials, keeps a badly injured player in the game, or deliberately lies about a player's eligibility. Such acts put winning the game before a concern for the well-being of the players and the spirit of fair play and therefore run counter to our philosophy.

John Wooden once confided that he never spoke about winning to his team; all he ever emphasized was playing well. This is a wonderful insight into the philosophy of this legendary American basketball coach and an example to us all.

At this point we invite you to consider your own position. What is your philosophy? What kind of coach are you? What kind of coach would you like to be? To what extent, if at all, do you share our philosophy? What you think and how you feel will have a direct bearing on how you actually behave as a coach.

Soccer Code of Ethics

In ethics, what matters is what one does, not what one thinks or says; an ideal has little value until it is put into practice. For this reason we now outline our personal code of ethics for everyone involved in soccer—players, spectators, and coaches.

- Certain fundamental concepts must be taught; the most important of these is good play.
- Good play is skillful, fair, and sporting; it does not include foul or abusive language.
- A good attitude on the part of players toward game officials is vital. The job of referees is to ensure that skillful soccer prevails. They may, and will, make mistakes, but players must be encouraged to accept all decisions without rancor, because dissent quickly destroys the atmosphere of any game.
- A game played in a fair, sporting manner will be more enjoyable for all concerned.
- Nothing is wrong with wanting to win; what is wrong is wanting to win at any cost. A person who loves soccer also cares about the way the game is won.
- An important task for all coaches is to encourage a love for the game in all who come into their sphere of influence.
- Coaches must educate parents and spectators about the importance of good play by both sides and encourage them to allow for mistakes, especially by younger players.
- Coaches must always put the welfare of players before the result of a game.
- Coaches are role models and should behave accordingly. They should never shout abuse at players or officials.
- Coaches must be continually vigilant to protect their reputations. Sadly, there are people in this world who use their influence over, and proximity to, young people to indulge in inappropriate behavior. In the United States, for example, the AYSO (American Youth Soccer Organization) requires that all coaches and volunteers have Safe Haven certification before they can run junior soccer teams. In the UK, all youth workers and coaches have to pass through the Criminal Records Bureau (CRB), which is a safeguard for all concerned.

In the following chapters we show how our coaching philosophy influences how we relate to and communicate with our players. We also discuss the coaching styles that are most effective in developing a love for the game and in encouraging players to enjoy both practice and playing.

2

Personal Coaching Strategies

• • • • • •

THIS CHAPTER PROVIDES an insight into coaching strategies that have been helpful to us and, we believe, should become second nature to every coach—almost irrespective of the sport. We believe that this chapter provides an insight into what might be called the basic principles of coaching.

Coaching Follows Observation

Our first strategy is that "coaching follows observation." Coaching is always retrospective; it is the exchange that takes place between you and your players after you have seen them perform. Of course, you may introduce a topic verbally or demonstrate what you want players to do, but this is only the beginning. Coaching only really begins when you attempt to change or develop what the players are doing, or put into practice your ideas and tactics.

If, when addressing individual skills with a group of players you are meeting for the first time, you start by telling them what you want them to do, you run the risk of underestimating their ability and wasting their time. It is very embarrassing to give a lengthy introduction to a skill only to find that some, if not all, of the players are already expert at it. It is much better to see players in action before you attempt to coach them. Only then can you choose a starting level based on their ability. This book provides many examples of warm-up activities and small-team games that will enable you to watch your players in action before you start to coach them.

The same advice holds true for coaching team tactics. You should base the work you do in preparing your team largely on your observation of the previous game, your observation of your opponents, or the strengths and weaknesses of your own team. In all cases, you are coaching after observing. A good way to start a tactical coaching session is to say, "In last week's game I noticed that . . . ."

Good Diagnosis

Our second strategy concerns good diagnosis. Like a doctor, you must be able to diagnose correctly before prescribing a cure. Soccer coaches often say, "If you can't see it, you can't coach it." This means that you must have the knowledge and experience to diagnose a problem to improve performance. Furthermore, you also have to know when to offer a physical cure and when to offer a psychological one. Because good diagnosis is so important, the eight chapters in this book on the coaching of skills (chapters 4–11) all carefully explain the key points of the basic skills they address. In addition, chapter 12 covers the principles of team play to help you diagnose how well your team is playing and identify weaknesses in your team's opponents.

Coach the Player, Not the Drill

Clearly, good diagnosis depends not only on your personal knowledge and experience, but also on your observations of what the player is actually doing. First, you must watch and diagnose what is happening. In soccer you never just coach a skill; you always coach a player on how to perform the skill. This brings us to our third strategy—the recognition that you coach the player, not the drill.

Some coaches think they can produce a successful coaching session simply by running players through a conglomeration of drills. This is wrong. Good drills are important because they help to isolate particular skills, but by themselves, drills never produce or guarantee success. Drills provide a starting point, but what matters more, much more, is how you progress the drill according to the ability and responses of your players. This leads to our fourth strategy, progressive practices.

Progressive Practices

The ability to start with a simple practice and gradually develop it into a realistic game situation is one of the hallmarks of a good coach. Drills must be progressive (and sometimes this means simplified) according to how the players respond. Throughout this book, we show how you can progress each drill according to the response of your players.

In this book, we give many examples of how to start with a basic skill and then progressively develop that skill into active, gamelike situations and practices. We also include all-star drills that will challenge even the best of players. The ability to develop progressive coaching situations leads directly to our next strategy—opening the mind of the player through good communication.

Good Communication

There is nothing worse than a player who won't or can't listen. Because successful communication with your players is crucial, it pays to have some insight into the field of knowledge called communication. This field of knowledge has much to teach us, including the fact that, although we all have the ability to receive as well as transmit messages, many of us—especially coaches—are more skilled at transmitting than receiving! We might improve ourselves as coaches simply by becoming better listeners! Also, we know that body language, posture, and gestures (nonverbal communication) are all very important in transmitting messages to others, especially messages of enthusiasm and commitment.

What we say or do usually carries with it an emotional message. For example, some people can convey intense anger with a softly spoken word or inject humor into the most violent-looking gestures. We want to highlight three types of communication that will enable you to gain access to the minds of your players. These three types, which are often combined, are verbal, visual, and physical communication.

Verbal Communication

As coaches, we probably use verbal communication more than any other method. We know from experience that talking with players, rather than at them, can be one of the most effective means of communication. When you tell players what to do, always consider how they will receive your message; try to anticipate their reactions.

Double Positive Approach

Receiving good news is always pleasant; we all enjoy being praised, provided that it is sincere praise. When you see a successful performance, stop the practice and explain and demonstrate why the performance is successful. We call this the double positive approach because you simultaneously reinforce the player for good play while establishing the correct points of technique for the benefit of all players engaged in the practice.

However, players do make mistakes. When coaching young players, who can be especially sensitive, try to correct mistakes without discouraging them. If you go directly to the negative—the failure or mistake—you can very easily make a player feel insecure to such an extent that he may avoid trying again. Instead, begin with a positive opening remark before you correct what the player is doing wrong (e.g., "Good try, but . . ." or, "Yes, that move was OK, but . . . ").

By giving an encouraging opening comment, you make the player feel secure and thus receptive. To be really effective, you must open the player's mind to advice. In this way you avoid creating the closed mind of the irritated or reluctant player, whose negative emotions might momentarily interfere with cooperation and reason.

In our view, the double positive approach is the most important of all of the strategies. If you can spend most of your coaching life looking for and positively reinforcing what is right, good, and correct, then you are much more likely to be a happy, successful, and respected coach.

Question-and-Answer Technique

We believe it is a mistake for any coach to continually tell players what they should be doing. You can often achieve far more by asking players rather than telling. We recommend what is known as the question-and-answer technique. For example, if you ask your players a question such as, "Who can tell me why that was such a good pass?" or "What defensive systems are our opponents using?" you will achieve two objectives. First, you will elicit the correct technical diagnosis; and second, by involving the players in the discussion, you will encourage them to develop their own powers of observation and critical analysis. Getting players to appreciate and develop their own knowledge of the game is surely at the heart of good coaching, and the question-and-answer technique enhances this process.

Visual Communication

Good visual communication—the ability to demonstrate well—is a priceless gift. Not only does a good demonstration provide a picture for your players, but it also adds to your credibility and prevents the boredom of long verbal explanations. Following are some important characteristics of a good demonstration:

- *Simplicity.* Emphasize only one major point and perhaps one minor point each time you demonstrate. Bring out additional features in the next demonstration.

- *Reasonable goals.* Your demonstration should always set goals that are within the ability of your players.

- *Appropriate body language.* If you want players to move quickly and urgently, demonstrate the correct pace and tempo of the movement. If you want to stress calmness and composure, let your body movements and your voice convey these qualities.

- *Talking while demonstrating.* This enables you to draw attention to key points while you are actually demonstrating them.

- *Refraining from overdemonstrating.* Restrict demonstrations to one or two repetitions. You may occasionally need to demonstrate a skill three times, but four or more demonstrations will usually bore your audience.

What if My Demonstration Goes Wrong?

You cannot afford to continually make errors in front of your students. How, then, do you handle a mistake when demonstrating? You may find the following strategies useful:

- Always try to rehearse in private. If you need a server, practice with that person. If the server makes a mistake in the actual demonstration, don't try to compensate; stop and try again.

- Before you demonstrate, say to the group, "I may need two or three attempts to get this demonstration right." If you alert the group to the possibility of failure, it won't be a disaster if you fail. Furthermore, this implies that the players too must be prepared for failure and that failure is not necessarily a bad thing. Of course, succeeding the first time is a bonus.

- Stop after your third unsuccessful attempt at demonstrating. Don't keep on failing! If you are not successful by the third attempt, start the players working with a comment such as, "Sorry, it's not going well for me today, but you can see what is needed!" No one is perfect, and the players would rather practice themselves than watch you fail. A sincere coach has nothing to fear from an occasional failure.

What Do I Do if I Simply Can't Demonstrate?

The ability to give good demonstrations is a priceless asset. There are limits, however, and no one who is seriously interested in coaching soccer should be discouraged by an inability to demonstrate. You would not, for example, expect every track coach to sprint 100 meters in under 10 seconds! What matters most is that you know what should be done and why and can get that knowledge across to your players.

If you do not feel confident enough to demonstrate, consider using a preselected demonstrator, the discovery approach, a group challenge, or visual aids.

- *Preselected Demonstrator.* Select a good performer, take him to one side, and have him rehearse the skill or movement several times. Then let this player demonstrate for the entire group.

- *Discovery Approach.* With this method you introduce the topic and start the group off without an introductory demonstration. For example, to coach accuracy in passing, you might start with the players in pairs passing to each other, or you might organize mini-games of 3v3. As the players pass, watch for players who pass accurately; then stop the practice and ask the accurate passers to demonstrate for the others.

- *Group Challenge.* This method is very useful when coaching restarts such as free kicks and corners. Give small groups of players the same task— for example, working out an attacking free kick. After a set period of time, let each group demonstrate in turn. In this way you will produce a number of tactical moves to discuss with the players. Further, you will have challenged your players' initiative.

- *Visual Aids.* Coaching videos, handouts, and charts are useful, but you must use them with care. Examine them in advance, and show only sections you want students to see. Showing a video of a complete game can often be a waste of time, for example—be selective.

Physical Communication

Physical communication, such as shaping, involves guiding players' limbs through the correct movement. This is more important when coaching younger players. Young children must discover how to perform new skills, and they learn more by doing and feeling the correct pattern or shape of the movement than by listening. Giving a player the feel of a movement can be a very productive approach, and sometimes it is the only approach! It is particularly valuable, for example, when teaching the correct positions for the foot and knee in the push pass, especially in the follow-through (chapter 5). Similarly, it is invaluable when teaching players to relax the foot or thigh when controlling the ball (chapter 4) or to tense the muscles in the neck and shoulders when heading the ball (chapter 9).

This technique affords a special advantage when coaching smaller children. To shape a movement, you often have to kneel in front of the player with your eyes on the same level. Youngsters really respond to being coached by someone who is literally on their own level rather than someone towering above them and perhaps talking down to them in more ways than one.

In this chapter we introduced a series of ideas and strategies that collectively provide a useful introduction to developing your own personal coaching style that players will find friendly and reassuring. It covered the methods and approaches that we have found, and still find, useful when approaching any coaching situation, especially with players we might not have seen in action before. The overriding strategy is really quite straightforward: observe the players, diagnose their strengths and weaknesses, and then select the methods of communication you think will best suit the group at that particular time. Then, depending on their skill levels, concentrate on making each drill a little more demanding than the previous one.

Group Coaching Strategies

3

• • • • • •

CHAPTER 2 DISCUSSED your individual relationship with your players. This chapter presents some of the strategies we have found useful when coaching groups. These include good preparation, the grid system of coaching, methods of selection, accommodating various levels of ability (matching), getting the group started, keeping momentum in a lesson, and planning a coaching session.

Good Preparation

Good preparation operates at two levels. First, it operates at a conceptual, or team management, level. This may include preparing a syllabus for a school or college, establishing a code of conduct for the team, introducing various systems of play, developing a policy for helping with the team chores, and determining a policy for including and dealing with parents and spectators.

Second, good preparation operates at a specific level in each coaching session. This includes preparing written notes; ensuring that the necessary equipment is both available and suitable; using the correct part of the field for the practice; organizing the practice in accordance with the number, ability, and development of the players; grouping the players according to ability; developing the practice to make the best use of the available time; and modifying the activities in relation to the mental and physical states of the players. If you take the time and trouble to organize in advance, you will be much more likely to succeed. A well-prepared group session has a clear objective; is well timed, progressive, and demanding; and involves every player for the maximum possible time.

Because good preparation is both general and specific, examples are best considered in relation to specific objectives and practices. For this reason, every practice in this book includes detailed advice on organization. However, we do recommend one general system of organizing large numbers of players into manageable groups. This is called the grid system of coaching and is worth examining in detail.

Grid System of Coaching

One of the most useful strategies for dealing with a large class is to subdivide the group into smaller, more manageable coaching units, ideally of similar ability. One of the best ways to achieve this in a soccer lesson is by using a coaching grid.

A coaching grid is an area on the field of any shape or size that is generally divided into 10-×-10-yard squares (see figure 3.1). As a general rule, small team games require a grid of approximately 10 square yards per player; thus a 3v3 game would be played on six squares comprising an area of 30 by 30 yards. However, the grid shape or size can vary according to the age of the players and the available space. Also, 1-yard circles, as shown in figure 3.2, at intersections make useful targets for players to both attack and defend depending on the drill and their role. On school fields, the grids can be permanently marked with chalk lines, but flags, cones, or other markers provide effective substitutes.

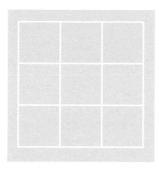

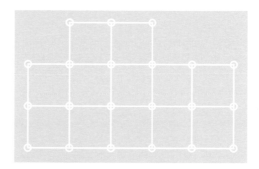

Figure 3.1
Sample coaching grid.

Figure 3.2
Coaching grid for a small-team game showing 1-yard circles.

The following sections describe several benefits of the grid system. Understanding them will help you gain maximum benefit from your practices.

Maximum Ball Contact Time

In a full 11v11 game, playing time is reduced by stoppages from 90 to 60 minutes (or a 2:3 ratio to the length of the game being played). This does not include the time lost when the ball is traveling between players. If every player were to have a fair share of the ball during the game, each player would get less than 3 minutes of contact! We know that such a distribution is impossible because some players monopolize the ball and others, such as the goalkeeper, touch it rarely. Using a grid to produce small-team games and arranging two or three players in each game automatically increases ball contact time. Because players learn largely by doing, the wisdom of this method is self-evident.

Easy Control of Time–Space Variables

The number of players and the amount of space they require can be easily controlled—the less able the player, the more time and space he needs to execute the skill. We continually use this time–space relationship. For example, when teaching a player to receive and control a ball (chapter 4), we delay the introduction of opposition. Or, in passing drills, we might start players in a 5 attackers versus 2 defenders situation to make the drill easier for the attackers. As the ability of the players improves, the ratio can be changed to, for example, 3v2 or even 2v3 for very proficient players.

Progressive Decision Making

Closely allied to the time–space variables is the advantage of progressive decision making. We do not take a novice driver on the freeway; similarly, we do

Small-Team Games

Small-team competitive games are the stepping stones to successful team play. Frequent use of these types of games during practice sessions develops individual skills in realistic situations; using fewer players (e.g., 5v3 or 3v2) increases the chances for players' success. Small-team games also provide the basis for introducing the principles of successful team play (chapter 12) and improving tactics and teamwork (chapters 14 and 15).

Another advantage of using small-team games is the fact that players enjoy them. In any sport, players enjoy practice more when it resembles a full-game situation that allows them to use their skills and talents without the restriction of the coach. However, you do want to influence the thoughts and actions of your players to ensure that they learn and improve. Small-team games offer a very useful compromise; they are an invaluable stepping stone between those twin objectives—learning and enjoyment.

Small-team games act as a bridge between learning skills and tactics and then applying them in the full-game situation. Acquiring new skills can be physically demanding, repetitive, and exhausting. What really matters is that the players experience a feeling of genuine satisfaction by the end of the session—that they have worked toward improvement, however minimal it might be. Small-team games can help you achieve this objective.

Always be prepared to modify a small-team game according to how well or how poorly the players are doing. If the game is too easy, the players may become bored; if it is too hard, the players are overchallenged and are unlikely to improve. The following guidelines may help:

- If the practice is too difficult (it keeps breaking down), increase the size of the playing area, remove some of the players, add extra players, change the balance of the teams (e.g., change 3v3 to 4v2), or modify the rules.
- If the practice is too easy, decrease the size of the playing area, introduce more players, remove players, change the balance of the teams (e.g., change 3v3 to 4v2 but coach the two players), or modify the rules.

not throw a young player directly into a full-game situation, especially if we want that player to learn how to make intelligent, composed decisions. To foster good decision making, we start players off in simple situations and in a friendly environment.

The coaching grid provides such an environment. For example, a player can begin to learn passing in a simple 2v1 situation on two grids. Then, by adding several adjacent grids together and having him play 3v3, he can graduate to a more difficult situation when he is ready. In the hands of the skillful coach, the grid system provides an excellent opportunity to develop the skills of players in a controlled manner.

Easily Identified Targets for Players

The lines of the grid restrict the area of play and can also provide targets and encourage positive attitudes in the players. A simple example is a 1v1 dribbling practice in which one player defends one of the lines of the square while a partner tries to reach, or cross, the line. As the ability of the players improves, you can also use the 1-yard circles in the coaching grid, as shown in figure 3.2, to provide smaller targets for the attacker (the smaller the target, the more the challenge) while at the same time making it easier for the defender to defend (when concentration is on the defender).

Better Use of Space

Finally, the coaching grid enables players to use the areas of grass that are away from the main playing field. In this way the match surface is protected against excessive wear and you make full use of the whole field. A word of warning, though: If you overuse the coaching grid, you may prevent your players from becoming familiar with the larger team environment. A good coach knows how to achieve a balance between the grid system and other situations, such as in the attack versus defense practice (page 268) and in the Silent Soccer (page 268).

Matching Players Within Groups

It's always difficult to accommodate the varying levels of ability that exist within a group. In soccer, you need to consider how to accommodate players of different ability levels in skill practices and how to select teams for small-team games so that all will have a reasonable chance of winning.

Selection for Skill Practices

In an ideal world, the strong help the weak to improve. However, pairing a good player with a weak player and expecting the one to help the other is usually a mistake. In reality, neither will derive much pleasure, nor make much progress. When coaching skills, try to match players or groups based on ability so that you encourage fair competition.

Selection for Small-Team Games

To encourage fair competition between small teams (e.g., 5v5), you must distribute your strong players and weaker players evenly to foster equal competition.

When selecting teams, never bring the best players to the front of the group and let them select team players in sequence. Those who are among the last to be selected will be terribly embarrassed and even humiliated. No youngster wants to be labeled a less able player, and you as the coach must ensure that no one is placed in this situation. Indeed, this situation is very easy to avoid—simply select teams in advance and read them off your notes, or select teams on the spot, relying on your experience to enable you to select balanced teams.

Strategies to Get the Group Started

When faced with wet, cold, or inclement conditions, you can do much useful preparatory work while the group is changing indoors. For example, you can tell the students who they are working with and how to start their first practice before they go out to the field. In normal conditions, however, after preparing the field and equipment in advance, you should begin coaching when the group is assembled on the field. In these circumstances, we recommend the following useful strategies.

Proper Positioning of the Group

Ensure that the players are grouped so they can see and hear you. Position yourself so that when your players are facing you, they are facing away from the sun or any distraction (e.g., another game). You don't want to find yourself talking to your team and having some, if not all, of them distracted by some other activity on the field (even a person walking across the field can be a distraction, let alone another game). The solution is to always position the group so that they concentrate on you and have their backs to any potential distraction.

Gaining Group Attention

Don't start until everyone is listening. If players are not paying attention, don't wait for them to become quiet because this wastes valuable time. Take the initiative. Bring them to attention by using any of the following techniques, which are listed in order of severity: a glance (eye contact is a marvelous thing), a raised finger, a quiet word or two (perhaps "thank you"), a spoken name, a firm command. Don't shout or blow your whistle. Shouting can destroy your credibility and may give the impression that you are uncertain of your authority. Save your shout and your whistle for emergencies.

Short Introduction

Keep your opening remarks as short as possible—two sentences if you can. For example, "I want to help you develop more accuracy in passing. Watch as I demonstrate." Certainly, you must tell the players what you intend to coach, but showing them is far more important (as discussed in chapter 2).

Keeping Momentum in Your Lesson

When handling a large group, you can easily lose momentum and interest when you have to stop the practice and move to another progression. To avoid long delays, we employ what we call the one-step-ahead technique.

While the class is working on the given topic, take a small group or even one player aside and rehearse the next skill. Then you can stop the main group and let the small group or player demonstrate the new task. Obviously, this method helps you avoid wasting time between activities, which can result in losing control of the class or group. By thinking one move ahead like a chess player, you save time between practices and keep up the pace and momentum in your practice. This is one of the hallmarks of a good coach.

Accommodating Various Rates of Progress

One way to achieve a reasonable balance of progress between the more and less able players in your group is to use what we call the five-stage strategy. The flowchart in figure 3.3 shows how to progress your coaching according to the presence or absence of a common fault or ability. The model may look complicated, but in fact it is a very simple concept to grasp and use. You will quickly appreciate how this strategy fits in with our other recommendations, such as preparing your next coaching point or demonstration in advance of stopping the group. The method also follows our general advice that coaching follows observation.

This method will help you achieve an optimum rate of progress for the group based on the ability of the average members. By ensuring that the majority can execute the skill reasonably well, you avoid going too fast or too slow.

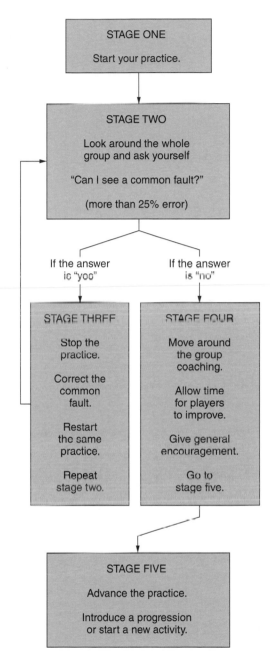

Figure 3.3
Five-stage strategy for group coaching.

Planning Your Coaching Sessions

One of the best ways to ensure that your coaching session flows (i.e., that each activity builds on the previous activity) is to use a flow diagram for your practice plan. One advantage of this well-known procedure is that you don't have to rearrange the groups or the equipment.

A simple way to create a flow diagram is to divide your practice session into three sections: the introduction, the main theme, and a game situation to finish. Allocate one sixth of the session to the introduction, two sixths to the main theme, and three sixths to the game situation. On a blank sheet of paper, draw three boxes horizontally connected by a line and numbered 1 to 3 from left to right. Now ask yourself, What is the main skill or theme I want to coach in this session? Suppose you want to coach the skill of supporting the player with the ball. Decide the best practice situation for developing this ability, and write it in box 2. In the case of support play, you will need a practice that involves both supporting and opposing players; a good example is 3v2 (or 4v1 for less able players).

Now ask yourself, How can I best develop the 3v2 situation into a larger gamelike small-team practice? Write the answer in box 3. In our example the answer might be 5v5 on a half-sized field, but it could also be a game such as Floater as described on page 94.

Finally, ask yourself, What activities can I use to start the session? Write the answer in box 1. In our case, this might be 4v1 Passing Outside the Square (page 68). Your diagram now looks like figure 3.4.

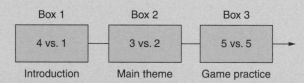

Figure 3.4 Sample practice plan.

The number of players in each activity depends on the size of your team. In our example, we have assumed that the number is divisible by 5. Also, as mentioned previously, in general, allow one sixth of the available time for box 1 (introduction), two sixths of the available time for box 2 (main theme), and three sixths of the available time for box 3 (small-team game).

Overall, this approach allows you to maximize the time you spend developing the chosen skills. It also ensures that at least half the available time is spent in active, gamelike situations in which the players apply the skills you have taught them.

PART II
· · · · · · · · · · · ·

Skills and Techniques

IN PART II we offer you our ideas on coaching the seven basic skills that, with the addition of goalkeeping, constitute the fundamentals of soccer. Some of the drills are well-known standards; some we have invented ourselves. We present these skills in a progressive sequence of four stages, which we hope you will find of particular value in relating them to the age and ability of your players.

We start with practices for beginners and then move to intermediates and then to advanced practices, many of which have been used with professional players. Finally, with the intention of inspiring every player to improve, we include special all-star practices to challenge your players to set their standards ever higher.

Being able to execute a skill in isolation is one thing; being able to execute it in a competitive game situation is another. The key is knowing how to develop the basic skills in realistic, competitive small-team situations. This is what we hope to share with you. Finally, we hope that you will also appreciate our ideas on how to open the mind of the player during these basic drills and situations. These early practices are forerunners to the chapters on tactics and teamwork in part III.

Collecting and Controlling the Ball

ARGUABLY, THE MOST important skill in soccer is the ability to control the ball. All players must be encouraged to develop this ability. It leads to confidence, satisfaction, and the freedom to execute the other skills of soccer effectively. All players must also be taught to appreciate that good control means one-touch control—whichever part of the body is used, one touch should be sufficient to control and redirect the ball as necessary.

Pelé, perhaps the greatest of all players, described collecting or controlling the ball as "the gentle art." We agree with Pelé; control is about gentleness, but there are circumstances in a game when a player adds pace to the ball, and this must always be controlled. To keep the ball close and within contact range, players have to absorb its force, and the key to this is relaxation. Overall tension—and particularly, tense limbs—repel the ball; relaxation contributes to the successful control of the ball.

Ball Juggling

Ball juggling, as shown in figure 4.1, is an excellent way to introduce young players to the ball and to encourage players of all ages to develop and retain a feel for, and mastery over, the ball. Even young players in professional teams' academies practice ball juggling continually; the skill some youngsters exhibit in keeping the ball airborne is impressive. They can flick the ball into the air and then use, at will, many parts of the body including, in particular, the platforms—the forehead, thigh, and instep. The constant touching of the ball develops finesse, balance, and confidence and encourages the use of many parts of the body, especially the platforms, which are so important in bringing the ball under control.

Figure 4.1   Ball juggling.

The secret to good ball juggling is practice. However, because formal practice time is limited, most coaches encourage their players to practice juggling on their own time. An inspiring example is Pelé, who as a boy used a grapefruit or a ball of rags tied together with string to practice ball juggling. To complement, and hopefully inspire, additional practice, many coaches start every coaching practice with a 1-minute competition to see who can achieve the most touches or keep the ball off the ground the longest. Because of this, we start this chapter with the skill of ball juggling and offer a number of techniques to help beginners learn and improve.

Drill for Beginners

With beginners, start simple! Beginners quickly lose interest if the ball bounces away from them, out of their control, every time they play. This is not only frustrating, but also embarrassing. This is why the following introductory drill, albeit basic, places so much emphasis on success.

Basic Ball Juggling

Equipment   One light ball for each player (such as a volleyball or a soccer ball at reduced pressure)

Organization   Individual players stand in free space.

Instructions   Players throw the ball into the air, let it bounce, and then play it once with the instep. Players try to keep the sequence going—that is, let the ball bounce, play it with the instep, let it bounce again, and so on.

Coaching Points
- Players should use the instep as a platform to lift the ball into the air.
- If the ball starts to spin, players should stop and start over (spin can make juggling more difficult for beginners).
- Players should hold their arms out wide for balance.

Coaching Progressions
1. Players make two touches with the instep for every bounce (play, play, bounce, play, play, bounce, and so on).
2. Players make three touches for every bounce.
3. Players try to score 10 touches before the sequence breaks down.
4. Players try to use different platforms (e.g., forehead, thigh).
5. Players try to use the platforms in sequence (e.g., head, thigh, foot, thigh, head).
6. Players set their own targets and hold competitions.

Drills for Intermediate Players

Any player who can consistently achieve 10 or more touches without losing control is ready to move to the intermediate level. However, we do not advocate simply achieving more and more touches or mastering the use of body parts such as the shoulder or the back of the neck to catch the ball. Such skills are fine for the circus performer, but the soccer player will benefit more from developing basic moves with the regular platforms of the instep, thigh, and forehead. These moves are best progressed using partner activities and moving situations, which are realistic rather than contrived and encourage effective soccer skills.

Continuous Heading

Equipment   One light ball (such as a volleyball or a soccer ball at a reduced pressure) for every two players

Organization   Players are in pairs of equal ability, 3 yards apart.

Instructions   Player A gently lobs the ball to player B, who heads the ball back; the drill becomes continuous.

Coaching Points
- Players' eyes should focus underneath the ball.
- Players should hold their arms outstretched to the side for balance.
- Players should head the ball upward back to their partners.

Coaching Progressions
1. Players aim to reach 10 or more continuous plays.
2. Players try to maintain sequences while moving sideways, forward, and backward. ■

Equipment   One light ball (such as a volleyball or a soccer ball at a reduced pressure) for every two players

Organization   Players are in pairs of equal ability, 3 yards apart.

Instructions   Players must juggle the ball and make at least three touches before returning it to their partners.

Coaching Point

- Players should achieve height on the ball between touches to give themselves more time to make contact.

Coaching Progressions

1. Players return the ball to their partners with either the foot or the forehead.
2. Players call out the part of the body their partners must use to return the ball. ■

Drills for Advanced Players

In the previous juggling drills, players remained relatively stationary. For advanced juggling, players are required to move while they juggle. The following drills progress from individual activities to partner practices.

Individual Juggling

Equipment   One ball for each player

Organization   Individual players stand in free space.

Instructions   Keeping the ball off the ground, players see how many yards they can cover while on the move (forward, backward, and sideways).

Coaching Points
- Players should try to achieve height on the ball each time they play to give themselves time to reposition their bodies and select which part to use to control the ball.
- Players should take plenty of time. It is better to move slowly forward, backward, or sideways than to rush a contact to gain distance.

Coaching Progressions
1. Players start from a basic position and see how far they can travel.
2. Players are given a specific distance and see how quickly they can reach the target and get back again. ▣

Partner Juggling

Equipment   One ball for every two players

Organization   Players are in pairs of equal ability, 3 yards apart.

Instructions   Players work in pairs 4 to 5 yards apart and juggle the ball between them. One player moves forward and the other player retreats as they juggle the ball between them.

Coaching Point
- Players should try to achieve height on the ball each time they play it.

Coaching Progressions
1. Players touch the ball only once.
2. Players touch the ball at least twice before returning it to their partners.
3. Players do not use the same part of the body twice in succession. ▣

Drill for All-Star Players

The following all-star drill is ideal when you do not have access to a net or tennis court. Also note that Head Tennis, described on page 167, can be adjusted so that it, too, can be an excellent alternative for developing juggling and ball control skills.

Team Juggling

Equipment   One ball for each group of two to four players

Organization   Create two teams of three players (could be reduced to two players, but never more than four); teams face each other 5 to 10 yards apart.

Instructions   One team throws the ball to the other team, which then has to juggle the ball at least three times with each player touching the ball at least once. The ball is then volleyed back to the opposite team in such a way that the receiving team can with reasonable effort gain control without the ball touching the ground. If this transfer is "unfair," the receiving team can restart the sequence.

Coaching Point
• Reiterate the basic coaching points, although it is often better with skillful players to just let the players perform the drill and learn by doing.

Coaching Progressions
1. Increase the distance between the players up to 20 yards.
2. Increase the minimum number of touches for each player in each team to two, or increase the number of touches for each team to six or more.

Basic Collecting and Controlling Techniques

There are almost as many ways of controlling a ball as there are parts of the body; however, not all of these ways are consistently effective. The basic techniques can be divided into three categories, or methods. Selecting which method to use is a matter of judgment and experience, but is largely determined by the way the ball is traveling (often toward the player) and the time and space the player has in which to complete the skill. For example, to control a high, dropping ball, the player could use the instep or thigh as a platform on which to catch the ball. With a flat, driven ball or hard ground pass, the player could use the chest or the inside of the foot as a cushion. The player could also use a wedge or angle, usually made by the foot or ankle and the ground, into which the ball falls as it drops to the ground during flight.

Platform

The three most common platforms are the instep, the top of the thigh, and the forehead. (other parts of the body, such as the chest, can also be used). By presenting a flat surface underneath the ball and withdrawing the surface on impact, the player takes speed or momentum off the ball. This is usually called taking the pace off the ball.

Instep

The raised instep (upper surface of the foot, usually around the boot laces) can be used to receive or catch the dropping ball. Ideally, the ball remains in contact with the instep throughout; at worst the ball stays within easy reach of the feet. Because the player must balance on one leg to execute the move, he may hold his arms out wide to improve his balance (see figure 4.2).

Figure 4.2   Controlling the ball with the instep.

Thigh

Depending on how vertically the ball is dropping, the platform of the thigh is raised between 40 and 90 degrees to receive the ball. Again, the arms are likely to be bent and to the side of the body for balance, but because the chest is tilted slightly forward, the whole body position is more compact and stable than it is with the instep method. Because of this stability and the much larger platform involved, controlling the ball with the thigh is both easier and safer than controlling it with the instep. Completed successfully, the ball drops straight from the thigh to the ground; an uncontrolled bounce away from the thigh indicates poor execution (see figure 4.3).

Figure 4.3 Controlling the ball with the thigh.

Forehead

Catching or controlling a dropping ball with the forehead is more difficult than with the thigh or instep. The key is judging the flight and focusing the eyes under the ball, which almost gives the feeling that the eyes, not the forehead, catch the ball. This ensures that the head is tilted back on impact, thus presenting the forehead as a platform to receive the ball.

The knees can help the head and shoulders cushion the ball by bending at the moment of contact. The feet should be about shoulder-width apart to allow the whole body to act as a shock absorber. Players often arrange their feet and bodies naturally as they adjust to receive the ball; if they do not, you should advise them on proper positioning! When this skill is executed properly, the ball drops to the ground or can be controlled again on the thigh (see figure 4.4).

Figure 4.4 Controlling the ball with the forehead.

Cushion

One-touch close control of a ball driven hard on a flat trajectory or along the ground is good play. It is achieved by positioning a part of the body in the ball's path and cushioning the impact as the ball strikes. Obviously, the larger the cushion presented as a target, the easier the control factor. For this reason, the chest, which can also be used as a platform (see figure 4.5*a*), and occasionally the abdomen, are two good areas to use (see figure 4.5*b*). Other areas that can be used as a cushion are the inside of the thigh when the knee is raised sideways (see figure 4.6) and the inside of the foot when it is square to the line of flight, as shown in figure 4.8*a* on page 37.

Figure 4.5
Controlling the ball with the (*a*) chest and (*b*) abdomen.

Figure 4.6   Controlling the ball with the inside of the thigh.

Wedge

With this technique the player makes an angle, or wedge, between the ground and the foot, allowing the ball to travel into this space. The most effective wedges are made with the sole and the inside or outside of the foot.

Sole of the Foot

With the foot lifted slightly from the ground, the toes are raised but the heel is held low to produce the sloping wedge shape. The arms are held wide for balance, and the upper body is often crouched (see figure 4.7). The player must gently control the ball with the sole of the foot. This maneuver may impart backspin to the ball, bringing it to the receiver's feet. Do not allow beginners to

Figure 4.7　Controlling the ball with the sole of the foot.

stamp on the ball when it is at their feet because the ball can shoot away them or become trapped under the foot, freezing the player in a static position and exposing him to incoming opponents.

Inside and Outside of the Foot

When faced with an angled and dropping ball and an onrushing opponent, the receiver must control the ball and move away from danger in the same movement. To do this, the player must use either the inside (most popular) or the outside of the foot depending on the intended direction of movement and perform a balanced body lean (see figure 4.8, *a* and *b*).

Figure 4.8　Controlling the ball with (*a*) the inside of the foot and (*b*) the outside of the foot.

Collecting and Controlling Drills

Again, the key to success in collecting and controlling is to start simple. You don't want your players to find it difficult to receive and control the ball. Rather, you want them to experience the feel of control and mastery of the ball when it comes to them—regardless of the speed, direction, and flight of the ball.

Drills for Beginners

We recommend four drills for teaching beginners how to control the ball. The first drill involves controlling the ball with the thigh, possibly the easiest method to learn, and the second involves controlling the ball with the instep. Both drills involve platform techniques and are ideal starters and confidence builders.

Self-serve practices are ideal for teaching beginners how to control with the inside and outside of the foot and how to use various parts of the body to cushion the ball, as we show in the third and fourth drills. Self-serve practices are useful because beginners can set their own targets; however, because such practices may not sustain motivation for an extended period of time, you should limit their use to 3 to 5 minutes. That is not to say, however, that a dedicated youngster will not spend hours playing against the garage wall at home and controlling the ball as it rebounds—good practice for both passing and controlling! Players can progress from these individual practices to the partner activities recommended for intermediates.

Equipment   One ball for every two players

Organization   Players are in pairs (one server and one receiver).

Instructions   The server stands approximately 2 to 5 yards from the receiver depending on ability level and, using both hands, serves a gentle underarm lob directly toward the thigh of the receiver. The receiver tries to catch the ball on the thigh, allowing the ball to fall directly to the ground, in order to pass it back to the server.

Coaching Points

- The ball should fall directly to the ground in front of the receiver.
- If the ball bounces upward off the top of the thigh, then the player has not absorbed the force correctly. In all probability the angle of the thigh presented to the ball is incorrect.

Coaching Progressions

1. The receiver initially catches the ball and then raises the knee up to it.
2. The receiver catches the ball with thigh and hands together (called the three-hands method).
3. The receiver uses the thigh only.
4. The receiver uses both left and right thighs in turn and so may have to move the feet to adjust to the varied service.
5. The server extends the distance of the throw and increases the height to just under head height.
6. The receiver returns the ball to the server with an accurate push pass.

Control With the Instep

Equipment   One ball for every three players

Organization   Players are in teams of three (one server, one receiver, one supporter).

Instructions   The server executes a gentle underhand throw using both bands, aiming directly at the receiver's instep. The receiver tries to keep the ball "tied" onto his instep while leaning on the supporter for balance.

Coaching Points

- The receiver can relax his foot by shaking it.
- The receiver should feel that he is hanging the foot about 4 inches (10 cm) above the ground.
- The receiver should turn his toes down.
- If the ball bounces forward off the receiver's foot, his ankle and foot are not relaxed sufficiently or the ball has hit his lower leg, not his relaxed foot.
- If the throw is accurate and the foot is relaxed, the ball will come to rest on the foot, and the receiver, usually an absolute beginner, will experience complete control over the ball—perhaps for the first time.

Coaching Progressions

1. The server moves farther and farther back, up to 10 yards depending on the skill of the receiver. The ball is thrown on a higher trajectory (approximately 6 to 10 feet in the air).

2. The receiver no longer leans on the supporter.

3. The receiver tries to control the ball with alternate feet. The service here must be accurate.

4. The receiver catches the ball on the instep and in the same movement turns around with the ball (only skillful players should attempt this). This skill can be used for advanced shooting practices in which the player stands in the penalty area with his back toward the goal, catches the ball, turns, and shoots (chapter 8). ▪

Control With the Inside and Outside of the Foot

Equipment   One ball for each player

Organization   Individual players stand in free space but must beware of others.

Instructions   Players throw the ball into the air, move to the point at which it lands (the pitch of the ball), and control it using the inside of the foot, as shown in figure *a,* or the outside of the foot, as shown in figure *b.* This practice is excellent for learning how to use the wedge method of controlling the bouncing ball.

Coaching Points

- Players must move quickly to the pitch of the ball.
- Players must achieve the correct angle with the foot and ankle to control the ball.
- Players must lean in the direction in which they intend to move the ball.
- Players must control the ball at the moment it first touches the ground, not after it has bounced or on the second bounce.

Coaching Progressions

1. Players throw the ball at various heights and in various directions but never so far or so high that they cannot reasonably get to the pitch of the ball. Players should set realistic goals.
2. Players decide which part of the foot (inside or outside) to use and try to stick to this decision.
3. Players try not only to control the ball but also to move or sweep it away in different directions as if beating an opponent.
4. Players start at a fixed point and see how far they can throw the ball and still reach and control it.

Equipment   One ball for each player and a large, smooth vertical surface

Organization   Individual players stand in free space.

Instructions   Players throw the ball at a wall or other surface and try to control the ball after it rebounds to them. This practice is very useful for teaching players the cushion method of controlling the driven ball and also how to use the forehead.

Coaching Points
- Players must watch the flight of the ball as it rebounds from the wall.
- Players should select the part of the body to control the ball as early as possible.

Coaching Progressions
1. Players increase the force of the rebound and vary the height and direction of the throw.
2. Players decrease the distance from the wall, thus reducing the time available to execute control.
3. Players preselect which part of the body they will use.
4. Players control the ball and turn away from the wall in one move.
5. Players move up and down alongside the wall, controlling the rebound at an angle—just like the wall pass (page 62).

Drills for Intermediate Players

For intermediate players, partner drills are excellent for developing the various methods of ball control. These drills permit servers to vary the service according to the ability of the receiver, and they also provide a very effective activity-to-rest ratio. They do require players to recognize and practice two attitudes—cooperation and competition—which is another important strategy when coaching new skills to players of different abilities. First, players are responsible for serving to their partners in a cooperative manner; players have a duty to provide a careful, accurate service to help their partners improve. Only when partners are mature enough should they begin to compete with each other; this should not be done too soon. You are responsible for deciding when to change from an attitude of cooperation to one of competition.

There are a number of interesting variations you can employ with the following drills. For example, a drill normally begins with the server facing the receiver, which allows the receiver to see and anticipate both the direction and speed of the serve and the incoming player. However, if the receiver starts with his back to the server and waits for the command "Now" before turning, the difficulty of the drill is increased considerably. Goalkeepers frequently use this backward starting position when working to improve their reaction time. Try it—it's good fun. Of course, the server must take care not to create impossible challenges for the receiver. Overall, this variation does a good job of reinforcing the difference between cooperation and competition.

Purpose To encourage players to move quickly to the bounce of the ball

Equipment   One ball for every two players; two markers, such as flags or cones

Organization   Players are in pairs of equal ability (one server, one receiver). Markers are placed 5 yards apart.

Instructions   The server throws the ball underhand alternately toward the two markers. The receiver moves sideways in response to the service, controls the ball using any suitable method (or in response to a predetermined method), and plays the ball back to the server.

Coaching Points

- Initially, the ball must be stationary before the receiver returns it to the server; the receiver must not play the ball back directly.
- Once the receiving player can regularly make the ball stationary, he should move the ball into a position with the first touch to return the ball to the server. Therefore, the ball is always on the move, just as it would be in an actual game.

Coaching Progressions

1. Players start with a simple, underhand throw.
2. Players increase the speed and difficulty of the serve (e.g., using spin).
3. Players serve the ball in the air so that it bounces at the point of control.
4. Players change to a one-handed (javelin-style) throw service to increase realism, which increases the distance of the throw.
5. Players progress to pressure training (page 355).
6. Players compete with each other (e.g., to see who can make the most perfect controls in 1 minute or from a designated number of serves). ◼

Goalkeeper

Purpose   To encourage greater movement and increase the difficulty of the control factor

Equipment   One ball for every two players; two markers, such as flags or cones

Organization   Players are in pairs of equal ability (one server and one receiver). Markers are placed 5 yards apart, as shown in the figure on page 45 for Alternating Targets.

Instructions   A server stands approximately 7 to 10 yards from a goal and tries to score from a pass along the ground. The receiver acts as a goalkeeper, defending the 5-yard goal without using his hands. Players take turns as the goalkeeper, which develops their ability to control a ball coming at them at various speeds and heights and from various directions.

Coaching Points

- The receiver should select the controlling method early, having read the speed and direction of the serve.
- The receiver should move the feet quickly if necessary to position the selected controlling surface behind the ball.
- The receiver should try to achieve one-touch control, placing the ball into a position so as to pass the ball back to the server with the second touch.

Coaching Progressions

1. Players cooperate before competing.
2. The server starts with a thrown ball before progressing to a volley or half-volley serve from the hand.
3. A variety of surfaces are required to control the ball as the various serves are delivered.
4. If the receiver really is a goalkeeper, he can roll the ball back to the server, who then shoots. The instant "first-time" return shot produces a very demanding challenge for the receiver. ■

Purpose   To stop the ball rebounding forward and away from the receiver

Equipment   One ball for every two players; two markers, such as flags or cones

Organization   Players are in pairs of equal ability (one server, one receiver). Markers are placed 5 yards apart, as shown in the figure on page 45 for Alternating Targets.

Instructions   The server plays the ball on the ground or as close as possible to the ground. The receiver stands 2 to 3 feet behind the goal line and controls the ball to prevent it from bouncing through the goalposts and across the goal line.

Coaching Points

- Players should use the cushion method, especially with the inside of the ankle.
- Players should judge the route and speed of the incoming serve.
- Players should select the controlling surface early and move the feet quickly to move into the line of the serve.
- Players should relax and withdraw the controlling surface on impact.

Coaching Progressions

1. The server starts with a push pass directly at the receiver.
2. The server plays the ball to the left and right of the receiver.
3. The server increases the speed and height of the serve according to the receiver's ability.
4. The receiver stands only 1 to 2 feet behind the goal line; the reduced space makes control more challenging.
5. Players see how many successful controls they can achieve in a set number of serves. ■

Drills for Advanced Players

Advanced players require active opposition to generate the realism of the game. Early opposition can be somewhat passive, but the later stages of advanced practices should always involve a high degree of healthy competition at match pace. For this reason, remember to match your players according to their abilities.

Receiving the Ball Under Pressure

Purpose   To develop control under pressure from opponents

Equipment   One ball for every two players

Organization   Players are in pairs, 5 yards apart.

Instructions   The server throws the ball underhand to the receiver. The server becomes the opponent and tries to dispossess the receiver. The receiver controls the ball and must either keep possession for 5 to 10 seconds or beat the opponent to a line behind the server.

Coaching Points

- The receiver can make the control factor easier by moving the ball away from the incoming opponent.
- The receiver can make the control factor more challenging by faking and disguising a dribbling move as the opponent rushes in.

Coaching Progressions

1. The server waits until the receiver actually touches the ball before moving in.
2. The server moves in while the ball is still in the air. A clever server may release the ball slowly and arrive at the same time as the ball. To rectify this, ask the server to challenge for the ball when it is, say, halfway between the players (marked by two cones). Then gradually move the cones nearer to the server so that he moves earlier toward the receiver after delivering the ball.
3. The server regularly varies the speed and flight of the service. ◼

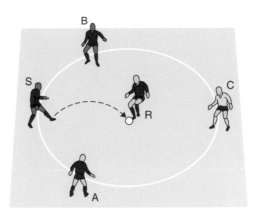

Purpose To increase the difficulty of controlling the ball under pressure

Equipment One ball for every five players

Organization Players are in groups of five (one receiver, one server, three defenders). The defenders and server form a 5-yard-radius circle (or larger for less skillful players) around the receiver.

Instructions The server serves underhand to the receiver. The defender, who is to tackle or put pressure on the receiver, is nominated by the server at the moment the ball is thrown. The server can nominate more than one defender as the practice develops. The server may also elect to be a defender. The receiver gains and keeps possession of the ball in the circle for a set period of time or controls the ball and breaks out of the circle by dribbling perhaps over a line or toward a target area. In this practice, the defenders can come from behind the receiver, which creates an exciting progression.

Coaching Points

- The receiver should always observe the trajectory and speed of the service, move his feet accordingly to present the chosen controlling surface to the ball, and then try to control and shield the ball from the incoming opponent.

- Knowing the position, movement, and intention of the opposing player will influence how the receiver controls the ball.

- The receiver must make an early decision, commit to the move, and move quickly to the ball.

- The receiver should control the ball away from the opponent or shield the ball from him by getting his body between the ball and the opponent.

Coaching Progressions

1. You can make this practice easier or harder for the receiver by having the server identify defenders who are out of the receiver's sight. For example, because attackers frequently have to play against two or more defenders (often with their backs toward the goal), consider the starting positions for the defenders:

   - Position A is easy because the receiver can see the defender and move both ways to avoid him.

   - Position C is harder because the receiver cannot initially see the defender and does not know which way to move.

   - You, or the server, can instruct up to three defenders to try to dispossess the receiver.

   - You can also make things easier for the defender by allowing the server to help the receiver, thus making the practice 2v1, 2v2, or 2v3. ■

Throw-Control-Pass

Purpose   To introduce more gamelike situations that involve players controlling the ball using a variety of skills

Equipment   One ball for every three or four players; four flags or cones

Organization   Players are in teams of three (or four) on a 30- × 20-yard (or 40- × 30-yard) mini-field marked by flags or cones.

Instructions   The aim of the game is to keep possession and to develop control skills, and it can easily be developed into a small-team game. Player A throws to player B, who controls the ball and passes to player C. Player C picks up the ball and continues the sequence with a throw to player A or B. The players must keep the sequence: throw-control-pass-pick up-throw.

   The player who picks the ball up may run with it before throwing. This opens up the game by increasing space and time.

Coaching Point

- Depending on the speed of the incoming opponent, the receiver must make an early decision about which way to control and take the ball.

Coaching Progressions

1. Players use a variety of throws (high, fast, low) and a variety of receiving skills (foot, head, thigh).

2. Given the primary aim of the practice (control), the receiver must pass the ball accurately using various types of passes (low, lofted, chip, and swerve, as discussed in chapter 5). The practice therefore broadens the technical requirements of the players in terms of both receiving and passing skills. ■

 # Turning With the Ball

All players, but especially midfield players and attackers, must be able to turn 180 degrees with the ball. This is one of the most important control and tactical skills for any player who has to receive the ball with his back to the opponents' goal because he is facing the wrong way. Turning toward the opponents' goal, therefore, becomes a vital skill, especially for an attacker in the opponents' penalty area.

The following basic drill is recommended when players are practicing turning. It is applicable to all levels of players and can also be used as a fitness training activity.

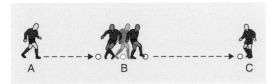

Equipment   One ball for every three players

Organization   Players are in teams of three, standing in line at least 5 yards apart.

Instructions   Player A push passes to the central receiver, player B, who controls the ball, turns in one move, and passes the ball to player C. Player C returns the pass, and the practice continues.

Coaching Points

- The proper sequence of movements used when turning with the ball are to turn sideways to receive the ball and offer a welcoming foot (see figure 4.9*a*), cushion the ball on impact, let it "run on" (see figure 4.9*b*), and take the ball on with the other foot (see figure 4.9*c*).

Figure 4.9   Turning with the ball.

» continued

Turning With the Ball » *continued*

- Players should turn sideways as the ball travels toward them and extend a welcoming foot to receive the ball—usually the foot farther from the ball, although not exclusively so.
- Players should cushion the ball and withdraw the foot (this controls yet maintains the momentum on the ball) and pass the ball with the other foot.

Coaching Progressions

1. Players turn and, with the first touch, direct the ball into a position to pass it to the receiver.
2. Players turn and drive with the instep to the receiver (distances between players obviously need to be extended to approximately 20 yards from the passer to next receiver).
3. Players turn quickly after allowing the ball to run between the feet and under the body. If there is not enough speed on the ball, players must add momentum with the inside of the foot.

Drills for All-Star Players

As players develop the fundamental techniques of controlling the ball, they should progress toward game-type, free-flowing scenarios in which they are required to observe and respond to events that are occurring around them. Such scenarios require that they look away from the ball to read the situation and control the ball according to the requirements of the situation.

All-star players must support the player in possession of the ball, take their eyes away from the ball temporarily, observe the position of fellow teammates, and control the ball so they can make accurate and efficient passes. These are the significant requirements of match play. All of the controlling skills addressed in the previous drills in this chapter now come into play.

Controlling and Passing on the Move

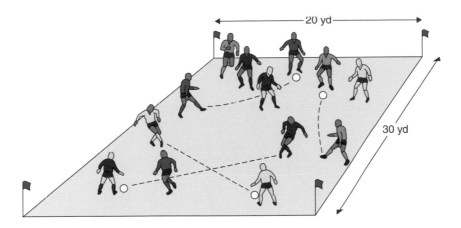

20 yd

30 yd

Purpose   To enable players to control and pass a ball in a variety of situations in which all players are moving and in the ever-changing variables of time and space that prevail throughout the practice

Equipment   Different-colored bibs for each team of three players (three, four, or five teams of three); one ball for each team; cones to outline the playing area

Organization   Create teams of three players. The playing area can be 30 × 20 yards for four teams of three players, or 40 × 30 yards for six teams of three players.

Instructions   The player in possession passes the ball (below knee height) to a teammate and moves to a support position to be available to receive a return pass. The two players not in possession of the ball must continually search for a position in which to receive passes from the ball holder. All teams play at the same time with their own ball.

Coaching Points

- When not in possession of the ball, players should support the player in possession by moving into the spaces created in and around the other players.
- Teams should spread out to create as much space as possible in which to receive the ball.
- When moving into a support position to receive, players should look away from the ball holder to observe the position of other team members.
- When moving to receive the ball, players must decide as early as possible which controlling surface to use, adjust the feet accordingly, and, with the first touch, place or direct the ball into a position that allows them to pass to a teammate. The space available to the receiver will be influenced by her own support position, the lines of the playing area, and the position of other players in the practice.

Coaching Progressions

1. Players control and pass the ball within two touches.
2. Players receive the ball with various surfaces of the foot.
3. Players receive the ball with one surface of the foot (e.g., inside) and pass the ball with a different surface (e.g., outside, heel).
4. Players receive with one foot and pass with the other.
5. In an expanded practice area, players deliver aerial passes, which require a variety of controlling skills (explained earlier in this chapter). ■

Control and Penetrate

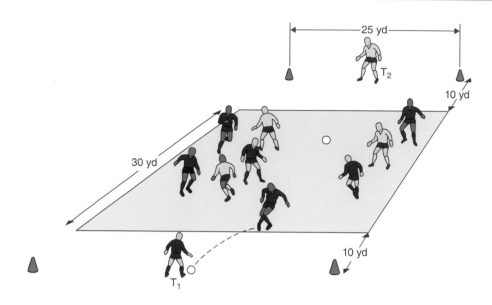

Purpose   To enable players to understand when to receive and pass the ball forward and learn why, if these opportunities are not available, their priority might be to protect the ball and keep possession

Equipment   One ball for each team of three players

Organization   Six attacking players and three defenders play in a 30- × 25-yard area. Additional target players are positioned 10 yards beyond each end line

Instructions

When in possession, the six attacking players are opposed by three defenders and must transfer the ball to the first target player (T1), to the second target player (T2) and back again as many times as possible in a certain time frame (e.g., 2 minutes).

Once they have successfully passed the ball to one of the target players, they should immediately readjust their support position to receive the ball from the target player who has possession and attack in the opposite direction. Should the three defenders gain possession of the ball, they should also pass to either target player, and the practice continues with the target player returning the ball to the six attacking players.

After the time period has expired, the defenders become attackers and three attackers replace them. Should the ball go outside the playing area, pass a ball to the attacking team to continue the practice.

Coaching Points

- Players are allowed only two touches of the ball (to receive and release the ball) per possession. This will encourages more economical and accurate game play.
- Players should control the ball into a position to pass the ball forward or to a free teammate or away from opponents.
- Requiring players to pass the ball below knee height challenges them to find support around and between opponents and to control the ball on the ground.

Coaching Progressions

1. The playing area is decreased to increase the difficulty in reacting to challenges.
2. The number of players is increased, and the two target players remain. ■

Passing

• • • • • •

5

SECOND IN IMPORTANCE to the ability to control the ball is the ability to pass the ball successfully. Good passing is the foundation of any team strategy and always involves at least two players—the passer and the receiver. Soccer players must develop both physical and mental abilities to pass successfully. They must possess the basic techniques of how to pass the ball, in addition to being able to decide where and when to pass the ball and how and where to support the receiver. You will see that there is an exciting difference between coaching physical skills and coaching the minds of your players.

Basic Techniques of Short Passing

This section deals with the three most common methods of short passing: the push pass, the outside of the foot pass, and the instep pass. The swerve pass is more advanced and is included in chapter 7.

Push Pass

The push pass is the most frequently used and therefore the most important basic passing technique. It is also the easiest to learn, which is why we coach it first.

The push pass is a sideways movement in which the knee is bent and the kicking foot is turned outward at an angle of 90 degrees so that it is square to the intended line of direction of the pass. As with many other sideways striking skills, such as the golf swing or the drive in tennis, a good follow-through along the line of flight is essential. Unlike golf or tennis, the back-lift is relatively short; the power of the pass comes from the muscles inside the thigh and from a firm, fixed ankle, which acts as a club or hammer on contact with the ball. Although the pass can be made in a variety of ways, it is best done with the player in a firm, compact stance with the center of gravity low and the arms held low. The stance has been aptly called the monkey stance to draw attention to the crouched body shape. Players need to acquire the slightly seated position of the monkey. See figure 5.1 for an example of a push pass.

Four common errors in the basic technique of the push pass are worth examining. The first is keeping the passing leg rigid, often with the toe pointed, which causes the leg to swing over and across the target line and slice the ball. The second error is raising the foot but not holding square to the target line, which plays the ball wide of the target. Third, the foot strikes the ball below its midline and causes it to lift, often with sidespin. Such passes are really kicks and are difficult for the receiver to control. And, fourth, there is no follow-through on the ball, which causes a stabbing action and fails to produce the important top roll and causes the pass to lose power. As a coach, you can work to correct all four of these errors by kneeling at the feet of the player and guiding his foot through the correct pattern to give him the feel of the movement. This is called shaping (for more information, see page 15).

Figure 5.1 Push pass.

Outside of the Foot Pass

The outside of the foot pass uses a different part of the foot than the push pass and also results in a different body shape. When using the outside of the foot, the player's body is often tall and upright; indeed, the player almost appears stately as he guides the ball past an opponent. Because of this body stance, however, this pass is much less powerful than the push pass and is best used over short distances and in tightly marked situations. Very often the ball is almost flicked away, although always with a firm ankle. See figure 5.2 for an example of an outside of the foot pass.

Figure 5.2 Outside of the foot pass.

Instep Pass

The instep pass is the most powerful of all the passes because it uses the movement that produces the most powerful kick in soccer—the instep drive. The instep pass comes off the instep, or laces, portion of the foot. The pass can be used over long distances, but because of the need for precise geometry between the instep and the ball, this pass is much more difficult to learn than the others. When used by beginners, the instep pass can be inaccurate, especially when compared to the much safer push pass. See figure 5.3 for an example of an instep pass.

Figure 5.3   Instep pass.

Short Passing Drills

Short passes are the bedrock of good team play. All players move and help each other. Passers release the ball at the right time, on the ground and at the right speed, and receivers continuously move into open positions to ensure the safe arrival of the pass. In confined spaces, especially when attacking in the penalty area, short, crisp, penetrating passes put the defense under pressure and often lead to a goal.

Drills for Beginners

We recommend the drills on the following two pages for beginners. In the first drill, the players are in a relatively static position, which simplifies matters for the players and makes coaching easier. In the second drill, movement adds realism and demonstrates to players the need for accurate, properly weighted passes that hug the ground and have no sidespin, making them ideal for the receiver to control.

Equipment One ball for every two players; one marker, such as a flag or cone, for each pair plus one extra marker

Organization Players are in pairs, facing each other, 8 to 10 yards apart. Markers are set up about 6 feet apart to form passing lanes.

Instructions Players pass the ball forward and backward to their partners using only the push pass. Players try to keep the pass within their lanes. They must control the ball before passing it back.

Coaching Points

- Review and check players' basic technique, as discussed on page 56.
- Encourage accuracy; the pass should be targeted to go to the feet of the static receiver.
- Encourage a quality pass; the ball should hug the ground because it has top roll. It should not bounce or have sidespin. This will be achieved by making contact through the horizontal center line of the ball.

Coaching Progressions

1. Players increase the speed of the pass.
2. Players reduce the distance between the cones.
3. Players return the ball without stopping it first (i.e., use a one-touch play).
4. Players increase the distance of the pass to 10 to 12 yards.
5. Players return to the basic starting situation but use the outside and instep techniques as variations.

Push Passing on the Move

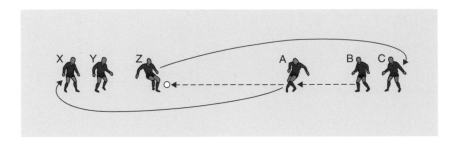

Equipment   One ball for every six or eight players

Organization   Players are in two teams of three or four, facing each other about 10 to 12 yards apart.

Instructions   Players use the push pass only. Player A dribbles the ball forward a few feet, and then looks for and passes to player Z. Player A then follows the pass and runs to the back of the opposite team. Meanwhile, player Z dribbles forward, passes to player B, and runs to the back of the opposite team. The drill becomes continuous.

Coaching Points

- In the early stages of the practice, the players should control the ball first, dribble a little, and then look before they pass.
- As players become more proficient, they should work to improve aspects of their passing in the following order: accuracy, appropriate weighting or force (not too hard or too soft), proper ball position (on the ground, top roll, no spin).

Coaching Progressions

1. Players progress to one touch only to pass the ball.
2. Players decrease the distance between each other.
3. Players increase the speed of the practice (i.e., the speed of the pass and the running between the lines of players).

Drills for Intermediate Players

As players improve and move to the intermediate level, the coaching emphasis changes from basic techniques to finesse and maintaining skill while moving. Often, the ability to cope with an irregular bounce of the ball or an uneven surface is a sign of improvement.

Give and Move Back

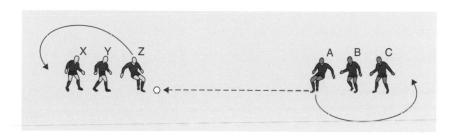

Equipment   One ball for every six players

Organization   Players are in two teams of three, facing each other 2 yards apart.

Instructions   Player A passes to player Z, but then quickly retires to the back of her team's line. Player Z passes to player B and retires to the back of her team's line. The drill becomes continuous.

Coaching Points

- Players should develop one-touch passing as quickly as their ability permits.
- Don't let them become discouraged if their early attempts fail, and teach them to impart top roll on the ball; players will soon realize that sidespin makes control difficult.
- Emphasize care and finesse; players should concentrate on and take pride in every pass.

Coaching Progressions

1. The teams move closer and closer together. This makes the practice really demanding and enjoyable.
2. The teams try to score more passes than their opponents in a given time frame (e.g., 30 seconds of one-touch passing). ■

Equipment   One ball for every six or eight players

Organization   Players are in two teams of three or four, facing each other at least 25 yards apart. One player (player W, who initially should be one of your better players) stands halfway between the teams and to the side by about 5 yards, to give a good passing angle.

Instructions   Player A dribbles a few yards, passes to player W, keeps running to receive a return pass from player W, collects the ball, dribbles, and then passes to player Z. Player A follows the pass to the back of the opposite team. Player Z repeats the sequence on the return. The drill becomes continuous.

Coaching Points

- The sequence for the player with the ball is control-dribble-look-pass.
- Each player should observe this sequence because this is the sequence that young players adopt in the game. You can encourage players to look before they pass by asking player W to move his position laterally.
- Players should strive for accuracy and correct weighting of the pass to the player W's feet.
- Player W should try to give an effective lead pass into the space ahead of the running player.

Coaching Progressions

1. Each player should take a turn as player W.
2. Players increase the speed of the practice while trying to retain accuracy and control. This is an excellent practice to develop into a shooting drill; the final pass becomes a shot on goal. ■

Drill for Advanced Players

For advanced players, the main objective is to keep both the passer and the receiver moving. For this reason, most advanced practices involve active opposition, although the following drill provides a useful introduction to them.

Layoff Passing

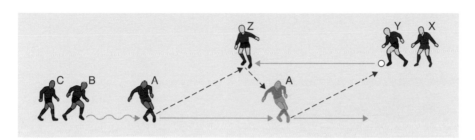

Equipment   One ball for every six or eight players

Organization   Players are in two teams of three or four, at least 25 yards apart, slightly set off from one another.

Instructions   Player A has the ball and, on command, players A and Z run toward each other. Player A passes to player Z, who gives an immediate one-touch return to player A. Player A controls and passes to player Y. Players Y and B follow the moves A and Z just completed. The drill becomes continuous.

Coaching Points

- Players must realize that skillful cooperation is vital.
- Player A should pass the ball accurately and firmly to the feet of player Z.
- Player Z should move to meet the ball and should work to develop a high degree of finesse with the pass to the space ahead of player A.

Coaching Progressions

1. This practice develops into a good shooting drill (chapter 8).
2. Players progress to one-touch passing.

Basic Techniques of Long Passing

The long pass is made, generally, when the ball is moving and the player has time and space to select her target for the pass. This often occurs when a midfield player is seeking to change the point of attack from one side of the field to the other, or when a winger centers the ball into the penalty area. Thus, the long pass requires both height and distance. The player achieves height with the pass by leaning back slightly, staying behind the ball, and kicking underneath the center line of the ball. The player achieves distance through a combination of factors: powerful swinging action with a high follow-through, a long lever (like a golf club), and an angled approach (approximately 45 degrees) to the intended line of flight.

When preparing for a long pass, the player lengthens the final stride to provide some forward momentum and to help with the long follow-though. Then, the player strikes the ball as it is moving, making contact underneath the center of the ball, with the leg straightening at the moment of impact and striking for distance rather than height and aiming for a high follow-through. See figure 5.4 for an example of a long pass.

Figure 5.4   Long pass.

Long passes are tactically important in several situations: making space by switching play from one side of the field to another, releasing a ball over the opponent's defense (or both), and when a winger crosses the ball into the penalty area. All of these situations call for accuracy, length, and height. A good long pass either lands at the feet of the receiver or is easily controlled by the receiver, or it lands on to the head of a forward. The problem with young players is that they may not have the power to make long passes. For this reason you have to help your beginners improve gradually. The following two drills, therefore, are for intermediate and advanced players. Beginners should concentrate on short passing and advance to long passing as their strength and technique improve.

Drill for Intermediate Players

We would expect an intermediate player to have reasonable accuracy and distance in long passing. To help with this, you can give him more time and space to prepare for the kick and omit opposition completely.

Long Passing

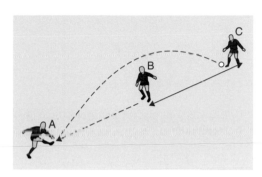

Equipment   One ball for every three players

Organization   Players are in teams of three, in a line with at least 15 yards between players, or they are on a coaching grid (see page 19).

Instructions   The central player (player B) has the ball. Player B rolls the ball to one of the end players (player A), who plays a long pass over the head (or past) player B to the far receiving player (player C). Player C controls the ball and returns it to player B. The practice is repeated, with each of the two end players practicing the long pass alternately.

Coaching Points

- Player B must always give a quality pass to players A and C. Such a pass requires a quality rolling ball with good top roll and no spinning or bouncing.
- Players A and C should concentrate on playing an accurate long pass that lands at the feet of the receiving player after a controlling touch to set up the ball for the pass.
- Players A and C must use a long-leg swing and follow-through. They should kick under the ball to gain height and keep their heads down.

Coaching Progressions

1. Player B tries to intercept the pass.
2. Players A and C pass directly to each other without player B playing the ball (i.e., 30-yard passing).
3. Players play the ball without stopping it first.
4. The passer tries to land the ball at the receiver's feet or a preordained target (e.g., the player's chest).
5. Players A and C use both feet. The ability to play a long, accurate pass with the weaker foot is the sign of a good player. ■

Drill for Advanced Players

To develop the long passing skills of advanced players, we have to introduce moving drills and practices and, gradually, opposition. For example, a winger might be required to sprint down the wing under pressure from a defending player and still cross the ball into the penalty area.

Long Passing on the Move

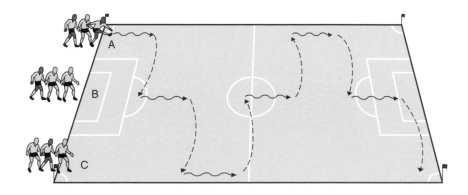

Equipment   One ball for every three players

Organization   For groups up to 12 players, players are in teams of three at one end of a soccer field. Players use the full width of the field. For groups larger than 12 (24 maximum), create two smaller areas by having players practice across the field, allocating one group to each half.

Instructions   Player A, with the ball, moves forward and then crosses or centers the ball to player B, who comes up to meet the ball. Player B controls, moves the ball forward, and gives a long, lofted pass to player C, who comes up to meet the ball. The drill becomes continuous as the players move along the field.

Coaching Points

- Players should lift their heads to know exactly where the receiver is and is moving to.
- Players should strike the ball with the toe down and hit through the bottom half of the ball to make it rise.
- Players should use a long swing of the kicking leg.
- Players should develop a high follow-through.
- Players should lean away from the ball.
- Players should keep the nonkicking foot well behind the ball.
- The controlling touch is vital in setting the ball up to deliver the pass to the next receiver.

Coaching Progressions

1. All three players move slowly and make the pass with the stronger foot.
2. Players use the foot that is farther from the receiver (i.e., the left foot when passing to the right and vice versa).
3. Players move quickly and deliver the ball as early and quickly as they can.
4. Players pass the ball with a first-time kicking movement (i.e., no time is allowed to control and dribble before kicking—this is a very challenging technique). ▪

Coaching the Mind of the Passer and Receiver

In a game players must decide and act for themselves. To help players learn how to make correct decisions, you should design realistic game situations that have the players acting as both passers and receivers. To do this effectively, you have to introduce decision-making situations through a series of small-team games (chapter 3).

Coaching the Mind of the Passer

When setting up small-team games for this level of coaching, you must create realistic situations involving support players and opponents. You can vary the numbers and the time–space variables, but the situations must be realistic.

Following are the three basic concepts you must get across to the passer:

1. *Control*

   The player must ask, Have I got full control of the ball?

2. *Look*

   The player must ask, Can I see a passing opportunity to a player who is in a better (safer) position to keep possession of the ball or use it more effectively? If not, the player should keep possession of the ball until a better opportunity arises.

3. *Pass*

   The passer must ask, Can I create a positive move by passing into an attacking space behind the opponent(s) for teammates to run into (i.e., make a killer pass between or through two or more defenders)?

Just as we do not take novice drivers onto the freeway, we do not put novice soccer players into situations that do not provide a reasonable chance of success. We have to introduce opposition gradually so that the passer can develop the correct sequence of control-look-pass. This sequence is the basis for most, if not all, of what you need to impart to your passers.

Drill for Beginners

The following is an excellent drill for coaching passing to the beginner in a realistic, gamelike environment. It provides a safety fence (a line or lines on the practice area over which defenders cannot cross) behind which young players can develop their confidence. Throughout this practice, beginners will need your constant encouragement and support as you tolerate their errors and manage their mistakes.

4v1 Outside the Square

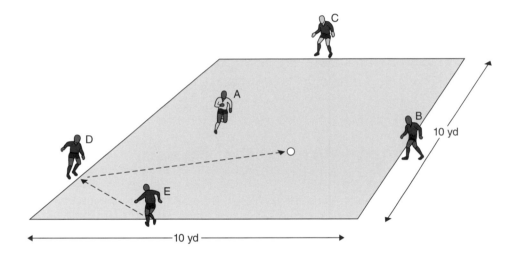

Equipment   One ball for every five players; four flags or cones

Organization   Players are in teams of five, and each team is on a 10- × 10-yard square. The defender (player A) is inside the square, and one attacker is on each side (players B, C, D, and E).

Instructions   The defender (player A) must remain within the square at all times and try to intercept the pass. The attackers (players, B, C, D, and E) may move sideways along their own lines, without the ball, to support each other. They may not step inside the square. The attackers try to pass the ball across the square to each other without interception by the defender. The defender is changed at intervals in rotation, such as after 10 successful passes by the attackers without interception by the defenders, after a preset time frame, or when the defender takes possession of the ball on three occasions.

Coaching Points

- Because the attackers cannot be tackled, they must be taught to show mastery over the ball and composure when performing.
- The attackers must lift their heads so they can read the situation before receiving the ball and when in possession.
- Players must use care and accuracy with the controlling touch to place the ball in a position that makes the task of passing the ball easier.
- The attackers must look for passing opportunities, or they must move the ball sideways to create passing opportunities.
- The attackers must execute quality passes with the appropriate speed and accuracy.

Coaching Progressions

1. The player with the ball has unlimited time to demonstrate control before making the pass.
2. The players have a maximum of two touches to release the ball to others.
3. Players waiting to receive a pass move sideways along their lines to create passing opportunities.
4. The player with the ball tries to feint or disguise a pass.
5. Players are challenged to use one-touch passes to other attackers if at all possible.
6. Players are encouraged to use various surfaces of the foot to pass the ball to other attackers.
7. Players pass to the player opposite wherever possible, not just to those on each side.

Drill for Intermediate Players

The next drill is an obvious and challenging progression from the previous drill. In this drill, certain passes may not be possible because of the positions of the defenders, so the player in possession must choose alternative passing options, which is the case in match play. Being able to notice the positions and movements of all other players in the practice, and act accordingly—always retaining possession of the ball—is the hallmark of an intelligent and improving young player. This drill again provides a safety fence (a line or lines on the practice area over which defenders cannot cross) behind which young players can develop their confidence.

2v4 Outside the Square

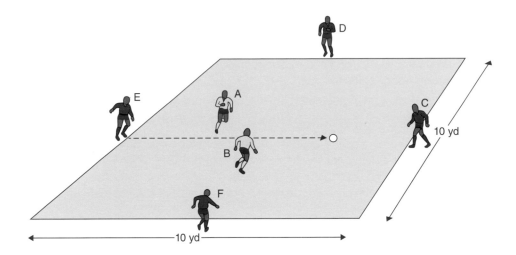

Equipment   One ball for six players; four flags or cones

Organization   Players are in teams of six, each team on a 10- × 10-yard square. Two defenders (players A and B) are in the square, and one attacker is on each side (players C, D, E, and F).

Instructions   The defenders (players A and B) must remain within the square at all times and try to intercept the pass. The attackers (players, C, D, E, and F) may move sideways along their own lines, without the ball, to support each other. They may not step inside the square. The attackers try to pass the ball across the square to each other without interception by the defenders. The objective is to deliver a killer pass (or through pass) between the two defenders if possible. The defenders are changed at intervals in rotation either after a certain time period or a certain number of passes from the attackers.

Coaching Points

- The player in possession should try to fake or disguise the pass and may have to dribble sideways to create a passing opportunity.

- All players should keep their heads up and notice the positions of other attacking players so they can look for the killer pass before receiving the ball and when in possession.

- The supporting attackers should try to make the killer pass possible through good movement and support positioning.

- While the drill is underway, move around the outside of the square and coach from behind the players. This way, you can speak quietly to players, reinforce good decisions, and see the same situation as the players, thus sharing their experiences.

- Repeat the key words: *look-control-look-pass.* Encourage players to remain composed during the practice, which will help them remain calm and make intelligent decisions as opposed to playing too anxiously or hurriedly.

- The players should attempt to move the ball quickly and accurately to each other so as to make the defenders change their positions frequently and so create the opening between the defenders through which the passes can be made.

Coaching Progressions

1. Players use one-touch passing whenever possible and if confident to do so.

2. Players use more advanced passes with the instep and outside of the foot; good players use swerve passes between and around defenders, although this may be difficult in a 10-yard square (if necessary, expand the area to 20 × 20 yards to ensure success). ■

Drills for Advanced Players

For advanced players, you can use the previous two drills, but remove the safety fence between the attacker and the defenders to add game realism and demonstrate the difference between passing directly to the feet of a supporting player and passing to a space into which the receiver must move. To further develop these skills with advanced players, use the small-team passing games explained in detail near the end of the chapter, beginning on page 84.

Coaching the Mind of the Receiver

A pass that is inaccurate or for some reason causes the receiver to lose possession is useless. Your problem is determining which player, if any, is responsible for the mistake. Did the passer pass too hard, too soon, or too late, or did the receiver fail to anticipate the developing situation? We now consider coaching the receiver; we will start by considering an old soccer adage, When not in possession, get into position.

Players who are not in possession of the ball should have only one thought in their minds—support. With younger players you might also use the word *help*. *Help* is a friendly term, and questions such as, "Chris, where can you go to help?" can allow you to get the message across clearly. Impress on players that a willingness to help is essential for good teamwork. Often, players have to make many unselfish runs without ever receiving a pass. The willingness to keep on running for the sake of the team is at the heart of every successful team; this attitude and spirit cannot be fostered too soon.

If players have the right attitude and are prepared to make unselfish runs, even if they do not receive the ball, you can help them to make correct judgments about where to support and show them how and when to move into position.

Where to Support

Basically, the supporting player moves as the game demands into a support position. That may be behind, to the side of, or in front of opponents (through 360 degrees in fact) so as to receive from the player with the ball. To make the correct decision as to where to support the player in possession of the ball, players must be able to read the play.

Reading the play is a skill like any other that can be learned. To take up the correct support position, the player must assess the positions and movements of other attacking players and opponents, and know the passing ability of the player in possession of the ball. If the player with the ball is closely pressed by an opponent and does not have the space and angle to play the ball through wide angles, then the supporting player should move to a position to the side of the pressuring opponent. This may well be slightly behind, or even in front of, the defender, but at an angle largely to the side of the defender.

If the player with the ball does have the space to play the ball forward, then the supporting player may take up a more advanced position, which could even be behind an opponent. These are relatively simple decisions to make, providing players are helped to recognize these situations. Following are a couple of scenarios to help your players understand the concept of support:

Situation: The attacker (player Z) is prevented by the defenders (players A, B, and C) from playing the ball forward. Player Z needs help.

Solution: Go behind. Support players need to help player Z by moving closer and to the side of defenders A and B, as shown in figure 5.5. If player Z then plays the ball back, the support players will be able to play the ball forward.

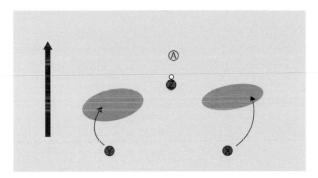

Figure 5.5   Support by going behind.

Situation: The attacker (player Z) has the ball with ample space to play the ball forward. If player Z dribbles the ball forward, he may commit the defender (player A). But the longer player Z dribbles, the longer the move is delayed and the more the ability to play the ball forward is lost. Player Z needs help.

Solution: Go in front. Support players must, in this case, run toward and take up attacking positions behind player A, as shown in figure 5.6. Player Z can now play the ball forward into positions behind player A.

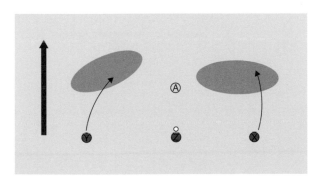

Figure 5.6   Support by going in front.

Safe Passing Angles

All players must know what is meant by a safe passing angle. Basically, this is a matter of geometry. For example, if the attacker (player A) is covered by the defender (player Z) and does not have the space to play the ball forward, the safe passing angle is backward and away from the defender (see figure 5.7).

Figure 5.7 Safe passing angles for a tightly marked attacker.

Alternately, if player A is not tightly marked and does have space to play the ball forward, then the safest and best pass may be forward, past the defender at a 45-degree angle, which is the safest position (see figure 5.8).

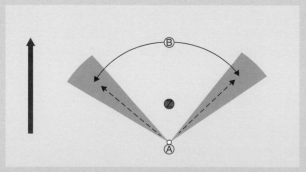

Figure 5.8 Safe passing angles for an open attacker.

As mentioned, an angle of about 45 degrees is the safest. A square (or sideways) pass is risky because if the defender intercepts it, at least two players are caught out of position—the passer and the intended receiver (player B), as shown in figure 5.9.

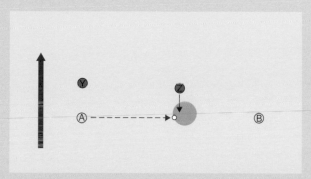

Figure 5.9   A square pass by player A is intercepted by player Z.

In figure 5.9, player A has the ball, but because he or she is contained by the defender (player Y), player A tries to make a square pass to player B. Player Z moves forward quickly and intercepts the pass. At this moment, players A and B are both caught out of position, and other team members, who should have been moving forward in support, are also likely caught out of position. Worse, the opposition has the initiative, and both players Y and Z can move forward and attack with confidence. In this situation, player A has several safer and better alternatives, such as the following:

- Make a much more positive attempt to beat player Y.
- Play a killer pass between players Y and Z for player C.
- Pass between players Y and Z for player B to move into beyond the two defenders, or receive support from behind from player B, who reads the pressure from player Y. In this instance, player A simply passes the ball backward to player B, who now has the space to play the ball forward past the defenders or over their heads. This is a very simple but very effective move.

How and Where to Move

Always be prepared to spend time showing your players where, when, and how to support the player in possession of the ball. Three basic attacking moves are the curved run, diagonal run, and blindside run.

1. *Curved Run*

    Here the player moves on a wide, circular arc that takes her out of sight and away from the defender and also increases the target area for the passer. This is often referred to as an overlapping run and is frequently employed by fullbacks moving beyond flank players (see figure 5.10).

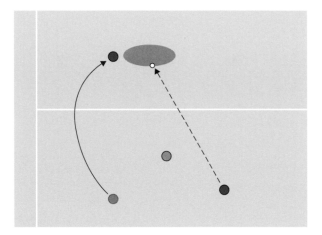

Figure 5.10 Curved run.

2. *Diagonal Run*

    With this run the player moves diagonally across the field of play and behind opponents as he moves. Such a movement, provided the player doesn't run offside, increases the chances of penetration, gives a forward target for the passer, and may also cause defenders to track the run thereby creating pass routes to other attackers. The run is a feature of clever and quick forward players looking to penetrate the opposition defense in and around the penalty area (see figure 5.11).

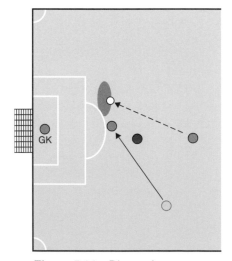

Figure 5.11 Diagonal run.

3. *Blindside Run*

The other popular name for this move is the backdoor run. The objective of the run is to take advantage of the unsighted defender by moving unseen behind her line of vision. Such a run increases the chances of penetration and provides the passer with an easier target. This run is frequently used by midfield players who run behind their midfield opponents on their journey to goal-scoring positions in the penalty box, especially from crosses from the flank (see figure 5.12).

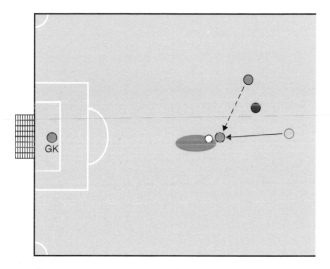

Figure 5.12   Blindside, or backdoor, run.

Drill for Beginners

When coaching receivers, we recommend games that involve three attackers against one defender—even for beginners. The reason is that using 4v1 can result in the four receivers standing relatively static in the four corners and simply passing the ball. This defeats the objective of teaching the receivers to think and move for themselves in relation to the movement of other players and the ball.

3v1 Piggy in the Middle

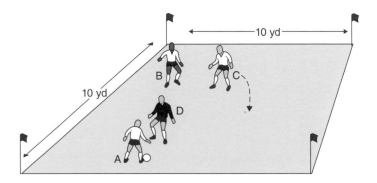

Equipment   One ball for every four players; four flags or cones; a bib for the defender in the square

Organization   Players are in groups of four (three attackers and one defender) according to their basic ability. Each group is in a 10- × 10-yard or 15- × 15-yard square marked by flags or cones.

Instructions   The attackers have to pass the ball and keep it away from the defender. They are given a goal, such as 10 consecutive passes without interception by the defender. When the defender intercepts the ball on three occasions, he changes places with one of the attackers.

Coaching Points

- Remember that you are coaching the receivers, not the passer.
- Receivers should look for and move into the spaces either to the side, behind, or in front of the defender.
- By using the full width and depth of the square, the attacking players will have more space and time in which to receive and decide on their next actions.
- Receivers should try to present safe passing angles quickly.
- Players should continually assess their best supporting position in relation to the movements of the passer, the defender, the ball, and other supporting players. Each player's key thought should be, Where, when, and how do I support?

Coaching Progressions

1. To emphasize the movement off the ball by the receivers, players can start by playing basketball but quickly change to soccer. They should play basketball with the ball always below head height until the attempt to score.

2. Use the playback system to highlight a good move by a receiver (see chapter 14 for more information).

3. If the players are not doing well, wait until one or both supporting players are caught in poor support positions, and then, using the double positive approach discussed in chapter 2 and the playback system you will learn about in chapter 14, explain the following: Player A has the ball. Players B and C are in those poor positions because neither can receive a pass from player A. Using a positive opening comment, such as, "You are running hard but . . ." show the players what is wrong, or let them tell you what is wrong, and restart the game with a correct move and pass. An even more powerful positive statement would be: "You are working very hard *and* if you were also to move into positions where you can receive a pass to your feet, that would be even better." Then, let player C move into his new and correct supporting position and let player A make a correct pass to player C. When the ball reaches player C, restart the game. This method of restarting a practice reinforces the importance of the receiver moving into position.

Drill for Intermediate and Advanced Players

Drills for intermediate and advanced players require either more players or a changed ratio between attackers and defenders. For example, the Piggy in the Middle drill, as described previously, can be increased to four attackers versus two defenders or even four attackers versus three defenders; these situations make it much harder for the receivers to find space and support the passer. Outnumbering the attackers provides even more challenge (e.g., four defenders versus three attackers) because the attackers really have to work hard to become good receivers. Of course, the dimensions of the playing area and the rules would need to accommodate the changes in numbers and the increased challenge. Following is a drill that has proved very successful at the college level. It is a one-on-one situation in which the attacker tries to make and receive passes from four static passers.

Corner-to-Corner Practice

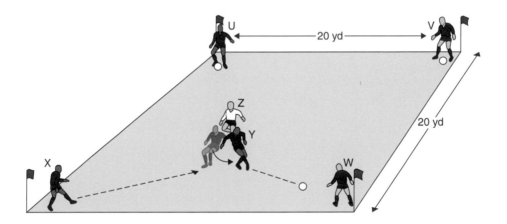

Equipment   Three balls for every six players; four flags or cones

Organization   Players are in teams of six, and each team is in a 20- × 20-yard square marked by flags or cones.

Instructions   A player stands in each corner; three of these players have a ball. The fourth player does not have a ball and acts as the first receiver. None of the corner players may move more than 2 yards in any direction from their corners. Of the two players in the square, one is the attacker (player Y), and one is the defender (player Z).

On command, player Y collects a pass from any of the three corner players with a ball, and then, by moving and dribbling, finds a way to avoid player Z and deliver a successful pass to the corner player without a ball (X). If the pass reaches player X successfully, then player Y immediately moves back into the middle of the square and invites a pass from one of the two remaining players with a ball (he may not get a return pass from player X). Having received this pass, player Y must again try to avoid player Z and deliver a successful pass to the player without a ball.

Coaching Points

- Concentrate on the attacker, not the defender.
- Player Y should create space to receive the ball by moving away from the defender with sudden changes of speed or direction.
- The receiving player should go to meet the ball while being mindful of the proximity of the defender.
- Attackers should, where needed, screen the ball (keep their body between the ball and the defender) to create time and space.
- Players should show composure and avoid panic.
- Attackers should see which corner is free before collecting the ball.
- Having made one pass, attackers should move immediately and quickly to receive another.

Coaching Progressions

1. The defender assumes a passive role to allow the attacker to learn the drill.
2. The defender becomes more aggressive as the attacker improves.
3. The defender forces the attacker to receive a pass from the corner farthest from the open corner.
4. The attacker plays continuously for up to 2 minutes (note that this can be physically demanding, especially for young players). ■

Drill for All-Star Players

As players develop technically and tactically, you should increase the challenge to simulate the game itself as closely as possible. All-star-rated players need practice at game tempo with all the elements present in the game itself. Also, because these players need to make gamelike decisions, the practice always needs opposition, direction, teammates, limits, and incentives. The following drill presents each of these factors.

Directional Possession Play

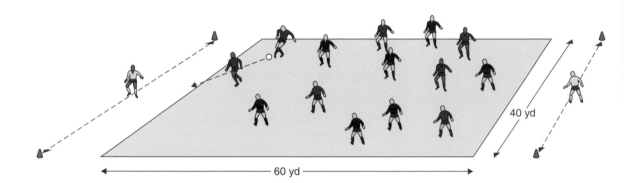

Purpose
To develop the ability to pass the ball in any direction but to prioritize the skill of passing forward toward a target (e.g., in a game situation to a striker or behind the defense for a receiver)

Equipment
Six soccer balls; different-colored bibs for each team and two additional bibs of a different color; cones to mark the dimensions of the playing area

Organization
Players are in two teams of equal numbers (e.g., six or seven on each team), and there are two target players, one at each end of the full playing area. The playing area is 60 × 40 yards in dimension but may be decreased if the players are of a high technical standard. The two target players are "neutral"; they play for whichever team has possession of the ball and never defend.

Instructions
A target player operating on each end line 10 yards behind the playing area may move anywhere along this line to receive the ball. He returns the ball to whichever team passed to him. The two teams of equal numbers may use the two target (neutral) players as they attack the opposition. The objective is for the team in possession to retain the ball as it progresses up the field to play it to the target player.

Any player can move anywhere to receive the ball, but it may help to give some structure to each team (e.g., two defenders, two midfield players, and two attacking players). Once the ball is played to the target player behind the opponents, then the successful team will receive a further ball from the target player playing behind their own team. Consequently, the practice is directional, with one team playing in one direction and the other playing toward the opposite target player. Work from the sideline and feed the ball into the practice when it leaves the field of play other than when it reaches the target players.

The goal is to be the team that is the most successful in passing to the target player in, for example, a 4-minute period. If the attack is successful and the ball reaches the intended target player, a further attempt can be carried out immediately by the successful team without the opposition ever having possession of the ball.

Coaching Points

- When in possession, the attacking team should disperse as widely as possible to create space and therefore time in which to receive the ball from teammates (dispersal meaning from end to end, from side to side, and in the central spaces created by this action).

- Before, or as, any player receives the ball, others must decide as early as possible what to do—to support the player in possession at the correct angle so as to receive the ball, to stay away from the player in possession so as to occupy opponents and therefore leave space for teammates in which to operate, or to make runs to drag opponents away from other possible pass receivers.

- In possession, the player must decide from a number of alternatives which pass is needed under the circumstance—one that simply retains possession but changes the point and line of the attack, one that sets a teammate free to make forward progress, one that penetrates the defense, or one that enables the passer to move forward quickly to receive the return pass (i.e., the wall pass).

- All of the passing and supporting techniques explained in this chapter will be relevant to and inherent in this practice. Your role is to help the player, if necessary, choose the most effective pass (tactical decisions) and to remind the player of the necessary details of delivering the chosen pass (technical efficiency). At all times you should observe the decisions made and the quality of the passes in terms of accuracy, timing, speed, and where necessary, disguise.

Coaching Progressions

1. Limit players to two touches of the ball (one if appropriate and possible).
2. All passes must be delivered below head height.
3. Passes to the target player must be delivered to hands raised above the head (passes may then be delivered in the air).
4. Passes to the target player can only be delivered from the attacking half of the field.
5. Choices of progression variations are endless; your job is to modify the practice conditions and rules to meet the needs of your players. ■

Small-Team Passing Games

This chapter has discussed the passer, the receiver, and the techniques of passing. In real games, the successful combination of all three of these elements, as well as successful decision making, is the hallmark of good play. An excellent way to combine these elements in practice is through the use of small-team games, which involve both opposition and supporting players and which, when we want to focus on a particular skill, can be conditioned to highlight a desired outcome. (*Conditioning* means imposing rules to meet the required outcome of the practice. For example, you may require one-touch control, require all passes to be below knee height, or not allow players to tackle. The conditions you can impose are limitless; their usefulness lies in allowing you to focus on a specific skill or desired outcome for the benefit of the players.)

The following games offer a variety of purposeful and enjoyable activities for players of all levels. However, remember the major principle—coach the players, not the drill.

Game for Beginners

The following game, Soccer Baseball, is appropriate for beginners. It is designed for younger players to emphasize that a pass has to be both accurate and forceful. However, note that it is also enjoyable for older players.

Equipment One ball for eight players; four flags or cones

Organization Players of equal ability are in two teams of four, each team on a 10- × 10-yard square marked by flags or cones.

Instructions The fielding team places one player on each base (players A, B, C, and D). On the command "Go," these players (starting with player A) pass the ball around

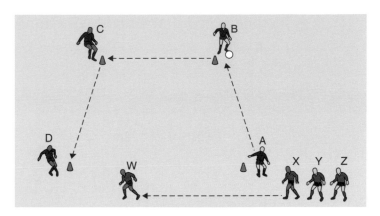

Figure 1

the outside of the bases and back to player A. The batting team players (players W, X, Y, and Z) stand at the corner of the square near player A. On the command "Go," the batter (player W as shown in figure 1) sprints around the square in the direction opposite the path of the ball. The batter scores a run if he gets back to the home base before the ball. Each player has one turn, and then the teams change. Any number of innings can be played. If the batter touches the ball or a player when running, he is out.

Coaching Points

- Batters should run quickly but also watch where the ball is. Fielders should pass carefully, accurately, and quickly.

- Fielders should aim at the feet of the receiver after making sure to use a first touch that helps them pass efficiently.

- Fielders should try to give quality passes—firm, fast, and with top roll to the feet of the receiver.

Coaching Progressions

1. The batters run around the square twice to score a home run (great training!).

2. The batters run once around the bases while dribbling a soccer ball, and at the same time the fielding team passes the ball both clockwise and counterclockwise around the bases.

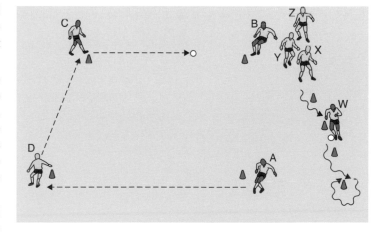

Figure 2

3. The batters, instead of dribbling around the bases, dribble in and out of four cones arranged as shown in figure 2. The number of cones for the dribbling team will vary depending on the ability of your players. ■

Games for Intermediate Players

The following small-team games progressively increase the physical and mental demands made on intermediate players.

Five Attackers Versus Two Defenders

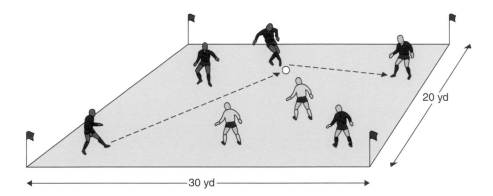

Equipment   One ball for seven players; four flags or cones; different-colored bibs for the teams

Organization   Players are in teams of seven (five attackers, two defenders), positioned in a 30- × 20-yard rectangle marked by flags or cones in the penalty area.

Instructions   Attackers keep possession and make as many successful passes as possible as the defenders attempt to dispossess them of the ball. Players changes roles at intervals (e.g., after 10 passes by the attackers, after three interceptions by the defenders, or after 30 or 45 seconds of high-intensity defending by the two defenders).

Coaching Points
- This game is an excellent starting point from which to develop team play. The generous ratio of attackers to defenders makes it fairly easy for players to combine successfully and produce effective passing sequences. (With young players, you can make the practice even easier by changing to 6v1, thus giving them even more time and space in which to think and act.)
- It is also a good idea to occasionally act as one of the defenders yourself. Your joining in always stimulates players and gives you an opportunity to help the weaker players. For example, you can control the situation in their favor by moving toward them, but not actually tackling—that is, by offering passive resistance. Be careful, though, when joining practice with youngsters because you have the physical advantage; consider any physical contact carefully and exercise control to prevent injury to the junior player.

Coaching Progressions
1. Players must pass below knee height.
2. Players are limited to two or three touches before passing.
3. Players develop specific passes (e.g., a killer pass or one-touch passing). ■

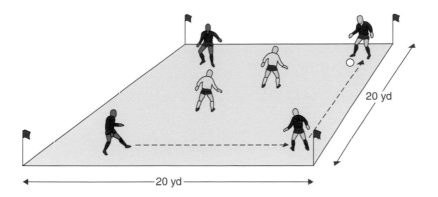

Equipment One ball for six players; four flags or cones; different-colored bibs for the teams

Organization Players are in teams of six (four attackers, two defenders), and each team is in a 20- × 20-yard square marked by flags or cones.

Instructions Attackers try to retain possession of the ball and attempt to score a predetermined number of passes or hold the ball for a predetermined time (e.g., after 1 minute or a total of 12 consecutive passes). Defenders try to win possession. Players change roles at intervals.

Coaching Points

- The passer should show composure and awareness in looking for the opportunity to pass before receiving the ball and also when in possession.
- The receiver should make as much space as possible to receive the pass.
- The passer should have two players at good supporting angles. Weak passers should continue to serve as attackers until they improve (they need more passing practice to improve).

Coaching Progressions

1. The player in possession screens the ball, and the players not in possession work hard to give good support.
2. The passing team may use a maximum of two touches, if possible.
3. Players have longer and longer periods of passing without losing possession (i.e., the challenge is to have 20 consecutive passes before an interception).
4. The passer screens the ball until passing opportunities arise. ■

Games for Advanced Players

In all small-team games it is important to demand high standards from your players. Insisting on a good response becomes increasingly important when coaching advanced players in small-team situations; realism and a competitive edge are vital ingredients.

Three Attackers Versus Two Defenders

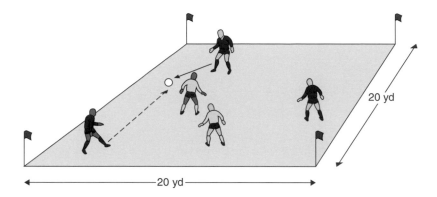

Equipment   One ball for five players; four flags or cones; different-colored bibs for the teams

Organization   Players are in teams of five (three attackers, two defenders), and each team is in a 20- × 20-yard square marked by flags or, preferably, cones or in the center circle.

Instructions   The game starts with the attackers in possession. The attackers try to retain possession or make a specified number of passes. The defenders try to win possession with and without tackling.

Coaching Points

- The passer should strive for increased control of the ball—encourage screening, feinting, and dribbling.
- Attackers should always seek the maximum space and good angles when supporting others in possession of the ball.
- Receivers should develop blindside moves.

Coaching Progressions

1. One of the three attackers is designated as a floater. When the defenders win the ball, the floater moves over to their side and those three players then become the attackers. Each person has a turn being the floater, so that all players get to practice passing.
2. Players have conditions, such as a having to use a specific type of pass or having to make only two touches when in possession. ■

Equipment   One ball for five players; four flags or cones; different-colored bibs for the teams

Organization   Players are in teams of five (three attackers, two defenders). A goalkeeper is positioned in the goal.

Instructions   To easily change the previous 3v2 game from small-team practice to an advanced tactical or team practice, we simply move the activity to the area just outside the penalty area. The three attackers now must beat the two defenders by maneuvering the player with the ball into the penalty area; this player finishes with a shot at the goal.

Coaching Point
- Increase realism by introducing direction and a goal. This immediately highlights the importance of close control and the ability to turn with the ball, dribble past defenders, and shoot.

Coaching Progressions
1. After the attacker gets into the penalty area with the ball, he then moves into a 1v1 situation against the goalkeeper.
2. Players must observe the offside rule when attempting to enter the penalty area.
3. The practice starts with different kinds of serves from the coach—lofted, ground pass, or volley pass. ■

Games for All-Star Players

As the standard of your players improves, you should increase the complexity and realism of the small-team games they play. By doing this, you maintain a high level of ball contact, which you would lose in a full 11v11 situation. At the same time, you highlight the particular passing skills and moves you wish to focus on. The following drill emphasizes how to keep or regain possession of the ball and then switch play.

Possession to Switch the Play

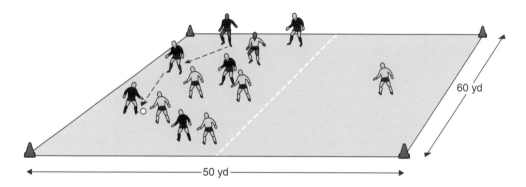

Equipment   A supply of soccer balls; different-colored bibs for the teams; marker cones

Organization   Two teams of equal numbers (e.g., 6v6) play on half of a soccer field or an area appropriate to the numbers available for the practice (e.g., 6v6 on an area of 60 × 50 yards) set off by cones or flags. One team positions one player in one half of the playing area and all other players in the other half of the playing area.

Instructions   One team receives the ball from you and attempts to retain possession for 20 consecutive passes. The other team attempts to gain possession and, when successful, transfers the ball accurately and quickly to its player in the other half. All players then move to the other half as quickly as possible except for one player from the team that had possession first, who remains behind, and the game continues.

Coaching Points

- The team in possession should disperse within its half of the playing area to create space and therefore time to pass the ball more comfortably and efficiently to reach the passing total.
- Constant awareness and adjustment of the supporting position is essential to success.
- Simple, quick, and well-timed passes will make it difficult for the defenders to gain possession of the ball.

- The defending team will likely be able to regain possession of the ball if the nearest defender presses the ball holder and if others support the "presser" by marking the attackers near to the player in possession and by anticipating passes. The least important opponent is likely to be the one farthest from the ball if pressure has been applied quickly and effectively and is well supported by others.

- On gaining possession, the now-attacking team should attempt to find its player in the other half of the area as quickly and accurately as possible. If the team members can't do so immediately, they should pass the ball quickly with the minimum of touches to find an opportunity to deliver the required pass effectively.

- Once the target player receives the pass, he will need quick support, as is the case in a full game situation. A number of passes can be accumulated before the opposition arrives to press and attempt to regain the ball.

Coaching Progressions

1. Each team positions two players in the half opposite from that occupied by the majority of the players.

2. The team in possession can pass using two touches or one, if at all possible.

3. All passes except those delivered to the target players must be delivered below head height.

4. Players can use combination plays (e.g., wall passes) and killer passes played through opponents to players behind them. These more difficult passes can be rewarded with double points in the quest for the 20-pass target. ■

Larger Game Situations

We now move to larger game situations, appropriate for advanced and all-star players, which require increasing mental and technical skills. Because they are played in a larger area, they are more similar to the full-game situation. Larger game situations require a wide range of individual responses from the players, who increasingly must think for themselves. Rotating Goalkeepers is a good example of a passing game that also requires players to react quickly to the need to act as goalkeepers.

Rotating Goalkeepers

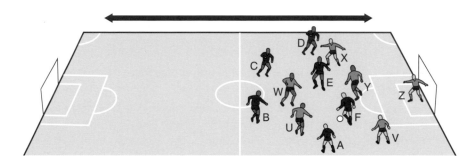

Equipment   One ball for 12 players; different-colored bibs for the teams; two small goals

Organization   Players are in two teams of six players of equal ability on half of a soccer field.

Instructions   The game starts with a throw or service from you. The team that fails to gain possession must immediately put one player in its goal (usually the nearest player to goal). When ball possession changes, so does the goalkeeper. Thus, the game always involves one goalkeeper plus 5v6. The team in possession always has the extra field player.

Coaching Points

- Players must see the breakdown point (i.e., when the ball changes possession) and react accordingly by attacking quickly toward the opponents' goal, if possible before the defense can recover and position to defend in numbers (i.e., counterattack).

- As attackers become defenders on losing possession, they have to close down quickly on their opponents or position themselves between the ball and their own goal.

- As defenders become attackers, they must move away from their opponents and look for spaces behind the defense or go wide.

- Players should think for themselves.
- Players should realize the importance of keeping possession and passing forward intelligently and accurately whenever possible.

Coaching Progressions

1. Players observe certain conditions, such as the offside rule or the use of two touches only when in possession.
2. On gaining possession, the attacking team must shoot at the opponents' goal within 8 seconds, for example, to encourage a counterattacking mentality. ■

Four Goals

Equipment   Four small goals; a supply of soccer balls

Organization   Players are in small teams of equal size and ability (e.g., 6v6) on a 50- × 40-yard area with goals positioned in the center of all four sides of the grid. Each team has two goalkeepers.

Instructions   Play progresses as for soccer, but players cannot be offside or score in the same goal twice in succession. Players change roles at intervals, acting as both goalkeepers and outfield players.

Coaching Points

- Do not overcoach. Players should discover for themselves what to do when they have to defend two goals or attack two goals.
- Coach individual players in mental skills and the art of reading the game.

Coaching Progressions

1. Attackers try to switch their attack quickly by using longer passes.
2. Defenders try to contain the attackers in a small area and prevent a direct shot at goal.
3. When possession changes or the ball is thrown into play by a goalkeeper, attackers try to look for open spaces while defenders move to cover and mark attackers in dangerous positions. ■

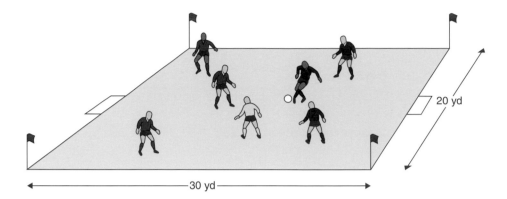

Purpose   To emphasize rapid reaction when a team gains or loses possession

Equipment   A supply of soccer balls; four flags or cones; two small goals; different-colored bibs for the teams plus a unique-colored bib for the floater

Organization   Players are in two teams of two to seven players, with one floater, in a playing area marked by flags or cones. Allow a minimum of 10 square yards for each player; for example, six players need 60 yards, or a 20- × 30-yard area.

Instructions   Play progresses as for soccer, and the floater always plays for the team in possession of the ball. When the ball changes possession, the floater changes sides. Teams try to make use of the floater where appropriate and benefit from the extra player. No goalkeepers (players who can use their hands) are used in this game. The team in possession should aim to complete 20 passes.

Coaching Point

- When players gain possession, they should use their extra player by moving out into wider, more open spaces and being prepared to run with the ball until they attract one or more defenders and can release the pass. This should create more space for the new receiver of the ball.

Coaching Progressions

1. Introduce goalkeepers. This immediately adds the problem of direction to the game with the game now becoming 4v4 plus a floater.
2. Players must observe the offside rule. ■

Dribbling

6

CLOSE DRIBBLING TO beat an opponent is probably the most excit-ing and creative of all the skills of soccer. Like all skills, it can be learned and improved, but dribbling is also an art, and players of outstanding ability always possess a natural flair or talent.

Dribbling involves a combination of physical and mental skills. Physical skills are needed to control the movement of the ball; mental skills are needed to know which movement to select and when and how to initiate it. The physi-cal skills are more easily listed; they require that the player do the following:

- Keep the ball within playing distance. This means that the player can reach out and touch the ball at all times while dribbling it.
- Remain balanced and able to move in any direction, even backward, when dragging the ball back and away from the opponent to create the time and space to execute a move.
- Have a series of practiced moves, which, once selected, have a reason-able chance of success.
- "See" the ball at her feet in addition to the developing situation, the other players, and the possible tactical opportunities, using peripheral vision. For beginners, developing this ability—to see the ball and the big picture—begins with drills such as Dribbling Pen (page 102). For intermediate and advanced players, seeing the ball and the situation is at the heart of the five basic ways to beat an opponent (see page 108).

The mental, or decision-making, aspects of dribbling are more challenging for the player to learn and for you to teach. Mental skills involve the following:

- Having confidence when in possession of the ball to initiate positive moves
- Watching how the opponents are positioned or are moving, especially their feet (more information about this can be found on page 105)
- Being prepared to react to the movement of an opponent, as well as to take the opponent on by making positive rather than negative decisions

Dribbling for Beginners

Beginners have to develop a sense of touch and control. Often, beginners kick the ball forward and run after it. To avoid this, they must learn how to play the ball forward gently with a relaxed foot. The next six practices encourage these skills and provide a rich variety of activities that will act as a springboard for many other games and activities of your own design.

Equipment   One ball for each player

Organization   Players are in a group of unlimited number in a designated area (e.g., the center circle).

Instructions   Players take the ball for a walk, jog, or run, keeping it as close to their feet as possible and not making contact with any other player or any other player's ball. Players cannot move outside the designated area.

Coaching Points

- Players should touch the ball gently, adjusting the angle of the foot to use the big or little toe and pushing the ball while relaxing the foot.
- Players should raise the head slightly rather than looking directly down onto the ball so as to see the other players in the dribbling area.

Coaching Progressions

1. The players respond to your whistle or call to start and stop the ball with their feet.
2. Increase the tempo of the game by reducing the time between the stop and start commands.

Follow the Leader

Figure 1

Figure 2

Equipment   One ball for each player

Organization   Players face the coach as shown in figure 1, or stand in a line as shown in figure 2.

Instructions   Players mimic your actions and follow your pathways.

Coaching Points

- Players should achieve a low center of gravity by bending their knees slightly, with their bodies slightly crouched and weight evenly balanced. Players should keep the ball close and hold their arms out sideways for balance.
- Players should use the inside and outside of the foot to change direction from side to side.
- Players should use the sole of the foot to pull the ball backward.
- Players should be alert to rapid changes of speed and direction.

Coaching Progressions

1. Increase the tempo of the movement. Players walk, then jog slowly, then move in various directions and at various speeds.
2. Fake moves by lifting your foot over and around the ball and exhibiting a variety of dribbling moves that the players must attempt to follow.

Equipment   One ball for each player; up to five cones

Organization   Players are in teams of three. Cones are set up at 5-yard intervals.

Instructions   Going one at a time, players use various methods of moving and controlling the ball between and around the cones before returning to the starting point.

Coaching Points

- Players should touch the ball as often as possible and should avoid kicking and running.
- Players should keep the ball close to their feet.
- Players should look ahead of the ball to see the position of the cones.

Coaching Progressions

1. Players increase the tempo of the dribbles.
2. Players engage in simple relays and competitions among themselves and between teams.
3. Players repeat the progressions with reduced gaps between the cones.

Ball Dancing

Equipment   One ball for each player

Organization   Players are in a designated area (e.g., the center circle).

Instructions   Using alternating feet, players touch or tap the top of the ball with the underside of their toes.

Coaching Points

- Players should tap or touch the ball gently and continuously—like running in place—to develop a rhythm.
- Players should hold their arms out for balance.

Coaching Progressions

1. Players apply pressure when touching the ball to make it roll gently backward.
2. Players make the ball go forward, sideways, or in the pattern of a square.
3. Players make other patterns, such as their initials.

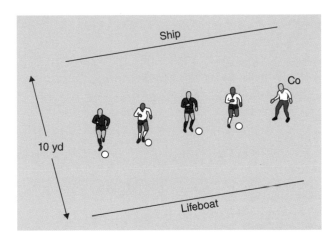

Equipment   One ball for each player; four flags or cones

Organization   Players stand in a line with about 2 yards between them. On either side of the line of players is a parallel line, marked by flags or cones; these two lines are about 10 yards apart. One is the ship; the other is the lifeboat.

Instructions   On the command "Ship" or "Lifeboat," players dribble their balls to the correct line. On the command "Freeze," all players put a foot on the ball and stop it. On the command "Goalkeeper," they fall on the ball and pull it toward their chest (this adds excitement and helps to improve reaction time).

After a period of time, the game then becomes an elimination game; the last player to reach the line is eliminated. However, all eliminated players then go to the back of the line of remaining players and continue to play the game. This keeps everyone involved until the game is over.

Coaching Points

- Players should keep the ball close to their feet.
- Players should stay alert and listen carefully to the calls.

Coaching Progressions

1. Sharpen players' wits by calling "Ship" when players are already on the ship line, or "Freeze" when they are already still.
2. Change calls with increasing rapidity.
3. Make the drill into a game of elimination—the last to respond is out.

Dribbling for Intermediate Players

Thought processes are the main difference between the beginner and the intermediate player. For the beginner, just thinking about the ball is challenging enough, but intermediate players should be able to divide their attention between the ball and what is going on around them. This skill is further developed as players improve. This section includes two drills for intermediate players.

Dribbling Pen

Equipment   One ball for each player

Organization   Players are divided into two groups—a working group and a resting and watching group. They are divided because, done properly, this is a strenuous activity (note that on cold days, you can have all players work). Players move freely within a designated area (e.g., the center circle).

Instructions   Players dribble the ball in the playing area, keeping it close. Give commands such as the following:

- Move freely about the zone in all directions, not just forward.
- Use the sole of your foot to drag the ball backward to make space in front, and the inside and outside of your foot to make forward, diagonal, and sideways directional changes.
- Use combination moves and sequences (e.g., quick two-footed movements when contacting the ball).

- See how far ahead you can look and still see the ball at your feet using peripheral vision. You should be able to see the ball while staying aware of the surrounding actions, such as where your opponents are and how much space is between them.
- Use feints and fakes before you contact the ball, exaggerating the fake by using your eyes, head, shoulders, and arms; by taking your body over the line of the ball; and by moving your foot over the ball.

Coaching Points

- Players should keep their heads up so that they can peruse the playing area while retaining sight of the ball.
- Players should relax the foot that is playing the ball and develop gentle control.
- Players should not kick and follow, but try to finesse the ball, always keeping it under control as they move.
- Players should develop an awareness of how far ahead they can move the ball while still keeping it under control according to the proximity of other players.

Coaching Progressions

1. Players look for and move into open space as the tempo of the practice increases.
2. Introduce opposition and develop confidence in your players. For instance, one player may enter the practice area and attempt to touch the ball with her hand at the feet of those dribbling the ball (e.g., using a specific number of touches in 30 seconds). ■

Purpose   To add realism to dribbling drills

Equipment   One ball for each attacker; one bib for each defender

Organization   Players are in groups or five to seven with one or two defenders according to ability. Players stand in the center circle.

Instructions   Attackers each have a ball, and defenders attempt to win the ball by gaining possession or playing or kicking the ball out of the circle. Attackers attempt to keep possession.

Coaching Points

- Players should be aware of the whole situation—the position of the ball, the other attackers, and the defender. Players should keep their heads up.
- Players should try to use and gain confidence in the techniques they learned previously.

Coaching Progressions

1. When confronted by a defender, the attacker should try to beat him, not just turn away and screen the ball for safety.
2. Each player has a ball. On command, players keep close control of their own ball while trying to cause other players to lose control of theirs. The last player in the circle is the winner, or players score a point each time they touch someone else's ball, with the highest scorer being declared the winner. ■

Dribbling for the Transition From Intermediate to Advanced Play

Real dribbling means taking on and beating an opponent, or better still, several opponents! For this reason, advanced drills should be based on 1v1 situations, but we believe there is a useful transition stage between the intermediate and advanced stages when you are introducing opposition. For this transition, we recommend drills that include a safety fence to allow players to develop the all-important qualities of composure and peripheral vision.

Safety Fence

Purpose   To introduce the concept of a barrier, or safety fence, between the attacker and the defender over which neither can cross

Equipment   One ball for every two players; two flags or cones

Organization   Players are in evenly matched pairs (one attacker, one defender), facing each other across a 10-yard line marked by flags or cones. The defenders are on the inside of the area, and the attackers on the outside.

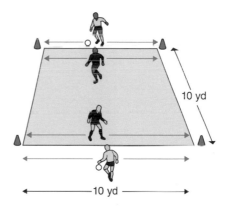

10 yd

10 yd

Instructions   The attacker has the ball and moves in various directions trying to avoid the defender. The defender has to react and keep his body directly opposite the attacker. Neither the players nor the ball can cross the line. The attacker is successful when he can trick the defender and reach one end of the line before the defender.

Coaching Points
- Players should try to drag the ball sideways with the inside of the foot.
- Players should lift the foot over the ball when faking moves and when changing direction with the outside of the foot.
- Players should use vigorous and convincing body movements to fake changes of direction.
- Players should practice faking by pointing in one direction but going in another.

Coaching Progressions
1. Players must work within a time limit.
2. The attacker practices all of the preceding moves with her back to the defender. This is a good introduction to screening the ball (page 114). ■

London Bridge

Purpose   To introduce the attacker to the skill of watching the defender's feet so that he can time the exact moment to play the ball through the legs

Equipment   One ball for every two players

Organization   Players are in evenly matched pairs (one bridge, one attacker).

Instructions   One player acts as the bridge, standing with his feet wide apart. The attacker dribbles the ball forward (figure 1), slips it through the bridge's legs (figure 2), and collects it on the other side (figure 3).

Figure 1

Figure 2

Figure 3

Coaching Points

- This practice ensures that the attacking players keep their heads up while approaching the bridge and develop a good sense of touch as they play the ball forward in small, controlled touches.

- Players also develop a sense of timing and accuracy as they slip the ball through the bridge and learn how to accelerate past the defender once they have played the ball forward.

- The attacker should not kick the ball and chase after it. Try to get the player to collect the ball 2 to 3 feet behind the bridge, which will place an emphasis on controlling the force applied to the touch under London Bridge!

- Encourage attackers to approach the defender (the bridge) while playing the ball with the front foot, dragging the ball with the rear foot, and playing the ball between both feet.

Coaching Progressions

1. The player acting as the bridge does jumping jacks to open and close the gap. The attacker must time the move through the gap; this is both realistic and enjoyable.

2. The bridge backs off slowly as the attacker approaches, using the correct jockeying footwork (i.e., one foot forward and back, at an angle to the player).

3. When the bridge is ready, he uses a small jump to reposition his feet from the correct sideways jockeying position to the incorrect square position (jumps the feet square) and thus invites the attacker through. The bridge must help the attacker by making a definite jump so that he lands with his feet square. This teaches the attacker to look and be patient and develops his confidence in holding the ball and waiting for the correct time to contact the ball. ■

Dribbling for Advanced Players

Skillful dribbling is a mixture of flair, composure, timing, and practice; dribbling is really an art form. All good dribblers employ five basic moves at some stage; these are well worth examining in detail. The methods are showing the ball, pretending to kick, creating space with the ball, forcing the defender off balance, and screening around the defender.

Showing the Ball to the Defender

Showing the ball is one of the first methods to learn for beating a defender. It usually involves a situation in which the attacker and the defender are facing each other in a relatively open space—for example, when a winger is approaching a defender. The player with the ball plays it gently forward toward the defender, but always keeping the ball within playing distance. The idea is to entice the defender to make the first move and lunge forward at the ball, at which point the attacker plays the ball swiftly past him.

Purpose   To attempt to draw the defender into making the first move

Equipment   One ball for two players

Organization   Players are in pairs of equal ability (one attacker, one defender).

Instructions   The defender slowly backs away as the attacker brings the ball toward him. The attacker should be encouraged to play the ball forward in a tantalizing manner, using his preferred foot. The attacker should present the ball to the defender in a manner that invites a tackle. As the defender lunges forward to strike, the attacker should play the ball past the defender or through his legs.

Coaching Point

- Observing the defender's movements, timing, and execution of the move is extremely important. The attacker must always keep the ball within touching (playing) distance and watch the feet of the defender while playing the ball toward him so he can anticipate the incoming tackle.

Coaching Progressions

1. Initially, the defender helps the attacker by making exaggerated, clumsy strikes.
2. As the attacker improves, the defender becomes more controlled.
3. Eventually, the attacker takes the ball directly toward the defender so that he is committed to tackle. That distance will be just outside the tackling distance of the defender. As the attacker improves in execution, timing, and confidence, he may take the ball within the defender's tackling distance before shifting the ball quickly away from the defender's challenge. ◼

Pretending to Kick the Ball

Pretending to kick the ball at the opponent aims to produce a defensive reaction. The defender, expecting the ball to be hit hard and fast, reacts by defensively raising up onto her feet, perhaps using her arms to protect her body. While the defender is in this upright and unbalanced position, the attacker can slip the ball past and move away. The advantage of this move is that it can be used almost everywhere on the field.

Pretending to Kick

Equipment   One ball for two players

Organization   Players are in pairs of equal ability (one attacker, one defender).

Instructions   The attacker takes the ball directly toward the defender at a controlled speed and pretends to kick it hard at the defender or to an imaginary teammate behind the defender. The attacker should make a vigorous fake kick at the ball with an upward lift of the head. This action must be sufficiently convincing to produce a reflex action in the defender, who will often think that the ball is going to hit him and move to evade or attempt to block or prevent the imaginary pass.

Coaching Point
- Some defenders will rise up on to their toes away from the ball and shield their heads; others will turn away from the action of the attacker; and others still will jump up in the air!

Coaching Progressions
1. The attacker brings the ball in fairly quickly at the defender, fakes the kick, and then pushes the ball forward and sideways off the front or back foot to go past the defender.
2. The defender cooperates at first and gives the desired reaction. As the attacker improves, the defender reacts normally. ■

Creating Space With the Ball

Attackers cannot expect good defenders to jump out of the way, but an attacker can move a defender sideways out of position to create space through which to dribble. One way to do this is to move the ball and make the defender follow, which is called creating space with the ball.

Creating Space

Figure 1

Figure 2

Figure 3

Equipment   One ball for two players

Organization   Players are in pairs of equal ability (one attacker, one defender).

Instructions   The attacker drags the ball to his left with the inside of his right foot, forcing the defender to move to his right. The attacker draws the defender even farther across and gets close to him (figure 1). The attacker now lifts his right foot over the ball (figure 2) or moves his right foot behind the ball (figure 3) before pushing the ball past the defender. The attacker pushes the ball with the outside of his right foot past the defender and through the gap that he created by moving the ball and the defender to one side (figure 4).

Figure 4

Coaching Progressions

1. The defender offers only token resistance.
2. As the attacker gains confidence and develops skill, the defender becomes more active. ■

Forcing the Defender Off Balance

An attacker can use body feints and disguise her intentions so that the defender makes a wrong move and gets off balance. For example, a defender who falls for the feint transfers his weight to the foot that is nearer the ball, which was the tackling foot. Tennis players call this having your foot in the hole.

Step-Over Play

Equipment   One ball for two players

Organization   Players are in pairs of equal ability (one attacker, one defender).

Instructions   The attacker fakes to go right, lifts his foot over the ball, and goes left by pushing the ball with the inside of his right foot (see figure 1, a-c). Next, the attacker drags the ball to the left, using his right foot. The attacker pretends to stop (as if to move in the opposite direction), but then continues left by dragging the ball with the inside of his right foot (see figure 2, a-c). Finally, the attacker makes a bold feint by stepping completely over the top of the ball with the front foot and then plays the ball forward with the back foot and accelerates forward (see figure 3, a-c).

Figure 1

Figure 2

Figure 3

Coaching Points

- The attacker must display confidence. He must give the defender the impression that he is in charge of both the ball and the situation.
- The attacker must be able to see both the defender and the situation that is arising (page 102).
- The attacker must be prepared to change or disguise both the point and the method of attack. Above all, the attacker must watch the feet of the defender.

Coaching Progressions

1. A useful start can be made by restricting the level of competition shown by the defender.
2. As the attacker develops skill and confidence, the defender can become more and more active. The attacker can bring the ball toward the defender at speed but is not judged to have beaten the defender until he has both passed the defender and stayed within playing distance of the ball. This is not a kick and run situation.
3. The more experienced attacker faces two defenders, one covering the other, with the second defender restricted to becoming active only when the first defender is beaten.

Screening and Turning

Screening is one of the most common techniques used by forwards who have their backs to the opponents' goal and a defender close behind them. When the ball is played to a forward in such a situation, ideally at his feet, he controls the ball while keeping his body between the defender and the ball. Then, keeping the ball at his feet, he maneuvers his body to turn around the defender, screening the ball away from her. Once around the defender, even partially, he can play the ball forward or shoot at goal.

However, this technique is not limited to attackers. For defenders caught in possession facing their own goal, this is a useful technique for relieving pressure. Overall, it is one of the most effective techniques for players to master.

Screening Around the Defender

Equipment
One ball for two players

Organization
Players are in pairs of equal ability (one attacker, one defender).

Instructions
The attacker moves the ball toward the defender and then turns his back to the defender and makes a wide screen, as shown in figure 1. The attacker drags the ball around in a circle, using his body as a screen between the ball and the defender.

Figure 1

Figure 2

The attacker has now moved around the defender and can make progress or release a shot, as shown in figure 2. The attacker may even start with his back to the defender in the early stages of this practice.

Coaching Points
- The player's arms are out wide to make his body shape as large as possible.
- The player must keep the playing distance between himself and the defender as close as possible.

Coaching Progressions
1. Without opposition, players receive the ball with the inside of the foot and move the ball in the same direction.
2. With a defender closely marking behind, but not aggressively, the attacker practices the same technique.
3. The defender is fully active with a target to aim at if the move is successful, either a shot at goal or a pass to a forward player. ■

Drills for Advanced Players

The following drills can be used to develop the five basic moves in dribbling, as described earlier in this chapter. The drills can also be developed as small-team games, as explained in chapter 3, because they create realistic situations in which to practice the basic moves. Coaching points are not included in this section because the player chooses which method to try; you should advise after the attempt.

Attacking the Square

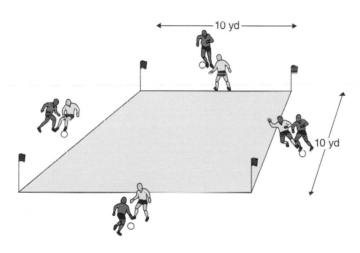

Equipment   Four balls for eight players; four flags or cones

Organization   Players are in pairs of equal ability (one attacker, one defender). Each pair stands outside of a 10- × 10-yard square marked by flags or cones.

Instructions   Each defender stands facing his attacker 5 yards from the line. Defenders may retreat as they are attacked but must not move back over the line. Attackers start 10 yards from the defenders; to beat the defenders, attackers must keep possession of the ball while taking it into the square.

Coaching Progressions

1. Players have a time limit.
2. The attackers rotate clockwise to play against each defender in sequence.
3. Players compete for the greatest number of successes.
4. Attackers take the ball into the square and, once inside, turn quickly to face the defenders and bring the ball back out of the square and return to the starting point. ■

Attacking the Corners

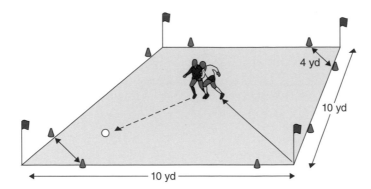

Purpose   To provide the attacker with alternative targets depending on the reaction of the defender

Equipment   One ball for two players; four flags or cones.

Organization   Players are in pairs of equal ability (one attacker, one defender), and each pair is in a 10- × 10-yard square marked by flags or cones. Small goals 4 yards wide can be placed in each corner as the target for the dribbling player.

Instructions   Starting in one corner, the attacker must control the ball passed to him by the defender from a 5-yard distance and take it to any of the other three corners. The attacker scores 1 point for reaching the corners to the left and right of the defender and 10 points for reaching the corner behind the defender. The defender tackles and tries to move the ball out of the square. Each player has five attempts before changing places and roles.

Coaching Progressions

1. The attacker must try, and keep on trying, to score 10 points.
2. Players have a time limit.

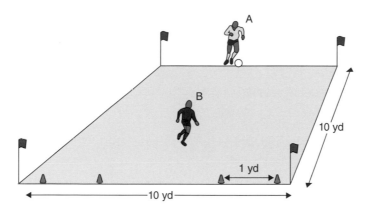

Purpose   To introduce directional alternatives that force the attacker to try to beat the defender and get past her.

Equipment   One ball for two players; four flags and four cones

Organization   Players are in pairs of equal ability (one attacker, one defender), and each pair is in a 10- × 10-yard square marked by flags. Cones are set to create two 1-yard-wide mini-goals along one side of the square.

Instructions

Play begins with the attacker (A) outside the square and the defender (B) inside. The defender passes the ball to the attacker from a 5-yard distance to start the practice before moving to engage the attacker. The attacker tries to score by dribbling the ball through either of the mini-goals. The defender defends both goals and wins by tackling the defender or playing the ball outside the grid. The defender cannot tackle until the attacker enters the square. The game continues until the attacker scores or loses possession.

Coaching Progressions

1. One goal is assigned more points.
2. Attackers have two or three attempts before the players change roles.
3. Players compete for the highest score or the first goal.
4. Attackers are restricted to a set time, such as 30 seconds, to score. ■

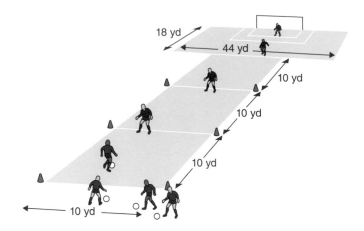

Purpose   To encourage the attacker to keep trying to dribble past opponents and, if possible, finish with a shot at goal

Equipment   Four balls for eight players; 8 to 10 flags or cones

Organization   Players are in groups of eight (one goalkeeper, three defenders, and four attackers—each with a ball) in 10- × 10-yard squares marked by flags or cones. One defender stands at the back of each square with the goalkeeper on the goal line.

Instructions   One at a time, attackers dribble toward each defender and try to maneuver the ball past the defender into the next square and, if successful, into the penalty area for a shot at the goal. Defenders must wait until the attacker enters their square before they can move from the line, and they must offer only the degree of resistance that you specify.

Coaching Progressions

1. On the first attempt, the attacker is allowed to beat each defender in turn and shoot at the goal upon reaching the penalty area. On the second attempt, the defenders are given a percentage at which they should resist (e.g., first defender, 10 percent; second defender, 20 percent; and third defender, 30 percent). The aim is to provide the attacker token resistance to permit a second shot at the goal.

2. As the attackers improve, the degree of difficulty is increased. This can be done in one of two ways. Either you specify the increased percentage resistance figure for each defender, or the attacker calls out this figure, thus specifying his own level of opposition.

3. The ultimate challenge for the attacker is to defeat the defenders and score even when all defenders give 100 percent resistance. ▪

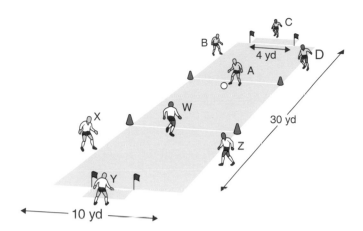

Equipment   A supply of balls; four flags; eight cones

Organization   Players are in pairs of equal ability (one attacker, one defender) in a 30- × 10-yard mini-field divided into three squares and marked by cones. Four-yard-wide goals are marked by flags.

Instructions   Each pair plays for 2 minutes (or less for younger players). Goals can only be scored when the attacker is in the square nearest the goal (this encourages dribbling, not shooting). When the ball goes out of play, the attacker takes possession at the point where the ball went out and the defender must retreat 4 yards to allow the attacker to restart play. There is no goalkeeper; players defend the goal, but they must not use their hands. Those not playing stand around the playing area at regular intervals and retrieve the ball to encourage maximum continuous play. Also note that this activity is a very useful way of handling the ball hog (see chapter 18 for more information).

Coaching Progressions

1. Players are paired according to their ability.

2. Players play a tournament using a round-robin or an all-play-all system rather than an elimination system, because those who are eliminated don't get any more practice and they are probably the ones who need it most. You may need more than one field of play.

3. Players play a straight elimination tournament, with a first-time losers competition in an adjacent area. With an elimination competition, use a handicap system to encourage the less able players; do this by handicapping the better players (e.g., player X starts minus 1 goal). ■

Dribbling for All-Star Players

Eventually, players must learn how to dribble under full match-play conditions. The techniques developed must be exposed to the decisions and movements of defenders operating as in a game. The following practice will give attackers the opportunity to test and develop their decision-making skills, their timing, and the execution of their chosen dribbling skills.

Sweeper

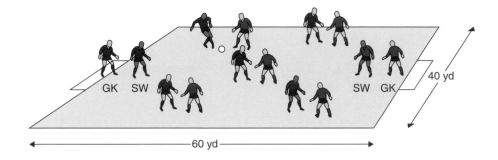

Equipment   Two sets of bibs; goals

Organization   Players are in two teams of seven players per team including goalkeepers. The dimensions of the playing area are 60 × 40 yards, but the size can be decreased as the players' skill level increases.

Instructions   Normal playing rules of the game apply except where explained here.

- Each team nominates a sweeper (SW), who is free of player-marking responsibilities and generally operates as the rear defender. Each team has a goalkeeper. All other players mark opponents on a man-to-man basis and are allowed to challenge only their own opponents in possession of the ball.
- Free kicks are given against any player violating the rule of challenging only one's own opponent.
- Should an attacker beat or break free from her opponent, only the sweeper may challenge her on her route to goal as her opponent recovers to defend.
- The sweeper is allowed only two (or three if needed according to player qualities) touches in possession of the ball before having to release it to others.

Coaching Points

- Because of the close and individual marking, each attacker should attempt to escape her opponent before moving to receive the ball from the sweeper or a teammate. This will usually involve quick changes of speed and direction to off-balance the opponent.

- On receiving the ball, if he has created space between himself and his defender, the attacker should turn as quickly as possible to face up to the defender before attempting to dribble past him.

- Once she has beaten the defender, the attacker should head directly toward the opposition goal, where she is likely to be confronted by the sweeper.

- If, on receiving the ball, the attacker cannot turn, then once again she should attempt to shake off the defender by either shielding and rolling around the opponent, shielding and moving with the ball across the pitch before a quick feint and change of direction, or feinting to pass or shoot before changing direction quickly.

- The attacker can use all of the techniques explained in this chapter, and others, if she becomes practiced to the point of being confident and fluent in her movements, outwaits the defender on occasion (literally waits for the defender to strike at the ball before moving the ball away quickly), and on other occasions directly confronts the defender by attacking her purposefully at pace with the ball.

- As the practice develops, the attacker can combine with other teammates in passing movements (e.g., wall passes) to keep the defender guessing as to whether the pass will be played or the attacker is feinting to pass before keeping the ball and going past the defender on a dribble.

Coaching Progressions

1. Players change roles every 5 minutes, and each becomes the sweeper in turn.
2. The goalkeeper initially can release the ball only to the sweeper, but as the game develops, she is allowed to distribute the ball to any of her own players. ■

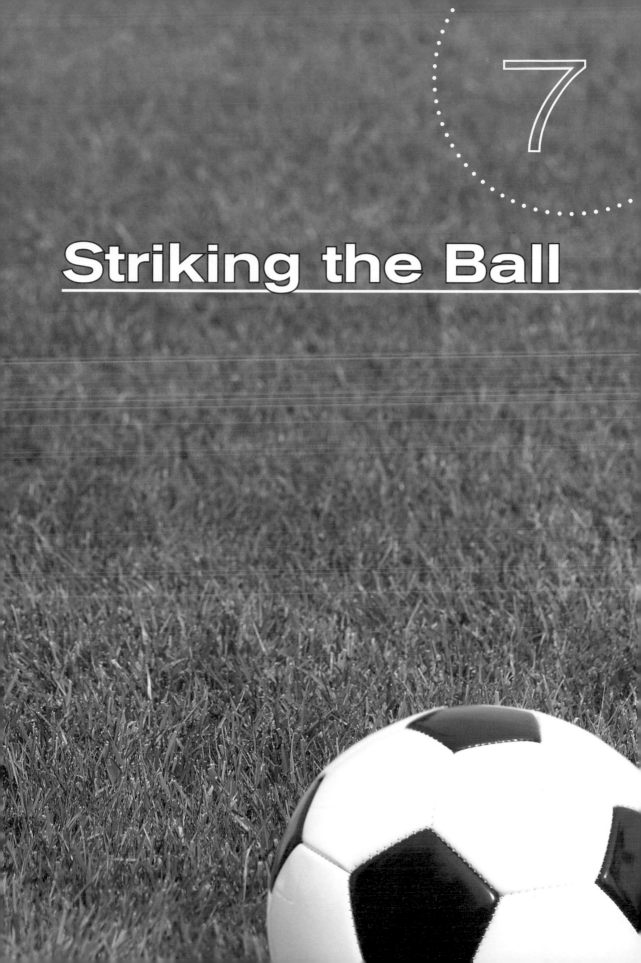

Striking the Ball

7

IN THIS CHAPTER we discuss the various ways of striking the ball, including the instep drive; volley and half-volley; chip; swerve, or banana, kick; and kick for height and distance. We start with techniques for players at beginner and introductory levels and end with a variety of drills that you can use with your all-star players during realistic competitive practices.

Lacing Soccer Boots (Cleats)

Many young players tie their boots in such a way that leaves large, loosely tied bows that interfere with the contact on the ball and may come loose during the game. The correct method of lacing provides a neat, flat kicking surface; the laces are securely tied off with the flat knot on the outside of the boot.

To lace boots correctly, first remove the lace completely. With the shoe on your foot, and using only one end of the lace in a surgeon's stitching action, do the following:

1. Go down into the top right hole and up out of the bottom left hole (figure 7.1a).

2. Continue stitching with the left end of the lace by going down into the holes on the right side and up out of the holes on the left side (figure 7.1b) until fully laced.

3. Tie off on the outside using a flat knot (figure7.1, c and d).

4. If necessary, adjust the length of the ends of the laces, or tighten the lace by pulling with the fingers on the next to bottom loop and working upward.

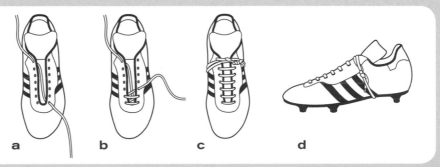

Figure 7.1   Proper method for lacing boots.

Basic Striking Techniques

The basic striking techniques that you will teach your players are the instep drive; the long, lofted kick; the volley; the chip; and the swerve, or banana, kick. These are discussed in the following sections.

Instep Drive

The instep drive (*instep* refers to the laces area) is one of the most powerful kicks in soccer. When used correctly, it keeps the ball low, which is most effective when shooting at the goal.

To use the instep drive, the player kicks the ball with the instep, which fits comfortably and almost vertically into the back of the ball. If this part of the geometry is correct, the rest of the body position is of secondary importance; however, several factors can improve the player's chance of success. For example, the toe must be down; the knee should be placed over the ball; the body should be compact and over the ball, not open or leaning back; and the follow-through should be short and in a straight line. All of these points can be achieved more easily if the nonkicking foot is placed alongside the ball, the head is kept down and still, and the body shape is compact. See figure 7.2 for an example of an instep drive.

Figure 7.2 Instep drive.

Long, Lofted Kick

The long, lofted kick, which can also include long-range passing, as we discussed in chapter 5, requires both height and distance. The player achieves height with the pass by leaning back slightly, keeping behind the ball, and kicking underneath the center line of the ball. The player achieves distance through a combination of factors, such as a powerful swinging action with a high follow-through, a long lever (like a golf club), and an angled approach (approximately 45 degrees) to the intended line of flight.

To prepare for a long, lofted kick, the player lengthens the final stride to provide some forward momentum and to help with the long follow-though. Then, the player hits through the ball with the leg straightening at the moment of impact, striking for distance rather than height and aiming for a high follow-through. Don't let the apparent ease with which professional players strike the ball fool you; like professional golfers, they have learned to time this action and produce what is called a kinetic chain. It's harder to do than it looks! See figure 5.4 on page 64 for an example of a long, lofted kick.

Volley Kick

The volley kick has a number of variations that all have two things in common: The ball is completely airborne, and it is usually struck with the instep, although the inside and outside of the foot can also be used effectively. Because the ball is airborne, it is light and responsive, making the volley a powerful kick. Balancing on the nonkicking foot and making perfect contact with the ball on the instep make this a difficult technique. Three things are essential: keeping the toe down, the head still, and the arms out for balance. See figure 7.3 for an example of a volley kick.

Figure 7.3 Volley kick.

Chip

The chip gets its name from the golf shot played with a wedge— it is a short, high, lofted kick with backspin. The player uses a sharp stabbing action, toes underneath the ball, with little or no follow-through. The ball is lifted almost vertically; when it lands, it remains almost stationary or, if very well played, spins backward. See figure 7.4 for an example of a chip.

Figure 7.4 Chip.

The Swerve, or Banana, Kick

No kick has had a more dynamic effect on modern soccer than the swerve, or banana, kick. It is now a priceless asset for attacking free kicks and is being used more and more in passing situations. It is an advanced skill, and even experienced professionals have difficulty controlling the amount and timing of the swerve. Nevertheless, the kick is important and is enjoyable to practice; even beginners can practice this kick if they use the kicking tee.

Depending on which way the player wants the ball to curve, the ball is struck on the outside or the inside of the ball with the inside or outside of the foot. The laws of physics control the movement of the ball after impact. See figure 7.5 for an example of the swerve, or banana, kick.

Figure 7.5 Swerve, or banana, kick.

Striking Drills

There is a natural hierarchy of ball-striking skills. A ball in the air is easier to strike than a ball on the ground; a moving ball is easier to strike than a stationary ball; and a spinning, bouncing ball is probably the most difficult of all to strike cleanly. The skill of striking a ball is further complicated by the combinations of speed, direction, and spin that can be imparted on the ball, both as it comes to a player and as it is dispatched. In this chapter we take careful note of these factors in the drills for all levels of play.

How to Make and Use a Kicking Tee

When teaching a beginner how to strike the ball correctly, or teaching an experienced player how to kick with her weaker foot, you can use a kicking tee. It is a simple coaching aid, but can really make learning to kick easier and safer. You can also use the tee when teaching advanced players how to swerve a ball or how to gain height and distance from a corner kick or a goal kick.

To make a tee, take a medium-sized plastic-coated cup and cut the bottom half away as shown in figure 7.6. Invert the top half of the cup to make the tee about 2 to 3 inches high, on which the ball is placed. Because the ball is now raised off the ground, the player can kick it correctly with the instep (the laces) without the fear of stubbing his toe. As the player improves, cut the tee down lower and lower until it is no longer needed.

Figure 7.6   Making a kicking tee.

Drills for Beginners

Before you begin teaching your players how to strike the ball, remember that for beginners, the easiest ball to kick is one that is airborne and captive, such as a ball held in a string bag or placed on a tee. Also, all players will find that a rolling ball is easier to kick than a stationary ball because it has less inertia. However, a spinning ball is difficult to kick because the contact zone is moving.

When teaching beginners, first give them time to prepare, to balance themselves before kicking, and then use the following sequence:

1. A ball that is rolled gently toward the player with no sidespin
2. A ball that is rolled gently away from the player (a lead pass) with no sidespin
3. A ball that is bouncing gently but not spinning

Instep Drive From a Tee

Equipment   One ball for each player (the ball must be of the correct size and pressure for the player); cones or flags for a target goal; a supply of kicking tees (unless they are made of plastic, they are easily damaged)

Organization   Players are in groups of up to six in a straight line with a minimum of 3 yards between them. The line should be parallel to and about 10 yards from a target goal. For larger groups, arrange a rotation system.

Instructions   One at a time, when called, players use the instep drive to strike the ball toward the target goal. Players must not lift the ball more than 4 feet off the ground.

Coaching Points

- Players should approach the ball in almost a straight line, although some find it helpful to make a slight curve on the approach run to the ball. Then, with the toe down and with a compact body shape (knee and head down at the moment of impact), players strike through the ball along the target line.
- The nonkicking foot should be approximately 6 inches (15 cm) away from but alongside the ball.
- Players should follow through in a straight line directly at the target.

Coaching Progressions

1. Players increase power and distance by moving farther away from the target.
2. Players practice with both feet to become proficient with left and right.

Lofted Kick From a Tee

Equipment   One ball for each player; a supply of kicking tees; a regular goal net or baseball cage

Organization   Players are in a straight line 3 yards apart, not more than 5 yards from the target or net.

Instructions   One at a time, when called, players kick the ball into the net, aiming for height and distance. A target can be placed in the net at which the players aim.

Coaching Points

- Players should keep the toe down and strike through the bottom of the ball and lengthen the final stride to give a long, high follow-through.
- Players should approach at an angle of 45 degrees.
- Players should keep the nonkicking foot to the side of the ball.

Coaching Progressions

1. Players progress from using the kicking tee to kicking from the ground.
2. Players try kicking from a tee with the nonpreferred foot.

Stationary Volley

Equipment   One ball in a secured net bag for each player

Organization   Individual players work in free space.

Instructions   Each player rests the ball on the ground (to ensure that it is both captive and still), raises it gently until it is at knee height, and then volleys using the instep.

Coaching Points

- Players should use the instep and keep the toe down.
- Players should keep their eyes on the ball and heads still.
- Players should follow through in a straight line.

Coaching Progressions

1. Players increase the force of the kick until the ball in the bag completes a circle.
2. Hold the ball for the player, who stands and volleys and then moves in and volleys.

Drills for Intermediate Players

Intermediate players should strike at a moving ball and increasingly generate power, accuracy, and distance. Then, they should try to strike a ball that is rolling away from them, and finally practice kicking a stationary ball.

Moving Ball

Equipment   One ball for every two players

Organization   Players are in pairs, 10 to 15 yards apart.

Instructions   A player push passes the ball to her partner using the instep drive and keeping the ball below 4 feet in height. The partner sends it back the same way.

Coaching Points

- Players should strive for accuracy and technique before power.
- Players should strike through the center line of the ball, not at it, and should generate power from the hips.
- The nonkicking foot should be alongside the ball and the toe down as the instep contacts the ball.

Coaching Progressions

1. Players stop the ball and play it forward before kicking.
2. Players drive the ball directly back to their partners (i.e., first-time kicking).
3. Players increase the distance between them. ■

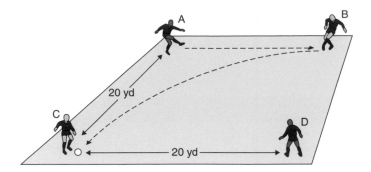

Purpose   To increase the range and accuracy of long kicking

Equipment   One ball for every four players

Organization   Players are in groups of four standing 20 yards apart in free space.

Instructions   Player A rolls the ball from his hands to player B, who plays a long, lofted kick to player C. Player C rolls the ball with his hands back to player D. The sequence continues with all players taking their turn to kick.

Coaching Points

- Players should keep their heads down until after contact.
- Players should go for a high follow-through and hit through the ball with a straight leg.
- Players should increasingly aim for distance rather than height (e.g., trying to play the ball over the heads of the receiving players).

Coaching Progressions

1. Player A passes the ball to player B with the foot, rather than rolling it, to create a more realistic service.
2. Player A serves an aerial ball with his hands. If competent, he can also serve the ball with his feet, which requires the receiver to control the ball before making the kick. ■

Purpose   To help players learn to balance on one foot while kicking with the other

Equipment   One ball for every two players

Organization   Players are in pairs, 2 to 3 yards apart.

Instructions   Player A gently tosses the ball to her partner (the server should always use two hands to serve), who volleys it back for the server to catch. In this drill, players learn how to balance on one foot while kicking with the other and how to develop finesse and timing. Players must be careful and gentle because the volley is a delicate skill—blasting off or not controlling the strength of the kick can be dangerous for the server (see figure 7.3 on page 126).

Coaching Points

- Players should keep the toe down and the head still.
- Players should hold their arms out to the side for balance.
- Players should use calculated and composed contact (finesse) on the ball.
- Players should keep the foot, ankle, knee, and leg in a straight line.

Coaching Progressions

1. Players work to develop the skill in both feet.
2. Players progress to volleying on the move: Player A moves gently backward while player B follows, serving and catching the ball volleyed by player A.
3. Player A moves forward and player B moves backward, still serving and catching the volley.

Players change to a serve over the crossbar, which the receiver volleys into the goal. ▪

Chip

Equipment   One ball for every two players

Organization   Players are in pairs (one server, one kicker), 5 to 8 yards apart.

Instructions   The server rolls the ball straight and gently to the kicker with no spin. The kicker chips the ball back to the server, who tries to catch it or bring it under control using different parts of the body (see figure 7.4 on page 127).

Coaching Points

- Players should use a short back-lift and a stabbing action, with the toe sliding under the ball at contact.
- The nonkicking foot should be placed close to and alongside the ball at the moment of impact.
- Players should use a short follow-through or none at all.
- Players should keep the head and the top half of the body down and over the ball.
- The body should jackknife downward as the kick is executed.

Coaching Progressions

1. Players change to a stationary ball.
2. Players work to chip for greater height (such as over the partner or an obstacle), which is achieved by using a quicker, sharper snap of the foot under the ball at contact.
3. Players try to get the ball to stop dead on landing or even to roll or spin backward.
4. Players try to chip a ball moving away from them, which is much more difficult. ■

Equipment   One ball for every two players; a supply of kicking tees; two flags

Organization   Partners stand facing each other on a straight line, 15 to 20 yards apart, with a flag placed in the middle to act as a target around which the ball must swerve.

Instructions   One player swerve-kicks the ball so that it moves away from the line but returns to land at his partner's feet.

Coaching Points

- Players should select the direction and then focus on the point of contact on the ball.
- Players should remember to follow through; this will not be in the direction of the pass but across the line of the pass as shown in figure 7.5 on page 127.
- Players should make contact underneath the horizontal center line of the ball to produce lift and outside the vertical center line of the ball to produce swerve or spin on the ball.
- The principles of contacting the ball off center apply whether the player imparts spin with the inside or outside of the foot.

Coaching Progressions

1. Players start using a kicking tee and then progress to a stationary ball.
2. Players work to increase swerve and distance and attempt both inswinging and outswinging kicks. ■

Drills for Advanced Players

For advanced players, the best progressions for teaching the instep drive are the shooting drills contained in chapter 8, which are arranged in a progressive sequence. One additional and enjoyable drill is a penalty competition in which the players must use the instep drive. For the long, lofted kick, advanced players should engage in two kinds of drills—striking a stationary ball in goal-kick, corner-kick, or free-kick situations; and practicing long kicking while moving. When teaching volleying to advanced players, Head Tennis, as described on page 167, is one of the best ways to develop advanced volleying skills. Or players can use chest control to catch a thrown ball, let it fall to knee height, and volley it back to a partner (see Partner Juggling on page 32).

Set plays provide effective chipping practice, but one of the best general drills for advanced players is the one attributed to the Dutch player Johann Cruyff, as described in this section. He is reputed to have practiced the chip kick over an empty goal, chipping the ball over the crossbar so that it spun back into the goal. In addition, because the swerve kick is so effective for attacking free kicks, the best practice situations are set plays just outside the penalty area (several excellent and safe drills are explained in chapter 16). The Cruyff Drill included in this section is also good fun for general practice and can motivate players to work on their own.

Cruyff Chip With Spin

Equipment   A supply of soccer balls; a regular goal without a net

Organization   Players work in pairs, facing each other, about 10 yards apart. If they are using an actual goal, then one stands on the goal line facing her partner. If you have a large number of players, some pairs may have to practice outside of the goal area.

Instructions   Players chip the ball over the crossbar in such a way that it spins back into the goal on landing. The backspin is imparted by the foot striking centrally and quickly underneath the ball.

Coaching Progressions

1. The server rolls the ball to the player who chips.
2. Players practice using a stationary ball.
3. Players hold competitions to see who can spin the ball back farthest or who can make the most successful chips in a set number of attempts. ◼

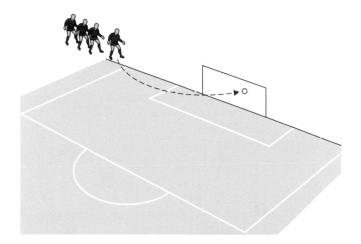

Equipment   Regular goals; a supply of soccer balls

Organization   Players line up at the corner post. If you are working with less powerful kickers, you can move the start position in, up to the penalty area line.

Instructions   Players swerve-kick the ball into the goal. Even for advanced players, successful corner kicks are usually, if not always, played with the stronger foot. This means that players will start their runs from different angles.

Coaching Points

- Players approach the ball from an angle and strike under the ball.
- Players use a long back-lift and follow-through, aiming for the ball to land on the penalty spot.

Coaching Progressions

1. Players use tees placed at the 6-yard line, the penalty yard line, and the corner. By increasing the distance, you also increase the length and therefore the difficulty of the kick.
2. Players use a stationary ball.
3. Players kick from both sides to develop inswing and outswing deliveries. ■

Drill for All-Star Players

The following practice incorporates all the skills explained earlier in an opposed practice situation.

Long-Range Kicking

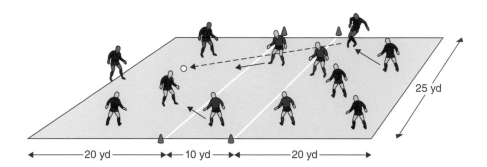

Equipment   A supply of soccer balls; two different-colored sets of bibs; cones

Organization   Eight attacking players are opposed by four defenders. The playing area is 50 yards in length and 25 yards in width, with a 10-yard central channel marked by cones separating the two 20-yard zones.

Instructions   Four attackers are opposed by two defenders in one area of 20 × 25 yards, and two resting defenders are located in the central channel. Four attackers are situated in the other 20- × 25-yard area with one (located on the end line) designated as the receiver of the passes from the opposed attackers.

Four attackers keep possession of the ball against the defending players until the opportunity is created to deliver the long pass to the designated target player, who is at least 30 yards away. As the ball is delivered to the distant target player, the two defenders in the central channel move to pressure the receiving team and are replaced in the central channel by the previous defenders, who now rest until the next transfer of the ball. Should the defenders gain possession of the ball on three occasions, they are replaced by the team of four players that conceded the ball on that third occasion. If the pass is inaccurate and leaves the playing area, you serve a ball to the team that should have received the intended pass.

Coaching Points
- The team in possession of the ball should spread out in the playing area to create as much space and time as possible to pass and receive the ball.
- While retaining possession of the ball, the attackers should be aware of the actions and movements of the defenders so that if the opportunity arises to receive and deliver the long pass, they can take it quickly.
- The controlling touch of the receiving player should assist him in setting the ball up to deliver the pass.

- Because the long pass may have to be delivered over or through the defenders in the central zone, appropriate skill must be used.
- Whether the pass is driven, swerved, chipped, or lofted, it must be accurate, and the speed or weight of the pass should make it easy for the receiving player to control.

Coaching Progressions

1. The receiving player is allowed a maximum of two touches to challenge the efficiency and speed of the receiving touch and the delivery of the long pass.
2. The designated receiver of the long pass has only one touch to release the ball to the next receiver—this will also place demands on the accuracy of the player making the long pass. ■

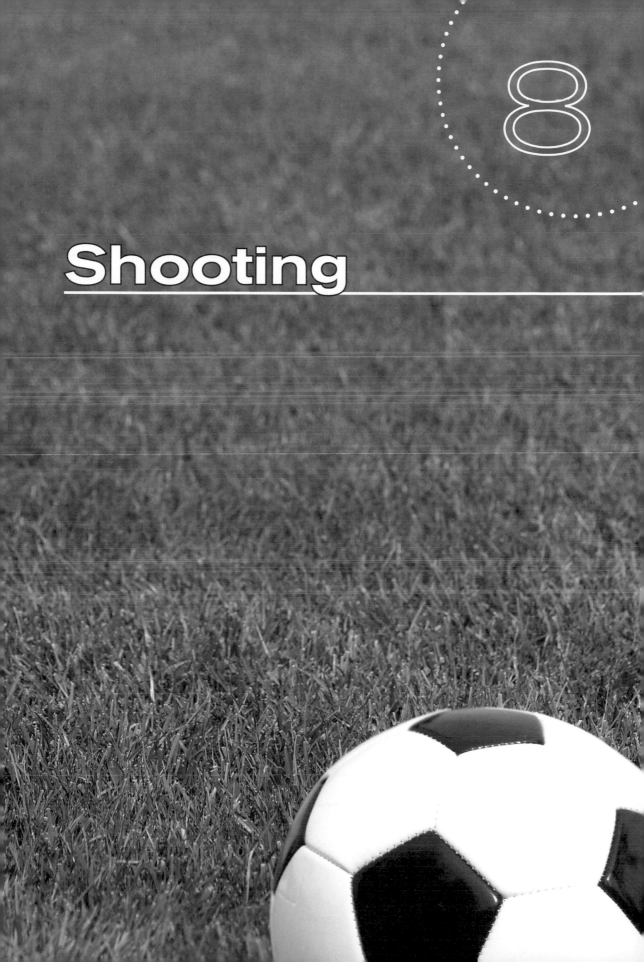

Shooting

8

THIS CHAPTER WILL help you develop shooting practices using the kicking techniques described in chapter 7. It also covers where and how to aim and how to encourage players to stay calm while shooting. Finally, it shows how to invent gamelike practices that emphasize the importance of shooting at the earliest opportunity yet also stress the need to remain calm and composed under pressure.

When to Shoot and When to Pass

Many goals are scored in the four corners of the goal, as shown in figure 8.1, because these areas are the most difficult for the goalkeeper to reach. Low shots along the ground close to the goalkeeper's feet and toward the far post are the most difficult for the goalkeeper to save when an attacking player gets into a shooting position from the front of the penalty area. Shots from the sides of the

Figure 8.1   Difficult areas of the goal to defend.

penalty area and at narrow angles are easier for the goalkeeper to save because the target area is so much smaller.

You can present these facts to your players by explaining to them the difference between the passing zones and the shooting zone. Your players should know that attempting a shot from a passing zone has a low chance of scoring (see figure 8.2). These zones are imaginary areas within the penalty area from which the chances of scoring are higher or lower—higher when in front of the goal with a wide target to shoot at; lower when you are toward the sides of the goal where the target area is much smaller, both because the shooting angle is reduced and because the goalkeeper can cover this smaller area more effectively. Goalkeepers are always told to "defend the near post" to improve their position and defend their goal more effectively.

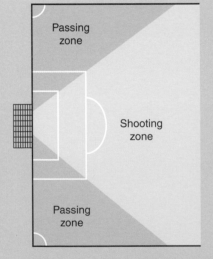

Figure 8.2   Shooting and passing zones at the goal.

Shooting for Beginners

The easiest shot at the goal is the instep drive, when the ball is rolling gently toward the player. Coaching this type of kick helps to develop a powerful shot that keeps the ball low. Accuracy is always the paramount feature of scoring, so you must communicate it positively in all shooting sessions. Players who opt for power over accuracy could spend much of their time practicing missing the target. The drills for beginners are arranged in a progressive sequence.

Instep Drive 1

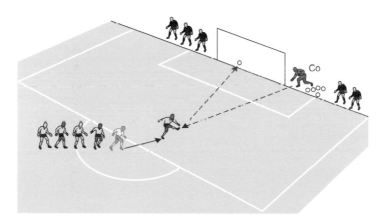

Equipment   A supply of soccer balls; a goal with nets

Organization   Players are divided into two groups of up to 10 players. One group stands behind the goal and along the end line to retrieve the balls; the other stands in a line outside the penalty area waiting for their turn. You stand at the side of the goal.

Instructions   For each player in turn, roll a ball gently forward toward the incoming player, who runs in, balances (adjusts his position), and shoots at the goal. Initially, players do not have a goalkeeper. When a goalkeeper is used, players must not shoot from less than 15 yards when using this technique of scoring (to protect the goalkeeper).

Coaching Points

- Players should not rush toward the ball, but should stay calm as they move forward and attempt to place the nonkicking foot alongside the ball.
- Players should use the instep drive and point the toe down to strike the ball through its midline to keep the trajectory low. Players should try to place the ball into the corners of the goal as their technique improves.

Coaching Progressions

1. Serve from the other post to the left foot of the player.
2. When a goalkeeper is introduced to the practice, players should note his position and attempt to take any advantage if he is poorly positioned.
3. Players should attempt to keep the ball low and aim across the goalkeeper toward the farther post if the goalkeeper is well positioned.
4. Players should always follow in their own shots in the event of any rebound.

Instep Drive 2

Equipment   A supply of soccer balls; a goal with nets

Organization   Players are in groups of six or fewer and work in the area in front of the goal on a standard soccer field.

Instructions   Stand about 25 yards from the goal and have a player stand with her back to the goal, close to and facing you. Roll the ball past the player toward the goal. The player spins, chases the ball, and shoots using the instep drive from a distance of about 15 to 18 yards.

Coaching Points

- Players should place the nonkicking foot alongside the ball at the moment of impact, striking the ball through its center line.
- Players should keep a compact body shape, stay down on the shot, strike the ball with the instep, and follow through toward the goal.
- Players should observe the positioning and movements of the goalkeeper before the strike at goal and shoot accordingly if she makes positional errors.

Coaching Progressions

1. Serve the ball over the head of the player and then require the player to shoot with the instep, possibly as the ball drops to the ground.
2. Now serve the ball to the player's feet and receive a return pass before supplying a through pass in front of the player's run as she moves to shoot at goal. This simulates the action of a forward player who lays off a pass to a supporting player before spinning to receive the next pass on her way toward the goal. ■

Shooting for Intermediate Players

Intermediate players should be given a simple control factor (e.g., a gently bouncing ball) before shooting to begin to achieve greater realism.

Instep Drive 3

Equipment
A supply of soccer balls; a goal with nets

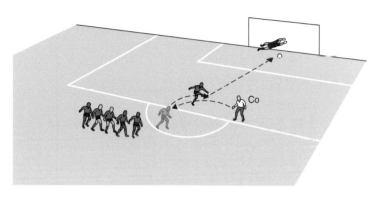

Organization
Regular goalkeepers are appointed. The remaining players are divided into groups of six. Six shooters stand outside the penalty arc as shown in the figure. The remaining players position behind the goal and along the dead ball line to catch balls until it is their turn to shoot. You stand on the penalty area line.

Instructions   You lob an aerial ball to the player, who heads it forward, follows it toward the goal, and shoots using the instep drive.

Coaching Points
- The simple act of heading the ball forward gives great realism to the practice.
- The header has to give players just enough time and distance to follow the ball and release the shot. If they head too hard, the ball runs too close to the goalkeeper. If they don't head the ball hard enough, they have to play it forward again before they can shoot, which destroys the drill.
- Players should head toward their best foot and retain their balance while adjusting their feet to strike the ball at goal.
- Players should pick a spot and aim carefully while looking at the contact spot on the ball. Even for a volley with the instep, this will once again be around the vertical center line of the ball.

Coaching Progressions
1. Players release the shot within 3 seconds of the first headed contact.
2. Players use the nonpreferred foot.
3. You set the target area (e.g., low right) as the player moves into the shot.
4. Players now control the ball into a shooting position with a variety of first touches (e.g., the chest, the thigh, the outside of the foot).
5. Players shoot using half-volley shots. ■

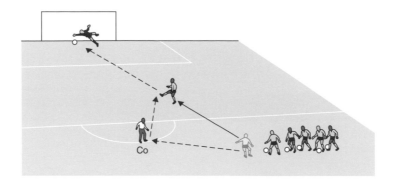

Equipment   A supply of soccer balls; a goal with nets

Organization   Players are divided into groups of six around the penalty area. You stand on the penalty arc with your back to the goal.

Instructions   Each player has a ball and dribbles, in turn, toward you. The player passes the ball to you from a distance of approximately 10 yards and then receives a return lead pass from you. The player then controls the ball and shoots on goal using the instep drive.

Coaching Points

- The pass to you must be firm and accurate; ignore a sloppy pass. The player must accelerate when giving the pass, but must be balanced before and when shooting.

- Players should observe the position and activity of the goalkeeper. If the goal-keeper positions way off center, then a simple side-foot, or push, pass of the ball into the exposed side of the goal is intelligent finishing and is to be encouraged.

- The emphasis of the drill must be on the instep drive. The drill is intended to highlight this skill and should be controlled accordingly.

Coaching Progressions

1. Play the ball to either side of the players as they approach.

2. Players who miss the target must retrieve their ball.

3. Play the pass with some lift or spin to make the shot more difficult, resulting in volleys and half-volleys with the instep.

4. Players must shoot at the goal on the first touch. They are not allowed a second touch of the ball to make the shot easier. ■

Equipment   One ball for every two players

Organization   Players are in two groups of equal number, with one goalkeeper, in one half of a standard soccer field. Group 1 is in the center circle, and each player is holding a ball. The goalkeeper stands in front of the goal. Group 2 stands behind the goal.

Instructions   A player from group 1 dribbles at speed into the penalty arc and releases a shot at the goal on, or very close to, the front penalty area line (the 18-yard line). The goalkeeper is restricted to the goal line until the player enters the penalty arc; then works to defend the goal. Players from group 2 retrieve and return the balls. This drill accustoms the players to dribbling the ball, at speed, immediately prior to a shot.

Coaching Points

*   Players should watch the actions of the goalkeeper, select the technique necessary to beat her, and place the shot accordingly.
*   Players should have a compact body shape, with toes and head down and the standing foot alongside the ball as it is struck toward the goal.
*   Players should strike through the ball, not at it, and follow through along the target line. After shooting at goal, players must be alert to any knockdown saves by the goalkeeper, which may result in a secondary scoring chance.
*   Leaning backward at contact can increase the likelihood of the shot rising and consequently missing the target; it may also result in a loss of power to the shot at goal.

Coaching Progressions

1. The time for the shot to be released is limited (e.g., shoot within 20 seconds).
2. Teams compete, with each team having 2 minutes to score as many goals as possible. Signal to players when they may attack the goal following the previous shot (this will usually be when the result of that shot is known). Record both team and individual player totals during each 2-minute period.
3. A defending player chases the shooter, who has a start of 8 yards. ■

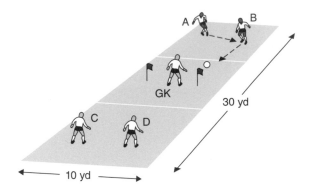

Equipment   A supply of soccer balls; two flags

Organization   Players are in one team of five, with one goalkeeper, on a 30- ×
10-yard playing area that is separated into three areas. The middle area includes a
small goal marked by flags.

Instructions   Player A plays the ball to player B, who shoots from the back half
of the square in which he is positioned (to shoot from the front line of the square would
mean that the shot was from about 5 yards from the goalkeeper). If the goalkeeper
saves, he returns the ball to player A, turns around, and invites a shot from player C
or player D. If the ball beats the goalkeeper, player C or player D retrieves the ball and
player A keeps shooting.

Coaching Points

- The first controlling touch is vital in setting up to strike the ball effectively.
- Players should remain composed, select a target, and place the ball past the
  goalkeeper.
- Players should not lean back, but should maintain a compact shape over the
  ball in order to strike the ball through the center.
- The shooting player follows in every shot to score from any rebounds from the
  goalkeeper.

Coaching Progressions

1. The shooting player takes a first-time shot.
2. The serving player gives different passes (e.g., from the front, from behind, and
   as the players improve, from the side) requiring a variety of controlling touches.
3. The server, after serving, becomes a defender.
4. Players take six shots each, and points are awarded as follows:
   - 3 points for a goal scored directly from the shot
   - 2 points for a goal scored from a rebound from a goalkeeper's save
   - 1 point for a shot at goal that is on target but saved by the goalkeeper
   - −3 points for a shot that is over the height of the goal made by the corner flags
   - −1 point for a shot that is wide of the goal ■

Shooting for Advanced Players

The drills that follow are ideal for coaching advanced shooting technique because they can be used to coach the mind of the shooter and can help you teach players how to make decisions on their own during a game. When under pressure from defenders, the shooter is denied the most essential element—time. Players under pressure can become anxious and take too long to shoot, shoot hastily, or make ill-judged decisions. Superior players always know where the goal is and look at the target while preparing to shoot or dribbling past defenders. The following practices develop the correct sequence of actions—maneuvering the ball into a realistic shooting position, glancing up at the target, and releasing the shot. These processes can be reduced to a simple sequence—control-look-shoot. As players improve, they can execute these tasks almost simultaneously.

Instep Drive 7

Equipment
One ball for every two players

Organization
Players are divided into two equal groups (one group of attackers and one group of defenders) and stand in two lines on a standard

soccer field. One goalkeeper is positioned in a standard-size soccer goal. You stand on the penalty line opposite the center of the goal.

Instructions
On command, the first attacker dribbles forward along the front of the penalty box, goes around you, and shoots for the goal. The first defender sprints along the goal line and tries to stop any shot that gets past the goalkeeper. Defenders cannot use their hands. The goalkeeper must remain on the goal line until the attacker has passed you. After the shot, the next player in line takes a turn.

Coaching Points
- Attackers must dribble quickly under control but avoid panic.
- When attackers pass you, they should glance up and pick a target.
- Attackers should concentrate on the correct instep drive technique, keep their eyes down, and follow the shot for a possible rebound from the goalkeeper.

Coaching Progressions
1. Players attack from the other side of the penalty area to develop shots using either foot as necessary.
2. Players are given a target time in which to move into position and shoot. ■

Instep Drive 8

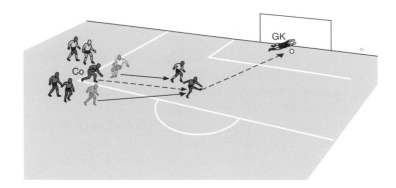

Equipment   A supply of soccer balls

Organization   Players are in two groups of equal number (one group of attackers and one group of defenders) and stand in two lines on a standard soccer field. One goalkeeper is positioned in a standard-size goal. Attacking players face the goal, and defending players have their backs to you. You stand at the corner of the penalty area, facing the goal.

Instructions   Serve the ball toward the area between the penalty spot and the 18-yard line and shout "Go." The first attacker chases the ball and tries to score. The first defender spins around and tries to catch and stop the attacker. After the play, the next players in line take a turn.

Coaching Points

- If the defender is quicker or more skilled than the attacker, the defender may be handicapped by 1 or 2 extra yards.
- The attacker should control the ball (if necessary), look at the position and actions of the goalkeeper, keep the eyes and toe down, place the shot, and stay cool.

Coaching Progressions

1. Change to the other side of the penalty area so players have to use their left feet.
2. Players have a set amount of time, such as 20 seconds, to complete the drill. ■

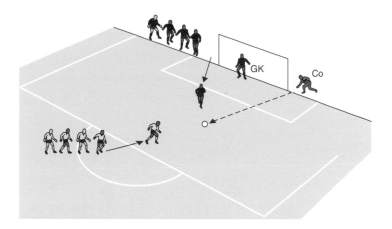

Equipment   One ball for every two players

Organization   Players are in two groups of equal number (one group of attackers and one group of defenders) on a standard soccer field. A goalkeeper is positioned in the goal. Defenders line up on the goal line outside the goal, and attackers line up centrally outside the penalty area. You stand on the side of the goal opposite the defenders with a supply of soccer balls.

Instructions   You roll the ball into the penalty area, and the first attacker moves into the area, controls the ball, and tries to score. At the moment you release the ball, the defender sprints to challenge the attacker.

Coaching Points

- Attacker should control, look, and shoot or, if under severe pressure from the defender, shoot immediately without trying to control the ball first.

- If the defender catches the attacker before she releases a shot, the attacker should be prepared to control the ball and try to dribble past the defender to create a shooting opportunity.

Coaching Progressions

1. Initially, the attacker has a clear advantage, which encourages shooting. Be sure to serve firmly and accurately.

2. As players improve, or with more advanced players, you can serve balls that bounce and are more difficult for the attacker to control.

3. Two attackers and two defenders play at the same time. ■

Shooting for All-Star Players

Finally, we offer a drill that covers shooting from a distance and involves supporting players following up the shot in case of goalkeeper errors. The drill also creates high-intensity situations (e.g., in the penalty area) which involve realism and competition.

Distance Shooting

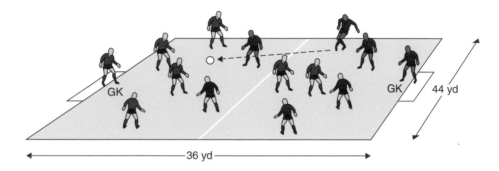

Equipment   A supply of soccer balls; different-colored bibs for teams; cones or small goals

Organization   Players are divided into two teams of seven players (goalkeeper included) in a 36- × 44-yard area (a double-sized penalty area.). Each team positions four players in the half of the area nearer its own goalkeeper (the defending half) and two in the attacking half.

Instructions   One goalkeeper throws the ball out to one of the four players in the defending half of the area, and the two forward players from the opposing team apply pressure. The player in possession should shoot at goal probably about 30 yards away at most; shots are typically taken from distances around 20 to 25 yards. If the player in possession cannot shoot because of the activity of the pressing opponents, he should pass to one of the other two teammates in the other half. The team in possession keeps the ball until a shooting opportunity arises.

   When the shot from distance is taken, the two players in the attacking half should follow those shots in at goal to collect any rebounds from the goalkeeper. If the goalkeeper saves the shot, he quickly distributes the ball to one of his own four players in the defending half and they shoot toward the other goal. If the shot that is taken misses the target, you or a designated server feeds a ball to the team whose goal has been attacked.

Coaching Points

- To receive the ball from the goalkeeper, the four players should spread out within the defending half to create space and time for themselves to control and shoot at goal.

- The receiving player must have an awareness of the position of the pressing opponents to direct the ball to a position to shoot at the goal with his first touch, although he may wish to shoot immediately at goal.

- After controlling the ball into a position to shoot, the player should observe the position of the goalkeeper and select the appropriate shooting skill.

- Accuracy is paramount whether the player opts for power in the shot using the instep drive or placement in attempting to swerve the ball by contacting it off center rather than through the center line.

- The shooting player may also choose to play the ball over the goalkeeper if he is poorly positioned. The ability to observe the position of the goalkeeper is an important requisite and should become almost habitual in all shooting situations.

- The two forward players should anticipate the shot from distance and move quickly to a position near the goalkeeper to collect the rebounds as they arise.

Coaching Progressions

1. The dimensions of the playing area can be reduced for younger all-star players.

2. Players in the defending half of the area can pass to the two players in the attacking half for them to turn and shoot, lay the ball back to one of the four coming forward to strike the ball at goal from the defending half, or combine with each other to create a shooting opportunity.

3. One of the defending players can move forward into the attacking half either with the ball or to support the two forward players who receive passes from the defending half, making the numbers three attackers against four defenders.

4. Two wingers for each team may also be positioned to the sides of the practice area, 10 yards outside the sidelines of the area on both sides of the attacking half. Players can pass to them to cross the ball into the scoring areas. ■

Shooting Games

Players never seem to tire of shooting practices, so this section includes some additional shooting games for all levels of players for your coaching repertoire. Use bibs or different-colored shirts to distinguish between the teams.

3v3 in the Penalty Area

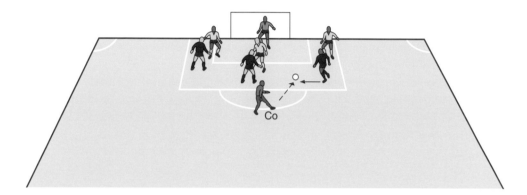

Purpose   To introduce realism and urgency in a restricted playing area

Equipment   A supply of soccer balls; different-colored bibs for teams

Organization   Players are in a group of seven (three attackers, three defenders, one goalkeeper) in the penalty area on a standard field.

Instructions   On command, the game starts and the players jockey for position. Hold the ball until an attacker moves into an open situation, then you serve the ball to that attacker. The team in possession tries to create a good shooting opportunity. Defenders and attackers switch roles at regular intervals.

Coaching Points

- Attackers should stay positive and take shooting opportunities early.
- Players should aim for accuracy before power and should stay calm.
- The player in possession should attempt to "sight" the goalkeeper, select which skill to use, and shoot at goal with precision and often at speed.
- If under pressure from a defender, a player may attempt to dribble and shoot or combine with other attackers to produce a scoring opportunity.

Coaching Progressions

1. If attackers are unable to get shots on target, reduce the number of defenders.
2. The player with the ball, when marked tightly from behind, tries to turn and beat the defenders.
3. Whichever player gains possession is joined by the other two. They become the attacking team, and others respond as defenders (the first player to the ball becomes the attacker).
4. You serve 20 times into the penalty box. Whichever team scores the most goals at the end of the practice wins. ■

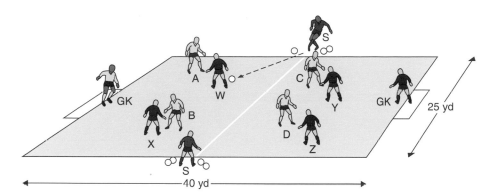

Purpose To increase the area in which players operate but also to introduce both the attacking and defensive roles as dictated by possession of the ball and, most important, to encourage players to react quickly when the ball changes hands and the attackers become defenders.

Equipment A supply of soccer balls; portable goals or flags; different-colored bibs for teams

Organization Players are in two teams of five (four players and one goalkeeper each), with two servers positioned at the halfway line of the practice area on a 40- × 25-yard mini-field. Teams are organized so that players of equal ability compete with each other.

Instructions The servers, with a good supply of balls, alternately deliver balls using a variety of serves. Goals may only be scored in the attacking half. Any player except the goalkeeper may move anywhere on the practice area.

Coaching Points

- All players should try to score when in the attacking half. Players should try not to shoot from the passing zone.

- When shooting, players should stay calm under pressure, take careful aim using low shots if possible, and follow in any shots that may rebound from the goalkeeper or the frame of the goal.

Coaching Progressions

1. Progress to one-on-one marking (e.g., only player X can tackle player B).
2. Temporarily remove one player from the winning side to restore the balance of the game. ◼

Conditioned Team Shooting Practice

Purpose   To work with all 11 members of your team at the same time and in a realistic and enjoyable situation

Equipment   A supply of soccer balls; different-colored bibs for teams

Organization   The goalkeeper and seven outfield players adopt their regular positions (three defenders—X, Y, Z; and four attackers—A, B, C, D). Two strikers (S) are positioned in, and restricted to playing in, the penalty area. The remaining defender (player W) must stay in the goal area with the goalkeeper until the ball enters the penalty area. Player W may then play however she feels is appropriate in defending against the two strikers.

Instructions   You start the game by passing to one of the attackers. Players A, B, C, and D combine to get the ball into the penalty area (which they cannot enter). Players X, Y, and Z defend as best they can outside the penalty area (which they cannot enter). Player W stays in the goal area until the ball enters the penalty area; then player W is free. The strikers remain inside the penalty area. When the ball arrives, the strikers try to score or pass to colleagues who must shoot first time. If the defenders (X, Y, or Z) gain possession of the ball, they should pass to the server as quickly and accurately as possible. The server then feeds the ball to the attackers immediately on receiving the pass.

Coaching Points

- Allow the players to think for themselves—don't overcoach.
- A variety of shooting situations will arise, each requiring a solution in terms of the choice and execution of the shot. Shooting success requires appropriate selection and accurate execution.
- Players receiving the ball in shooting positions under pressure from the defender should decide either to create a shot at goal or provide a teammate with a better scoring opportunity.
- Players should always be aware of the offside rule. They should be aware of the position and movements of the defender while also making sure they are not offside when they offer themselves for a pass.

Coaching Progressions

1. Players can change positions to sustain interest (i.e., defenders become attackers and vice versa).
2. Attacking players outside the penalty area can play the ball directly to one of the strikers to achieve penetration. ■

Heading

9

• • • • • •

FOR MANY YOUNG players, learning how to head the ball can be a painful experience—and nothing is more counterproductive for beginners. But it doesn't have to be painful. Introduced correctly and developed through a series of sensitive progressions, heading can be a very rewarding skill to master. Certainly, as players improve and develop both power and direction, this skill adds an essential dimension to their overall soccer ability. In addition to techniques for beginners, this chapter also deals with attacking and defensive heading for intermediate, advanced, and all-star players and introduces the game of head tennis.

Basic Heading Techniques

The keys to powerful heading are tensing the muscles of the neck and shoulders and striking the ball with the forehead the way a hammer strikes a nail. The key to accurate heading is looking at the intended target with the eyes, which ensures that the ball goes where it is intended. If a player is "flicking the ball on" to a player, usually behind him, however, knowing where that player is or will be at the time of contact is invaluable. Unfortunately, many beginners not only close their eyes on impact but also tilt their forehead downward and let the ball land on the top of their head, which can be very painful! Indeed, this combination of faults makes many learners frightened of heading the ball.

You can help your players overcome the fear of injury in several ways. Most coaches use a light, soft ball such as a volleyball or small, underinflated soccer ball in heading practice. This chapter describes two heading techniques—the diving and the standing technique. Regardless of the ball you use or the technique you teach, keep in mind that even with the best coaching and a strict adherence to safety factors, heading practices are challenging, so they should be frequent but short.

Diving Technique

For beginners, we strongly recommended that you teach heading using a simple diving movement from the kneeling position. In this technique the player heading the ball kneels, with his trunk upright and arms bent slightly (see figure 9.1*a*). A server gently lobs the ball through the air using both hands, so that it lands approximately 2 feet in front of the player heading the ball (see figure 9.1*b*), who dives gently forward putting weight on his hands, with his eyes open, and pushes his head through the center of the ball with the flat part of the forehead (see figure 9.1*c*), sending the ball directly back to the hands of the server.

Because the server holding the ball stands above the player heading the ball, the forehead is correctly aligned; the dive of the player ensures that the head strikes the ball. When the ball is headed correctly, it goes straight back to the hands of the server. On the other hand, a ball that is headed too soon rises up in an arc; a ball headed with the eyes down simply hits the ground; and a ball headed with the head down simply makes contact with the top of the head and once again arcs through the air. Therefore, when using the diving technique, both you and the player get instant feedback about how well he headed the ball. As the player gains confidence, the dive will become more adventurous; the server can develop this by serving to the side or conducting the practice in front of goal so the player can develop the full diving header.

Figure 9.1 Diving technique for heading.

Standing Technique

The more conventional way to coach beginners to head the ball is by using the standing technique. Here, a server gently lobs the ball, using both hands, and the player heading the ball stands and heads the ball on a flat trajectory back to the server. To do this, the player heading the ball should stand with one foot forward, arms out to the sides, eyes open, and watching the ball as it comes toward the forehead (see figure 9.2a). The player heading the ball should strike the center of the ball with the forehead, keeping the neck muscles firm, and move the upper body forward at the time of impact to add power (see figure 9.2b).

Figure 9.2 Standing technique for heading.

Attacking and Defensive Heading

Once the basic heading technique has been established, you can concentrate on the two basic situations in which heading occurs in the game—that is, in attacking and defensive situations. The differences are easily recognized. When heading defensively, the emphasis is on gaining distance and adding height on the ball. This usually occurs in the penalty area to clear a potential threat on goal and gain time. Attacking heading is just the opposite. Here, attackers are trying to score goals, usually from close range in the penalty or 6-yard area.

Attacking Heading

Many attacking headers require the ball to be directed downward and away from the goalkeeper at the areas of the goal that the goalkeeper has the most difficulty defending (page 142). Thus, the player has the problem of directing the ball past the goalkeeper and controlling both the accuracy and the force of the strike at the same time, which is not easy!

Drill for Beginners

A good way to introduce attacking heading to beginners is using the triangular system of serving and heading, as described in the following drill.

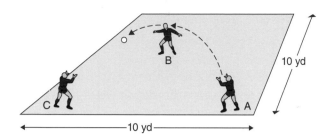

Equipment   One volleyball or soft soccer ball for every three players

Organization   Players are in groups of three in a triangle, about 4 yards apart in a 10-yard square.

Instructions   Player A throws to player B, who heads to player C. Player C throws to player A, who heads to player B. The sequence continues with each player heading in turn.

Coaching Points

- The server should serve in front of the header, who heads down.
- Players heading the ball should strike the ball rather than letting it hit them.
- Players heading the ball should place their feet apart to form a good base, move their feet to position themselves to head the ball, let their eyes direct the ball to the target, keep their neck and body muscles firm, and use their arms to increase power.

Coaching Progressions

1. Players move about the playing area, slowly at first, continuing the sequence of throw-head-catch.
2. Gradually increase the distance between the players until the services are approximately 6 to 8 yards in length.
3. The drill can be further developed into an opposed practice by introducing a defender. The three attackers throw, head, and catch the ball as they move it among themselves. Anyone can throw to any other player, but everyone must follow the throw-head-catch sequence. The defender can attempt to intercept the ball and, when successful three times, replaces one of the attackers. The defender can intercept the ball with her hands, or if a change of rule is preferred, she can only take possession of the ball by intercepting a throw with her head or a header with a catch, thus following the throw-head-catch sequence.

Drill for Intermediate Players

This next activity is one of our favorite drills. Players of all abilities find it a very enjoyable way to learn attacking heading. It provides an opportunity to practice their attacking heading skills without opposition. This noncombative situation greatly helps players develop their skills.

Doubles Heading

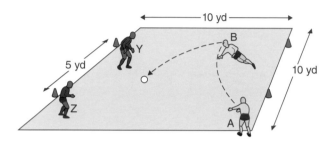

Equipment   One ball for every four players; four flags or cones

Organization   Players are in two teams of two players each, in an area 10 yards square with 5-yard-wide goals.

Instructions   Player A serves to player B, who tries to head past players Y and Z to score. Players Y and Z act as goalkeepers, and when they save or catch the ball, it is their turn to become the attackers. The first team to score 10 goals wins.

Coaching Points

- The serve must always be in front of the header.
- The player heading the ball should use the forehead, strike the ball hard, tense the neck and shoulder muscles, and direct the ball past the goalkeepers by knowing where the target is.

Coaching Progressions

1. The header progresses to a diving header (which is made possible by a careful serve).
2. The header moves in and jumps up to head the ball at goal, as an incoming forward would in a game. ■

Drills for Advanced Players

Advanced players must have a proper goal to aim toward, must play with a goalkeeper, and must learn to contend with opposition and a ball played at varying heights and distances. Such drills are best built up in stages, starting with a simple throw or serve to an incoming player without arranging opposition and then varying the speed and direction of the serve. Then, and only then, introduce opposition. We show this in the following drill.

Heading at Goal

Equipment   A supply of soccer balls of regular size and pressure

Organization   Players are in groups of five (one server, one goalkeeper, three headers) on a standard soccer field.

Instructions   The players form a line at the penalty spot. The server stands to the side of the goal and throws gentle, helpful serves. Each header takes a turn, aiming for the corner of the goal away from the goalkeeper, who does his best to save the attempt.

Coaching Points

- The player heading the ball starts 5 yards from the point at which he is likely to make contact (note that accurate service is required for this to happen).
- The player heading the ball moves toward the service and is prepared to jump or dive as appropriate, when making contact with the ball.
- The player heading the ball aims to generate power with direction, making contact on, or just above, the center line of the ball in order to direct it downward and past the goalkeeper.

» continued

Coaching Progressions

1. The players heading the ball must dive at the ball wherever appropriate, and again, accuracy of the service is important.

2. The ball is served over a greater distance from the side of the goal, possibly with an overarm throw using a flat trajectory.

3. The ball is delivered from a stationary position into the penalty box from a position down the side of the penalty box, as would be the case in an actual game.

4. With good players, wingers and fullbacks can dribble the ball and cross it into the goal-scoring areas for the attackers, who start their runs from a position 10 yards from the front of the penalty box.

5. Defenders try to stop goals and must be positioned according to the skills and developmental stage of the attackers. Always create situations in which the attackers can be successful, although they should have to earn that success under varying degrees of pressure.

Defensive Heading

Before you coach defensive heading, your players should have mastered the basic skills of heading, especially heading for height and distance. What they now must develop are the power and courage to meet the ball regardless of the challenge from the attacker. Indeed, the courage to attack the ball is a characteristic of both attacking and defensive heading, and it cannot be emphasized too soon.

A good defensive header has three qualities. The first is height; height gains time and safety and allows the defense to regroup. The second quality is distance; this really clears the ball away from the goal. The third quality is width; the ball must be directed out toward the wings and thus away from the shooting zone so it does not fall at the feet of an attacker.

Drill for Intermediate Players

Drills for intermediates are best taught without opposition. Intermediate players are typically still building confidence, and developing their skills and contending with an opponent too soon can be counterproductive. The drill on page 166 allows players to practice defensive heading without becoming frustrated or overwhelmed.

Defensive Heading in Threes

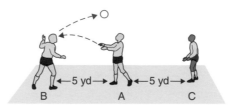

Equipment   One ball for every three players

Organization   Players are in groups of three, standing in a line with 5 yards between them.

Instructions   Player A throws to player B, who heads the ball over player A to player C. Player C controls the ball and returns it to player B. It then becomes player C's turn to head the ball. As the drill progresses, all players take turns serving the ball.

Coaching Points

- The player heading the ball stands with feet apart and uses the ground for leverage.
- The player heading the ball attempts to strike under the center line of the ball to gain height and uses the arms to pull the chest forward to add power to the contact.
- The player heading the ball keeps the neck and body muscles firm and is aggressive.
- While standing with the feet apart, the player heading the ball must be ready to adjust his feet according to the flight of the service in order to shift his body to make the required contact.

Coaching Progressions

1. Players increase the distance between them.
2. The player heading the ball increases the height of the clearance.
3. The player heading the ball runs in, jumps, and heads.
4. The next receiver becomes a moving target for the player heading the ball.
5. The server, having served, becomes an opponent. ■

⚽ Head Tennis

This game can be used with players of all abilities by modifying the rules to suit their skill level. It is very popular with all levels of players and makes an enjoyable break from normal training. It is realistic, involves players making decisions about which types of heading are required, and is very useful in building team spirit. It is a fun game that provides an enjoyable conclusion to a session on heading and can accommodate players of all abilities. The rules of the game can also be modified to include the development of ball control and juggling skills. For example, each player has to juggle the ball at least twice before returning it over the net or passing it on to another team member (see chapter 4).

Equipment   One soft volleyball; one net approximately the height of the tallest players

Organization   Players are in two teams of up to eight players on a volleyball or tennis court where a net can be erected. If a net is not available, the drill can be played in the center circle of a soccer field or in any area on the field; leave a space of no less than 3 yards between the opposing teams. This space acts as the net and becomes a central out-of-bounds zone between the teams. The scoring system is similar to that of the game of table tennis except that service changes hands on every point.

Instructions   Beginners head the ball directly over the net *or* catch it and serve it to a team member, who tries to head it over the net or the out-of-bounds zone. Intermediate players head the ball directly back *or* head it to a team member, who heads it back over the net or zone. Advanced players head the ball directly back *or* head it among team members no more than three times before heading it back over the net or zone.

For all levels, the rules of the game are as follows: The game is scored like table tennis. Each team has five serves. The first team to score 21 (or another number of your choice) wins. A point is scored if the ball bounces on the opponents' side or if it is not returned properly. A point is lost if the ball fails to clear the net, bounces out of court, or is not played over the net according to the rules. The rules can be modified to allow the players who receive the ball to use any body surface to keep the ball off the floor and distribute it to other players, but the final touch to return the ball over the net must be a header.

Drill for Advanced Players

Advanced drills for heading, both attacking and defending, must contain realistic conditions—such as opposition and variety of service—to develop commitment and the courage to move in and attack the ball regardless of the challenge of other players. These elements are best introduced in stages. For example, start with a serve that gives the performing player a clear advantage in terms of space and time. Then, gradually reduce these advantages until both players have equal opportunities; you can even favor the opponent in the final stages of the drill.

Headed Clearances

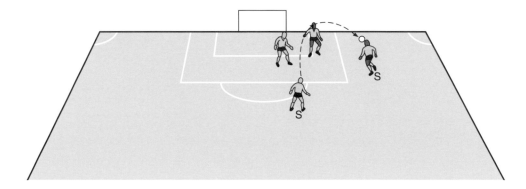

Equipment   One ball for every four players

Organization   Players are in groups of four (two headers, two servers) on one half of the penalty area.

Instructions   The first server accurately serves a high ball to a predetermined header. The player heads the ball to the second server, who stands outside the penalty area and at least 10 yards away. Having caught the ball, this player returns a throw to the second header, who heads the ball back to the first server, making the drill continuous.

Coaching Points

- The player heading the ball should initially head the ball with both feet on the ground to generate power. Movement of the feet is vital to do this.
- The player heading the ball should then time the jump to head the ball at the highest possible point. The service is important here to enable the header to watch the flight and calculate just where and when to attack the ball at its highest point.
- The player heading the ball should use the neck and shoulder muscles to generate force.
- The player heading the ball should strive for height, distance, and accuracy—in that order.

Coaching Progressions

1. Servers vary the height and trajectory of the service.
2. One player becomes a defender in front of the header, opposing her first passively, then actively.
3. Practice takes place in the area in front of the goal. A goalkeeper is added to develop a functional practice with a center back opposing a central striker.
4. Two defenders oppose two attackers, and a goalkeeper is added. Crosses are delivered from fluent situations in wide positions. Two strikers commence their runs to attack the ball approximately 10 yards outside the penalty area. These runs are matched by the defenders, who adopt the appropriate marking and defending positions to clear the cross, often as a result of heading the ball.

Drill for All-Star Players

The drill included here is used with competent players from U16 all-star teams to professional teams. The drill is ideal for all types of headed contact from both the defensive and attacking viewpoint and is ideal for the introduction and development of heading on the move in gamelike situations.

Throw-Head-Catch

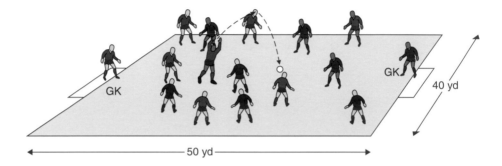

Equipment   Full-sized goals (or modified to suit the ages of the players); a supply of soccer balls; different-colored bibs for teams

Organization   Two teams of an equal number of players with goalkeepers play on a 50- × 40-yard playing area. These dimensions will accommodate teams with eight players each or fewer; adjust the size of your playing areas according to how many players you have.

Instructions   The game starts with a tip-off as in basketball. Teams play the game to score against each other with the final strike at goal being from a header. A team makes progress toward the opponents' goal by throwing to a teammate, who must head to another teammate, who then catches the ball and throws. Consequently, the sequence is throw-head-catch for the team to progress.

The opponents can regain possession only by using the same sequence (e.g., by heading a pass that has been thrown by the opponents, or catching a ball that has been headed). Should the ball fall to the ground, the first player to the ball should secure possession for his team and commence the sequence of throw-head-catch.

Should a player from the defending team break the sequence in his own penalty area, then a penalty results. This is taken by a server (one of the attacking players) throwing the ball from one side of the goal for an attacker to dive and head past the goalkeeper. The attacker must start on the penalty spot, and the goalkeeper must be on the goal line. Obviously, the size of the playing area will dictate the location of the penalty spot.

Players off the ball can move freely around the playing area, but the player in possession is not allowed to take more than three steps while holding the ball. All goals must be scored from a headed attempt at goal. If the ball leaves the field of play, then, as in an actual game of soccer, play is commenced by the use of a throw-in, a thrown corner, or a throw from the goalkeeper as opposed to the normal goal kick.

Coaching Points

- Players should search for support positions that enable them to receive the ball under as little pressure as possible.
- Players should know the positions of teammates before the ball arrives from the throw and attempt to accurately pass with the head to those teammates.
- Headers at goal sometimes must be taken under pressure; calculating how to beat the goalkeeper may not be possible. However, the attacker should make every attempt to keep the ball low by making contact at or above the center line of the ball. On other occasions the attacker may have the time to observe and judge the goalkeeper's position and thus be able to direct the ball past him.
- Defenders will often be under pressure to clear the ball, but there may be occasions in which the ball can be headed to a teammate rather than simply cleared with height and distance.

Coaching Progressions

1. Goals may only be scored with two feet off the ground (this will encourage diving headers and players attacking the ball early at its highest point in flight rather than waiting for the ball to arrive).

2. All services must be below head height except for the service for the final attempt at goal.

3. All goals must be scored from a cross from the attacking third of the field. ■

10

Goalkeeping

• • • • • •

THE GOALKEEPER IS arguably the most important position on the field. A good goalkeeper not only prevents the opposition from scoring, but also inspires the defense, and by using various distribution methods, contributes to the attack. In addition, modern goalkeepers must have "two good feet," meaning that they must be able to contribute to defensive tactics by being able to make safe, long, upfield kicks when defenders play balls back to them. Many coaches neglect their goalkeepers during practice situations, partly because the position can be difficult to coach and partly because they devote the majority of their time to the majority of their players, who are outfield players.

In short, a well-organized team should have two regular goalkeepers plus at least two other players who are capable of goalkeeping. Indeed, we believe that all players should try the goalkeeper position at some time in their development. There are three reasons for this. First, by engaging everyone in goalkeeping practice, you are better able to identify natural talent. Second, you have a responsibility to give all young players a comprehensive soccer education, and this includes goalkeeping. Third, goalkeeping practice gives everyone a personal insight into, and knowledge of, the requirements of the position and thus encourages an appreciation of and respect for whoever plays in goal, especially when she makes a mistake.

Goalkeeper Safety

Not all experienced goalkeepers like to wear protective clothing or devices such as knee and elbow protectors. Perhaps goalkeepers aren't required to wear these during a game, but in practice sessions, we advise the use of protective clothing. Sweatpants, long-sleeved uniforms, and pads should all be a part of your team equipment and should be provided for the goalkeepers—prevention of injuries is always better than cure.

You have a special duty to your goalkeepers. To ensure safety, enforce good player discipline in the penalty area. No player should ever be allowed to simply shoot at random at the goal, and two or more players should never shoot simultaneously. Practice should always be supervised and operated under clear and well-understood rules.

Also, no goalkeeper should have to practice in a worn, rutted, perhaps muddy area in front of the goal. You need to provide the best possible practice surface for the goalkeeper; often this is found in the area under the goal net. To expose this area, simply reverse the goal net and have players shoot into the goal from the back. You then have both a goal net to stop the ball and a safe surface for your goalkeeper. If you have portable tubular goals available, these can be easily moved into well-grassed areas of the field to provide your goalkeeper with perfect conditions. Ideally, every school or club should have a least one pair.

When choosing a goalkeeper, in addition to technical and tactical abilities, you should also look for desirable physical characteristics; there is no doubt that height is an advantage to a goalkeeper. Other qualities are also important, such as gymnastic ability, flexibility, speed of reaction, a sense of position, and courage. These are all desirable qualities and are essential for top-class players. Discovering natural goalkeeping ability can be very enjoyable for all concerned. Use a practice as shown in on page 188 of this chapter to help develop natural goalkeeping skills in all of your players.

The best way to help your goalkeepers improve their skills is to provide them with at least one special session a week. This session should be 35 minutes long (or longer) and can be held before regular practice begins or at a separate time in the week. If an assistant coach is available, he may be able to work with goalkeepers during regular practice, but if not, you may be surprised at just how willing outfield players can be to attend special sessions for goalkeepers.

Goalkeeping Warm-Ups

Goalkeepers, like outfield players, should follow a careful, individually designed, and systematic warm-up program. Prior to a coaching session, we recommend the following sequence of activities:

1. *General Jogging*

   Goalkeepers can jog with the outfield players because the aim is the same—to increase heart rate, raise the body temperature, and stimulate the circulation prior to strenuous exercise. Of course, this varies with regard to the climatic conditions and the work that will follow.

2. *Rolling*

   Next, goalkeepers roll on the ground in all directions mostly in the sitting or tuck position with the hands clasped around the knees and the chin down. In this safe sitting position, players can roll in various directions—forward, backward, and side to side. In addition to being a quite enjoyable activity, this exercise familiarizes goalkeepers with the ground and prepares them for the more demanding saves that require serious contact with the ground!

3. *Stretching and Mobilizing*

   Goalkeepers should not use any excessive bouncing or ballistic exercises at the start of the warm-up sequence, so they should stay seated on the ground and use progressive static stretching (see chapter 17) to work on the groin, spine, neck, arms, legs, and shoulders. Next, they stand up and continue working on the groin, hamstrings, and arms and shoulders. They can then gradually and very gently begin to flex and extend the spine and finally involve the arms and shoulders and begin swinging movements to extend the range and speed of their move- ments. At this point they are ready to being more explosive dynamic stretching activities.

4. *Explosive and Jumping Movements*

   Powerful, explosive, springing movements are essential in goalkeeping for diving saves and for dealing with high balls. Players must therefore train for these movements, but they should start gently with actions that employ about 40 to 50 percent effort. Vertical jumping using one-footed takeoffs, with one or both arms raised simultaneously as if catching or punching a ball, are ideal. Then players can work on increasing the power of their movements—jumping to block a ball thrown just over the crossbar (as in volleyball) is a good example. Also, the goalkeeper can practice pressure training to catch high balls thrown at short intervals toward various parts of the goal, perhaps by two or more servers. Catching a series of balls 2 feet above normal stretch height is good, hard training and is very skill related.

5. *Diving Movements*

   Goalkeeping warm-ups should be completed with simple diving-type movements to safely introduce the necessary body-to-ground contact, but should include more "falling on the ball" activities than actual diving. The goalkeepers, fully protected, simply toss the ball into the air and fall on it when it lands, hugging it to the body. As the activity progresses, encourage them to throw the ball higher and farther away so that they have to move several yards to get to the bounce of the ball, always trying to fall on it vertically. Finally, encourage them to roll after smothering the ball. The full sequence is throw-move-fall-roll; this provides a very demanding yet satisfying drill. Note that at this stage no full sideways diving movements are made—these should come later in a practice.

Basic Goalkeeping Techniques

The goalkeeper spends a major part of the game dealing with shots at goal. This involves both catching and diving and intelligent decision making about positional play. The goalkeeper's work can also be risky, so good discipline in shooting practices is essential.

Basic Stance

Like the receiver in tennis, the goalkeeper must be able to react quickly in any direction. To achieve this, he should assume a slightly crouched body position, with feet about shoulder-width apart, weight forward on the balls of the feet, and hands just above waist height with palms forward and fingers spread (see figure 10.1). The goalkeeper's body should be still at the moment the attacker shoots, and his eyes should be fixed on the ball.

Figure 10.1 Goalkeeper's stance.

Catching the Ball

Although the hands catch the ball first (included later are practices for catching the ball with the hands only), complete safety is ensured if the ball can then be clutched into the chest or the abdominal area as a second safety barrier (see figure 10.2). Teaching this method first highlights the vital skill of getting as much of the body into the path of the ball as possible, which requires good footwork. This double barrier, hands and body, can be emphasized by drawing attention to the two sounds made by a perfect execution. The first sound is the slap of the ball into the hands; the second is the sound of the ball being pulled into the body (see the drill Pingers on page 189 to practice this technique).

Figure 10.2 Two-sounds catching.

Figure 10.3
Proper hand position
for catching a ball
above chest height.

Figure 10.4
Collecting a gently
rolling ball.

Catching the Ball Above Chest Height

A ball that arrives high up on the chest or just under the chin can be awkward to hold. The goalkeeper can use an overhand grip, with one hand above and one below the ball (see figure 10.3), or can simply bend at the knees and drop the bodyweight just before contact with the ball, in order to raise the hands into a position in front of the head and absorb the speed and catch the ball.

Ground Shots

Shots along the ground range from those that roll gently toward the goalkeeper to those that are driven hard over a possibly bumpy, uneven surface. To collect balls that roll gently toward the goalkeeper, he simply bends from the waist, bends both knees slightly, places the feet slightly apart just in case there is an awkward final bounce, and lets the ball roll up into his hands, which are positioned behind the path of the ball (see figure 10.4).

The technique for a hard-driven shot is more involved. The goalkeeper should turn sideways to the ball just before it arrives (see figure 10.5a), drop down on one knee and place it close to the other foot so that no space exists for the ball to go between the feet, and make a cradle with the hands and arms in front of the body (see figure 10.5b). Now, if the ball comes awkwardly, the goalkeeper has at least two effective barriers against making a mistake.

Figure 10.5 Collecting a hard-driven ball.

Diving Saves

Diving saves are the most spectacular and enjoyable of all the goalkeeper skills. When goalkeepers are taught to dive correctly, they love making these types of saves. Diving saves do involve an element of danger, and therefore courage, so you should note the safety precautions provided earlier in this chapter and progress your goalkeepers slowly and carefully through the following practices.

- *Sitting and catching.* The player sits with legs straight but spread for the purposes of balance. When the ball is thrown, the player catches it (see figure 10.6, *a* and *b*) and rolls sideways.

Figure 10.6 Sitting and catching.

- *Kneeling and catching.* The player, kneeling, stretches to the side with both hands, catches the ball (see figure 10.7, *a* and *b*), and rolls sideways. The player should not land on the point of the elbow but should turn the shoulder underneath for safety at the moment of impact with the ground.

Figure 10.7 Kneeling and catching.

- *Punching.* Now the goalkeeper is ready to dive for balls that are beyond catching reach. He has to learn to deflect with the hand and punch with the fist, which gives the greatest distance on the *stretch diagonal* (the line through the body from one foot to the opposite arm and hand). Starting in the kneeling position, goalkeepers can reach farther if they use the higher hand for the aerial shot (see figure 10.8*a*) and the lower hand for the ground shot (see figure 10.8*b*). Note that the ideal width of the goals for this practice is twice the height of the goalkeeper. Players love this practice and usually forget that they are diving on what could be quite a hard surface. Further, they begin to make decisions for themselves, which is what goalkeeping is all about.

Figure 10.8　Punching: aerial shot (*a*) and ground shot (*b*).

Only when your goalkeepers enjoy and are competent in the simple diving practices described previously should you teach the full dive. When teaching the full dive, first find a soft surface and then follow these steps:

1. The goalkeeper crouches, facing away from you. Hold the ball and stand at body length distance from the goalkeeper—5 to 6 feet away (see figure 10.9*a*).
2. Make a loud, sharp command, such as "Now!" or "Go!" at which point the goalkeeper turns and dives to take the ball from your hands at full stretch (see figure 10.9*b*).
3. The goalkeeper dives for the ball at full stretch in a sideways-on position and then turns in flight to trap the ball against the ground with his hands over the ball to secure it (see figure 10.9*c*). Trapping the ball on the ground can also cushion the impact of the goalkeeper's landing.

By using this method, the goalkeeper learns how to react to a sudden command; in the general excitement, thoughts of injury or discomfort when

diving never occur. Also, the goalkeeper learns how to use the ball to break the fall. After this practice, put the goalkeeper into full-size goals, continue the normal shooting practices, and encourage the full dive whenever appropriate. Remember, however, that the goalkeeper enjoys the shots he saves, so control the service to benefit the goalkeeper, not the shooters.

Figure 10.9
Goalkeeper's diving practice.

Crosses

Many goalkeepers love to demonstrate their skill at catching a high ball crossed in or centered from the wings. This is a spectacular move that requires a high degree of positional sense and perfect timing of the jump to ensure that the ball is taken confidently at the highest possible point of that jump.

To gain maximum height, the player must take off from one foot, ideally after a short run toward the ball, so that the nontakeoff leg can also generate lift with a powerful upward movement and a bent knee (see figure 10.10). The player should take the ball with both hands spread in a W formation around the back of the ball and the fingers spread wide. As the player's arms and fingers reach upward, his eyes must fix on the ball. Indeed, fixing and keeping the eyes on the ball throughout the complete sequence is the key to success. Once the goalkeeper is committed to the move, he must not allow anything to distract the actions of looking at and catching (or punching) the ball.

Figure 10.10
Positioning for a cross.

Diving at the Feet of an Attacker

Diving at the feet of an attacker is the most difficult of the goalkeeping techniques; it requires skill, timing, and courage. Diving at the feet of an attacker is used to deny a scoring opportunity or dispossess the player. Keep in mind that this skill is for advanced players only; practicing it requires careful coaching to impress on the attacker that she is there to help the goalkeeper, not to score at any cost.

To practice diving at the feet of an attacker, the goalkeeper moves to the correct distance (which obviously will vary according to the starting position of the attacker and her speed and direction of approach) from goal and competes 1v1 against an attacker who has broken through the defense. The goalkeeper tries to jockey and position to force the attacker to move in a certain direction (players typically move toward their right side because they are more confident with their right foot). Once the goalkeeper forces the attacker to move in a sideways direction, the goalkeeper, when the time is appropriate, dives at the feet of the attacker and smothers the ball. The practice has four stages, in which the goalkeeper has four decisions to make.

First, the goalkeeper must determine the exact moment to start moving out of the goal toward the attacker. If the goalkeeper moves too soon, the attacker can simply chip the ball over him into an empty goal. If the goalkeeper moves too late, the angle is not reduced and the attacker has a very wide target at which to shoot. The goalkeeper should move forward slowly and under control, observing the actions of the attacker and being mindful of the space between the goalkeeper and the goal. With young goalkeepers it could be helpful to explain that they should defend the space behind them until the attacker crosses the penalty area line and then make a decisive, controlled, but balanced move forward (see figure 10.11a). The attacker may of course be under pressure from a recovering defender, which will influence the decision of the goalkeeper, or the pass intended for the attacker may be overhit, which will also be a major factor in deciding whether to leave the goal and gather the ball.

Second, the goalkeeper must try to force the attacker to move sideways away from the direct line toward the goal by offering no obvious and early targets for the attacker to exploit in the goal. Usually, the goalkeeper can achieve this by approaching the attacker along a line directly between the ball and the center of the goal (see figure 10.11b). Third, as the distance between the attacker and the goalkeeper decreases, the goalkeeper must then time the start of any dive toward the ball by waiting until the attacker plays the ball sideways (see figure 10.11c). And fourth, the goalkeeper must then time the actual dive for the ball in such a way that the hands and arms contact and gather the ball at the same time the body is positioned in as long a barrier to the attacker as possible (see figure 10.11d).

Figure 10.11   Diving at the feet of an attacker.

There are also two important positional skills for the goalkeeper to learn. These are narrowing the angle and supporting the defense.

Narrowing the Angle

When the goalkeeper moves off the line and goes forward to meet the attacker, we call this narrowing the angle. By moving forward, the goalkeeper reduces the target area between himself and the goalposts, as shown in figure 10.12, into which the attacker may direct a shot at goal.

Figure 10.12   Narrowing the angle of the shot by moving forward toward the ball.

Supporting the Defense

The goalkeeper should always be at the correct supporting position behind the defense, whether his team is attacking or defending. This distance is largely determined by the location of the ball, the space between the deepest defender and the goalkeeper, and whether pressure is being applied to the ball holder. The crucial factor is that the space behind the defense must be managed by the goalkeeper and the rear defenders, who may drop deeper to protect this valuable area.

When the distance between the goalkeeper and defenders is too great, intelligent attackers will play a through or overhead pass to get one of their players behind the defense, which results in a 1v1 situation with the goalkeeper. To counter this move, you must decide with your defenders and goalkeeper how this area will be protected. Much depends upon how far up-field play is taking place. For instance, if the ball is in the attacking third of the field approximately 80 to 100 yards away from goal, the goalkeeper may be positioned on the edge of, or even a few yards outside, the penalty box. If the ball is around the halfway line, then the goalkeeper will be around the penalty spot, and if the ball is central in the defending third of the field, the goalkeeper will not be too far from the 6-yard line.

These distances are merely guidelines, but are the foundations on which the goalkeeper bases her positioning. The goalkeeper continually adjusts her support position as the ball moves around the area, positioning herself on a line between the ball and the center of the goal. From this position, the goalkeeper can give information to her defenders, organize their actions, act as an extra defender and, if necessary, come forward to intercept any over-hit passes from the attackers. She can also play constructively on gaining possession by passing to a teammate or, for safety, by kicking the ball forward with height, distance, and accuracy if the situation demands.

From his support position behind the defense, the goalkeeper decides when to come forward and away from the goal line if an attacker breaks through the defense. As explained earlier, the more the goalkeeper comes forward from his line, the smaller the space is for the attacker to score between the posts and the goalkeeper; however, the opportunity to score by lifting the ball over the goalkeeper and under the crossbar increases. In a 1v1 situation in which the forward has broken through, the goalkeeper must come forward from the line but under control, in the basic goalkeeper's stance as explained earlier. He must also be ready for any strike at goal from an attacker who decides to shoot rather than take on the goalkeeper in a 1v1 situation. Because this circumstance is not uncommon, goalkeeper practice time should be devoted to this vital aspect of the role both with and without the full defense in position. Only by practicing and getting intelligent advice from you will the goalkeeper and the defenders be able to decide on a strategy for handling this situation.

Judging Angles When Shot-Stopping

In shot-stopping situations, the goalkeeper always moves into a position between the attacker with the ball and the center of the goal and is forward of the goal line (how far will once again be decided by the location of the ball) in the basic shot-stopping stance (see figure 10.13). The goalkeeper is continually moving her feet to change her position as the attacker changes the position of the ball.

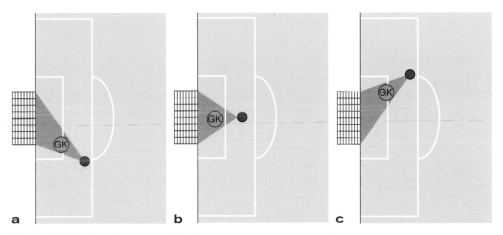

Figure 10.13   Goalkeeper positioning to protect the near post.

An excellent way to teach the young goalkeeper to find the correct angle in which to position himself is to use a piece of cord 20 yards long. Tie the ends to the bottom of each post and take the apex of the triangle toward the ball; the resulting lines tell the goalkeeper exactly the angle in which to position herself when shot-stopping.

Distributing the Ball

The goalkeeper needs to be able to distribute the ball both by kicking (for distance and accuracy) and throwing (for speed and accuracy). She must also know when to use the various techniques to set up an attacking move quickly (often by switching play) and when to wait with the ball until team members have moved forward into balanced attacking positions.

Distribution by Kicking

The goalkeeper, whenever possible, should be encouraged to take all goal kicks to relieve other players from this duty because it is primarily the goalkeeper's responsibility. The goalkeeper must also be expert at the volley and half-volley kicks (sometimes called the "drop kick" where the goalkeeper gently throws the ball forward and strikes it just as it bounces), to increase the range and accuracy of distribution skills. When volleying, the goalkeeper must also be taught that a kick that produces a ball dropping vertically down is much harder for the forwards to control than a ball with a flatter trajectory. Forwards much prefer balls approaching with flat trajectories, either to control or to play backward behind the defense. However, at times the kick with the high and lengthy trajectory is valuable because it can cause the defenders many problems in contacting and clearing the ball accurately.

The trajectory is affected by the way the goalkeeper strikes the ball, which is affected by the manner in which the ball is thrown by the goalkeeper before striking the ball. Simply tossing the ball into the air in front of the body and kicking it with an upward swing of the foot is likely to produce a high trajectory that is difficult for players to control. Feeding the ball slightly to the side of the body and striking it as with a "side-volley" produces a flatter trajectory, which is easier for the receiver to control. Many top goalkeepers playing today use this side-volley action to produce a flat and accurate delivery.

Additionally, the half-volley kick will assist the goalkeeper in achieving a lower trajectory. The ball is struck with the laces at the moment it rebounds from the ground after the goalkeeper drops it ahead of his favored kicking foot. If the goalkeeper's toe is turned down and the knee is over the ball at contact, provided the upper body is not leaning excessively backward, the ball should follow a low trajectory if contacted through the center line. All goalkeepers should spend time practicing their distribution skills using a variety of kicking techniques and both feet. Aiming at and hitting both close targets and distant targets provides useful practice. It is largely a matter of developing a clean contact on the ball.

Also, when a defender under pressure passes the ball back, the goalkeeper can then distribute the ball, possibly with a long kick upfield or an accurate pass to one of his own players over a short distance. Because the defender passing the ball back to the goalkeeper may pass it to either the goalkeeper's left or right foot, the goalkeeper has to be able to kick, with confidence, with both feet. This is an important feature of a recent rule change which prevents the goalkeeper from handling a ball that is passed back (unless it is headed back).

On a regular basis, the goalkeeper should be included in all passing practices, in which he should be obliged to both receive and release the ball with his feet. At the highest levels of the game, goalkeepers are increasingly dealing with the ball at their feet. For this reason, you would do well to heed this requirement and begin to develop excellent footwork both with and without the ball at an early stage in a goalkeeper's development.

Distribution by Hand

Goalkeepers can use three popular techniques for distributing the ball by hand: the javelin throw, the overhead throw, and the roll. The roll is very accurate over short distances and is easy for the receiver to control because it has no sidespin. The technique is similar to bowling because the ball begins and ends its journey on the ground. Its weakness is that it can only be used over shorter distances. The more common techniques are the powerful javelin and overhead throws, as discussed in the following sections.

First, however, it is worth noting that with all thrown distributions, the goalkeeper should call out to inform the receiver of the possibilities available on receiving the ball (e.g., "turn" or"plenty of time"), and with the shorter-range throws, actually move in the direction of the receiver into a support position for any return pass if necessary.

Like outfield players, goalkeepers—often prior to receiving the ball—should be aware of the tactical options available to them so they can make early and quick decisions about instant throwing or delaying the release of the ball. The modern goalkeeper is now an integral part of a team's attacking and defending game and must be included in practices with the defending and attacking units as the team rehearses tactics. The goalkeeper must be accurate when distributing the ball and must master the art of all distribution skills in order to play her full part in the attacking game.

Javelin Throw

The javelin throw for soccer is similar to a throw used in baseball and cricket. The ball is thrown hard and flat, with the elbow leading the throwing action. The ball is supported and then delivered by one hand only. More pace and distance can be applied to the service when the hand is behind the ball with the palm and fingers spread at the point of delivery. The goalkeeper must practice until he can make this throw preferably from either hand without imparting sidespin, which complicates the control for the receiving player.

Overhead Throw

The overhead throw is similar to the hook pass in basketball or to bowling the ball at the wicket in cricket. The goalkeeper stands almost sideways to the intended target with the front foot reaching ahead of the body and acting as a fulcrum for the delivery. The goalkeeper uses a long, high, and quick windmill arm action to achieve sufficient height to clear opposing players and sufficient distance to reach the receiver and follows through with the throwing arm and body moving toward the target.

Goalkeeping Drills

Above all, goalkeepers need courage and confidence. They need the confidence to make the right decisions, especially about when to go out from the goal line to catch or punch a ball coming into a crowded penalty area, or whether to stay on the goal line and watch and wait. Moreover, once they have made their decisions, goalkeepers need the courage to carry them out. They have to be prepared to make mistakes that can cost the team the match—and also saves that win the match! In this section we present drills and realistic situations that can help goalkeepers at all levels of ability develop both courage and confidence.

It is worth mentioning, however, that drills for goalkeepers often serve a dual purpose; what is a learning experience for a beginner can be a warm-up drill for an experienced goalkeeper. A good example of this is the very popular drill called Pingers, so named because of the sounds made when the server volleys the ball and when the goalkeeper takes the shot in the hands. When the drill is done well, the two pings are most impressive.

Drills for Beginners

When introducing basic goalkeeping skills to beginners, you should, ideally, already have preselected two or three potential goalkeepers from the team. However, a good case can be made for teaching all members of your team how to keep goal. First, you never know when an outfield player might have to take over the goalkeeper's position because of injury, and second, learning how to keep goal is part of your players' soccer education. It also makes them more sympathetic when their goalkeeper makes a mistake!

Basic Goalkeeping

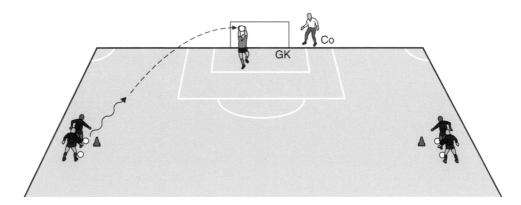

Equipment   A supply of soccer balls

Organization   One player acts as a goalkeeper and stands on the middle of the goal line. The remaining players take up positions on the flanks, each with a ball.

Instructions   The goalkeeper takes up a central position inside the 6-yard box so he can see the ball delivered from the attacking player. Taking turns alternately from the left and right sides, the flank players, on your instruction, touch the ball forward and then deliver it into the penalty area. The goalkeeper moves toward the ball and takes off from one foot, bringing the other knee up high to add vertical lift. The goalkeeper takes the ball at the highest possible point in flight, using both hands in the W formation (fingers spread and facing upward behind the ball, with the thumbs almost touching). Upon landing, he secures and protects the ball by enveloping it in his chest area as described earlier in this chapter. The goalkeeper then returns the ball to the kicker and turns to receive a ball from the other side.

Purpose   To allow the goalkeeper to become accustomed to receiving hard shots to the body

Equipment   One ball for every two players

Organization   Players are in pairs (one server, one goalkeeper) in free space standing 8 to 10 yards apart. The closer the players are, the more difficult the drill will be for the goalkeeper.

Instructions   The server volleys the ball toward the goalkeeper's upper body. The goalkeeper positions herself behind the line of the flight and takes the ball with the hands only. If the server is unable to volley inaccurately, then she should throw the ball at the goalkeeper's upper body.

Coaching Points

- The goalkeeper should use good footwork, with her weight forward, and keep her hands in the W formation.
- The goalkeeper should allow the ball to come to her rather than reaching forward to collect it.
- Even though the goalkeeper takes the ball with her hands, she should try to get her body into the line of flight.
- When the service is lower into the midriff, the goalkeeper may be unable to make the first contact with her hands. In this case, she should allow the ball to come past her hands and into her abdominal area, rapidly wrapping her forearms and hands around the ball to secure it.

Coaching Progressions

1. Progression with this practice depends on the service. To increase difficulty, decrease the distance, vary the height, and increase the force of the serve.
2. The goalkeeper begins in a position to the left or right of the intended shot and must move into the line of flight.

Clock Shooting

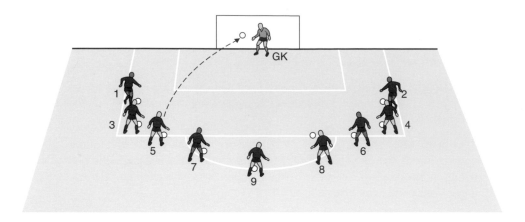

Purpose   To train the goalkeeper to move the feet rapidly and prepare quickly for the shot

Equipment   One ball for each player

Organization   Players are in a group of unlimited number in a semicircle around the penalty area of a standard soccer field. The shooters are numbered alternately from each end inward as shown in the figure. The goalkeeper stands approximately 6 yards in front of the goal.

Instructions   The shooters shoot as you call their numbers. The goalkeeper positions himself for each shot. Make sure the goalkeeper has time to position himself between shots.

Coaching Points

- The goalkeeper should position himself correctly in terms of narrowing the angle for each shot.

- The goalkeeper should be balanced and still and in the basic shot-stopping stance at the moment he takes the shot.

- The goalkeeper must decide what technique to use to save each particular shot—they will all differ. Some shots can be held and secured using the techniques explained earlier. Some will have to be deflected outside the goal and behind the goal line, whereas others will have to be deflected over the crossbar.

- The goalkeeper must recover to make a second save if he does not succeed at holding and securing the first shot—it may fall to an attacker following up the shot at goal.

Coaching Progressions

1. The shooters increase the speed at which they release their shots.

2. Two players on opposite sides of the penalty area work together. One shoots on your command, and the other rebounds for any shots that rebound off and away from the goalkeeper.

Drills for Intermediate Players

For intermediate players, you can use any of the previous beginner drills, but you must move farther and farther away to increase the height and distance of the service. This leads to the ball being volleyed or kicked across to add to the realism. As the goalkeeper improves, additional opposing players are introduced, which leads to the next section for more advanced players.

Alternate Shots

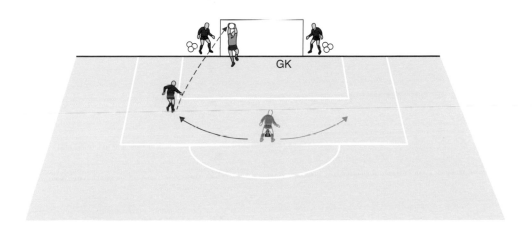

Equipment   A supply of soccer balls; one flag or cone

Organization   Players are in teams of four (one goalkeeper, one shooter, two servers) on a standard soccer field. The shooter operates from an area just inside the penalty area, from behind a central cone or flag. The servers, with a supply soccer balls, stand by each goalpost.

Instructions   The server serves the ball to the shooter along the ground. From her position behind the flag or cone, the shooter moves to receive the service and shoots at goal. She should follow up or rebound the shot for any secondary scoring opportunity. The server can alternate between an aerial serve or a ground serve, and should alternate right and left. Once the shooter has taken the shot and rebounded, she returns to her position behind the flag or cone.

Coaching Points

- The goalkeeper should move quickly into position as the ball travels toward the shooter.
- The goalkeeper should be still and balanced in the shot stopping stance just before the shot is released.
- You should help the goalkeeper select the appropriate shot-stopping technique.
- The goalkeeper should recover quickly and readjust her position if necessary to make a second save attempt if the first attempt does not secure the ball.

» continued

Coaching Progressions

1. Increase the tempo of the drill by reducing the time between shots. This also places an increased demand upon the shooter.

2. Introduce a second shooter, who, when called, has to dribble a ball into the area, dribble past the goalkeeper, and score. This forces the goalkeeper into a 1v1 situation and requires that she not only narrow the angle but also dive at the feet of the oncoming player as well as make saves from shots. You should obviously allow the goalkeeper to make the first save and any second save from a rebound before calling for the second attacker to dribble at the goalkeeper. ■

Drills for Advanced Players

All advanced goalkeeping drills require partner activity. The server can, from various ranges and at various speeds, roll, pass, throw, kick, volley, and dribble the ball to the goalkeeper, depending on the technique the goalkeeper needs to improve. To progress such drills, change them into pressure training (for more information, see chapter 19). Also refer to the chapters on shooting and tactics at corner kicks and free kicks (chapters 8 and 16), which contain many excellent situations for realistic goalkeeper training.

Remember that the introduction of more players, both attackers and defenders, into the drills makes the actual technique of catching the ball more difficult, because the goalkeeper is now in a crowded situation and may not have a clear route to the ball. It also requires the goalkeeper to make gamelike decisions. The two most important decisions are (1) leaving the goal to try to reach the ball versus staying in the goal to see what happens and (2) catching the ball versus punching it away.

As always in goalkeeping, the ability to make quick decisions and react at speed is crucial. The following two drills highlight these requirements in different circumstances. Goalkeepers enjoy these activities because they specifically challenge their capacity to deal with crosses and shots at goal.

Crosses and Shots

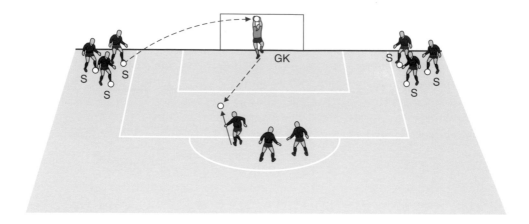

Equipment   A supply of soccer balls, at least one for each player

Organization   Players are in groups of 10 (six servers, three shooters, one goalkeeper) on a standard soccer field. Three servers are on each side of the penalty area, and three shooters are in the penalty arc. The goalkeeper is in the goal.

Instructions   The goalkeeper collects a high cross from one of the servers and then distributes the ball to one of the shooters, who takes an immediate shot at goal. The goalkeeper now has to deal with a cross followed quickly by a strike at goal. The goalkeeper should be given a rest after about 12 repetitions.

Coaching Points

- The goalkeeper must position correctly in the goal area for both the cross and the shot.
- The goalkeeper should anticipate both the cross and the shot and read and react to the flight of both.
- The goalkeeper should constantly adjust both the feet and the hands to either catch or deflect both crosses and shots.

Coaching Progressions

1. A shooter moves forward to attack the cross, and the goalkeeper must now decide whether to stay in and defend the goal or move to take the cross.
2. A player making a cross tries to float the ball into the goal and score.
3. A player making a cross aims for the far-side servers, who become strikers.
4. The goalkeeper has defenders: initially a center back, then two backs, then a full defense.
5. Players progress to wave attacks (see chapter 14 for more information).
6. Players practice tactics at corners (chapter 16 for more information). ■

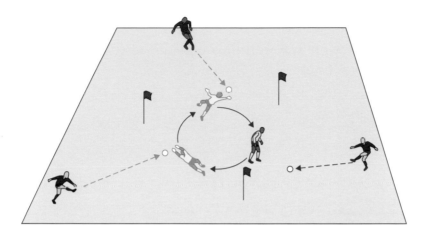

Purpose   To develop the agility of goalkeepers so they can adapt to various situations

Equipment   A supply of soccer balls for each shooting player; three corner flags

Organization   Players are in teams of four (one goalkeeper, three shooters), and the flags are about 8 yards apart forming a triangular goal. The shooters are approximately 15 to 20 yards from the goal depending on the age and ability of the players.

Instructions
The goalkeeper moves to each side of the goal in sequence and reacts according to each shooter, whose only instruction is to score. The shooters may elect to shoot or to dribble. The shooters should keep in mind that their aim is to get the goalkeeper to make a good save. They are there to bring out the best in their keeper, and they should shoot accordingly. Shooters should take shots at your command, so the goalkeeper can have time to recover from the previous strike at goal and reposition to make the next save in the adjacent goal.

Coaching Points
- Along with you, the goalkeeper should determine the correct distance off the goal line when facing up to the shooter as well as the correct angle prior to the shot.
- The goalkeeper must move his feet quickly to maneuver to each shot and from goal to goal, but not as the shot is being taken.
- The goalkeeper should always attempt to be balanced, still, and in the shot-stopping stance before reacting to the shot, but he must prepare quickly.

Coaching Progressions
1. Players increase the speed of the practice by your giving the goalkeeper less time to prepare for each shot from the different attackers. He must move more quickly between the goals and into position.
2. Number the shooters and call out the numbers at random causing the goalkeeper to move into position according to the location of the attacker and not in a predictable sequence. The goalkeeper should face six consecutive shots before resting and recovering for the next round of strikes. ■

Drill for All-Star Players

The following drill, although primarily designed to coach and train the goalkeeper in collecting and distributing the ball from crosses, can easily be enhanced by integrating a shooting challenge into the work.

All In

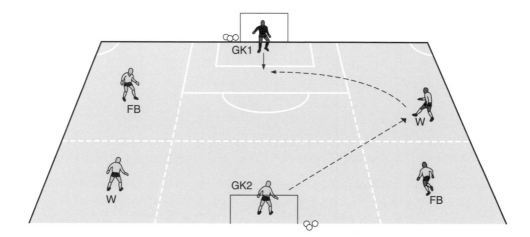

Equipment   A supply of soccer balls behind or to the side of each goal; cones to mark the width of the playing area (44 yards and from the goal line to the halfway line on a standard soccer field)

Organization   Two goalkeepers are standing in opposite goals, and four wide players (two wingers and two fullbacks) are in each area as illustrated.

Instructions   Goalkeeper 2 throws the ball to the winger, who receives the ball, as illustrated in the figure. Within two touches (if possible) the winger crosses the ball for goalkeeper 1 to collect. Once goalkeeper 1 has collected the ball, he throws it to the winger on the other side of the area. The action is repeated toward goalkeeper 2. The winger must be in the attacking half of the playing area on receiving the ball. At your call, the players change sides so that the goalkeeper can collect crosses from both the left and right sides.

Coaching Points

- When distributing the ball, the goalkeeper should move forward from the goal and communicate with the wide player about what he is going to do.
- With your help, the goalkeeper should continuously move his position according to the location and movement of the ball ahead of him.
- You should constantly monitor, and correct if necessary, the goalkeepers' distance from goal and their positioning to attack and collect the cross before and as it is delivered.
- The distribution of the ball will be influenced by the distance of the intended receiver, whether the delivery is from the hands or feet. Monitor the goalkeeper's decision making and technique of collecting the cross.

Coaching Progressions

1. The goalkeeper can distribute the ball to the winger, who must be overlapped by the fullback, who will then cross the ball from a more advanced position, nearer to the end line of the pitch.

2. The ball can be delivered to the fullback, who passes to the winger and overlaps. This forces the goalkeeper to constantly adjust his position according to the location of the ball as it is passed and then moved into a position to be crossed.

3. The ball can also be distributed to the fullback, who, within two touches, must cross the ball from a distant and deeper position, thus altering the angle of the delivery into the box.

4. You can introduce two attacking players at each end of the pitch 20 yards from goal who contest the cross. Either or both of the two attacking players challenge for the cross with the goalkeeper, who must decide to catch, deflect the ball over the bar, or punch the ball to safety. Should the goalkeeper catch and secure the ball, he can throw to the two attackers in the attacking half, who will turn and shoot or dribble the ball at the other goalkeeper in an attempt to score. They may also combine their play—possibly in the form of a wall pass or a pass and overlap movement—before a shot is taken at goal, with both players rebounding the strike at goal.

5. More players can be introduced as the practice is built up to resemble the competitive match. In addition to the defenders included in coaching progression 4, a defender may be introduced in the wide channels to pressure the winger or fullback, whoever is in possession, and also defend against the combined play of the winger and fullback. Most of the goalkeeping skills (shot-stopping, dealing with crosses, defending in a 1v1 circumstance, and distributing the ball) are embodied in this practice. Of course, the outfield players are also involved in developing their positional skills.

 **Goalkeeper Game**

Goalkeeper Game is an excellent goalkeeper practice, for players at an intermediate level and above, because it provides an enjoyable environment in which players can develop most of the skills discussed in this chapter, from kicking and throwing to narrowing the angle and dealing with shots.

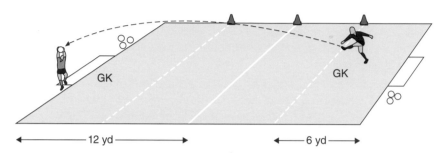

Equipment   A supply of soccer balls; two portable goals or sets of flags

Organization   Two goalkeepers practice against each other, protecting two opposing goals 24 yards apart.

Instructions   The game starts when one goalkeeper takes a dead ball (stationary) kick or throw from the 6-yard line and tries to score past her opponent. This kick also restarts the game whenever a shot misses the goal and the ball goes out of play or when there is a dispute of any kind not covered in the rules. The receiving goalkeeper catches her opponent's shot and can then shoot back by using a volley or half-volley from the point at which she made the catch. If the receiving goalkeeper parries the shot but fails to catch it, then she takes a 6-yard kick. If the ball rebounds over the center line, the goalkeeper loses possession (this encourages the goalkeepers to pounce on any ball they cannot hold). If a ball rebounds from the goalposts, the goalkeeper takes a 6-yard kick. The players can set any number of goals as the target or play for a predetermined time.

11

Tackling and Defensive Skills

• • • • • •

ALL PLAYERS MUST develop good defensive skills, which includes more than just being able to tackle correctly. Good defenders are able to out-think their opponents and can often win the ball or force an error without coming into contact with the attacker. Defenders must be able to anticipate the play, play aggressively (but fairly), and position themselves correctly. When these mental and physical skills are combined with courage and determination, you have a real defender. This chapter begins with mental strategies for advanced players who already know how to tackle. However, if you are coaching beginners, you should start with the section beginning on page 219, which deals with coaching the basic tackles.

First and Second Defenders

Every defender must be able to recognize whether she is the first or second defender. The first defender is the player who is nearest the opponent with the ball and whose main duty is to stop the attacker from advancing unchecked, playing the ball forward, and possibly shooting a goal. The second defender must support the first defender, but must also think about the developing tactical situation. When defenders are confused about which role they should be playing, they are most vulnerable. Players cannot be taught too soon that, generally speaking, the nearest player goes to oppose the player with the ball.

First Defender

As mentioned previously, the first defender is the player nearest the opponent with the ball. Because his primary duty is to stop the attacker, the first defender must know how to close down an attacker and jockey, win the ball by good positioning and interception, stop the attacker from turning with the ball, force the attacker one way, and recover when beaten. Let's look at these actions in more detail.

Closing Down on an Attacker

The first defender must always go toward the attacker with the ball. If the attacker is close, the first defender has only a short distance to cover. However, when the attacker is some distance away, the defender must move quickly yet cautiously; to rush at an attacker who is in full possession of the ball is asking for trouble! Young players can be taught to close down on attackers in the following four stages:

1. *Initial Approach*

   The defender runs quickly and with a normal running action while the ball is traveling toward the attacker but is not yet under his control. See figure 11.1 for an example of approaching the attacker.

Figure 11.1   Approaching the attacker.

2. *Split Step*

   To slow down or sometimes halt the running action, the defender executes a split step by stopping sharply with one foot forward and one backward and the knees bent; the body assumes a crouched position to aid balance. This should be done about 3 to 5 yards from the attacker as he takes control of the ball. See figure 11.2 for an example of the split step.

Figure 11.2   Split step when approaching the attacker.

3. *Close In*

The defender now closes in on the attacker cautiously and in a threatening manner, edging forward step by step. The intention is to force the attacker to look down at the ball to see where it is in order to protect or manipulate it, or to cause the attacker to turn away from a forward-passing or running-with-the-ball option. The moment the attacker's eyes go down, he is a reduced threat. See figure 11.3 for an example of closing in on the attacker.

Figure 11.3   Closing in on the attacker.

4. *Jockey*

Having contained the attacker and prevented a penetrating move, the defender should jockey and wait for the right opportunity to try to win the ball or force the attacker away from the danger zone. See How to Jockey on page 203 for more information on jockeying.

How to Jockey

Jockeying, the skill of keeping between the attacker and her intended target (usually the goal), requires the defender to slow down or delay the attacker while at the same time trying to force an error or make a successful tackle. The jockeying stance is similar to that of a boxer; the body is sideways, the feet are apart, and the weight is on the toes to allow quick movement in any direction. The eyes watch the ball and, in the peripheral vision, the midline of the attacker's body, not her head or shoulders. In this way, sudden upper-body movements do not throw the defender off balance.

The key to good jockeying is footwork. The defender's feet should move like a boxer's, as shown in figure 11.4a, but must never be caught square to the line of attack, as shown in figure 11.4b.

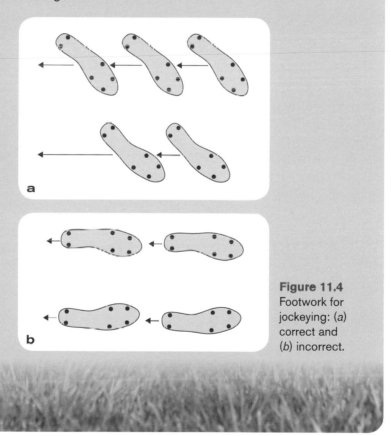

Figure 11.4 Footwork for jockeying: (a) correct and (b) incorrect.

Winning the Ball by Good Positioning and Interception

Clearly, good positioning and interception go hand in hand; good positioning helps the defender to win the ball by interception. However, these elements differ in an important way. The decision to intercept comes at the moment the ball is actually passed to a player and requires a split-second decision and reaction, whereas the thought processes that control good positioning occur before the release of the ball and over a period of time and in relation to the tactical movements of other players.

This difference is worth developing with your advanced players, and you can start with the two examples, shown in figures 11.5 and 11.6. Figure 11.5 shows a perfect example of how the defender (player A) ensures winning the ball by good positioning behind player C. If the attacker (player B) plays the ball over or past player A, player C loses the race to the ball because player A has read the delivery and dropped early to turn and win the race to the ball. If the ball is played to player C's feet, player A, by good positioning and reading the intention of the passing player, intercepts the pass, if possible. If this is not possible, he simply stops him from turning with the ball and in this way gains more time. This is good defending.

In figure 11.6, the ball is played to the attacker (player C) from midfield. The defender (player A) is now in a position to read and anticipate the pass and win the ball by interception. Reading the play and anticipating the likely event are important defensive skills for any player.

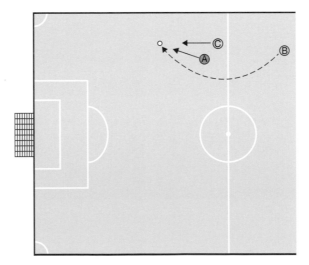

Figure 11.5   Good positioning by a defender.

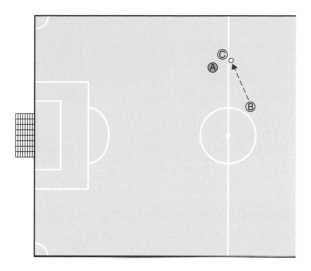

Figure 11.6 Defender in a position to intercept the ball.

Stopping the Attacker From Turning With the Ball

If interception is not possible, excellent defensive players stop the attacker with the ball from turning comfortably and facing the defender's goal. Such defensive play counters three potential dangers: the shot at the goal, the pass forward, and the attacking dribble.

Stopping the turn is a hallmark of good defense by individual players and by the defense as a whole. It is an advanced skill, however, because it requires confidence plus the self-control to avoid tackling from behind and risking giving away a free kick or, worse, a penalty kick. See figure 11.7 for an example of stopping an attacker from turning with the ball.

Figure 11.7 Stopping an attacker from turning with the ball.

Forcing an Attacker in One Direction

In addition to slowing an attacker by jockeying and backing off, a good defender can often force the attacker one way. By positioning to one side of the attacker, the defender can force the attacker away from a danger zone and toward other, supporting defenders, or onto the stronger tackling side of the defender or the attacker's weaker foot.

Perhaps the best example of forcing an attacker to move in the least dangerous direction occurs when the fullback directs, or invites, the winger to play down the sideline, thus stopping the winger from attacking directly toward goal.

Recovering From Being Beaten

"What do I do if I'm beaten?" This is not the kind of question a player is likely to ask a coach because the answer might be a rebuke: "Don't think about being beaten—think positive!" However, players do get beaten, and they must know what to do when it happens. Players should be taught the following four stages of recovery. Either individually or collectively, these stages provide the beaten player with clear guidelines about how to react in the best interests of the team, give immediate chase, use a recovery line, get goalside of the ball, and stop and cover.

- *Giving immediate chase.* Inexperienced or poor players often throw their heads up or cry out in anguish if they make a mistake; this wastes valuable time. The first thought in the player's mind must be to recover and get back into the game.
- *Using a recovery line.* Unless a player is the last defender, she seldom chases directly after the player who has the ball, because the cover defender will be chasing that player. When beaten, defenders should run hard along their recovery line (for more information, see Recovery Lines).
- *Getting goalside of the ball.* The player must continue to run hard along the recovery line until she is closer to the goal than the ball or until she is required to pressure an attacker from behind who may be running with the ball toward the goal.
- *Stopping and covering.* Having reached this point, the player reassesses the situation and normally becomes the second defender (for more information, see figure 11.9 in Recovery Lines).

Second Defender

The second defender must, whenever possible, support the first defender who has gone to meet the attacker with the ball, unless she is marking an opponent. The way the second defender moves to give this support is vital to good defensive play; a player who moves too soon or too late can be easily

Recovery Lines

All defenders have recovery lines. These are pathways along which players run if they are beaten. Players who are beaten on the sides of the field run back toward the nearer goalpost. Players beaten in the center of the field run back toward the penalty spot or the middle of the goal (see figure 11.8).

The four stages of recovery are shown in figure 11.9. In this example, the first defender (player A) has been beaten by the attacker (player C). The second

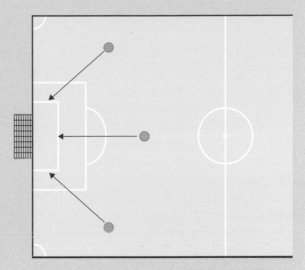

Figure 11.8   Recovery lines for a beaten defender.

defender (player B) moves from a cover position to engage player C, slow his progress, and prevent him from having a clear run at goal. Player A now recovers by turning quickly and sprinting back along the recovery line shown until he is goalside of the ball. Once player A has recovered goalside of the ball, he acts as the second defender.

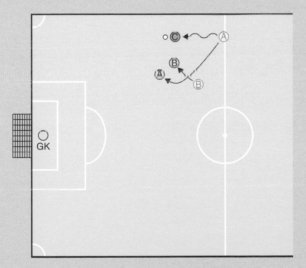

Figure 11.9   Four stages of recovery.

bypassed. So how should the second defender cover and support, and what other tactics can she employ to foil an attack? This section deals with covering and supporting the first defender and setting the offside trap.

Covering and Supporting

The basic covering position for the second defender (player B) is about 4 to 6 yards from the first defender (player A), at an angle of 45 degrees and on the most dangerous side (usually the goal side), as shown in figure 11.10. Exact measures such as 4 to 6 yards or 45 degrees can never be absolute: they will depend on the circumstance and the distance from goal, but they do provide a useful starting guide for two reasons. First, a defender who positions square to the first defender does not provide support because the attacker can beat both defenders in one move (see figure 11.11). Second, if the second defender stands more than 10 yards behind the first defender, the second defender is not providing effective cover. The attacker has ample space and time, having beaten player A, to gain momentum and attack player B in a 1v1 situation. The second defender must be close enough to apply pressure quickly to the attacker if the first defender is beaten.

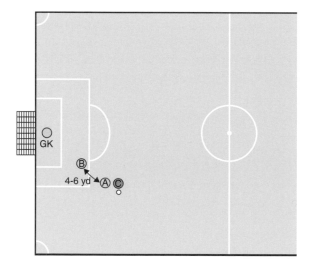

Figure 11.10   Basic covering position for the second defender.

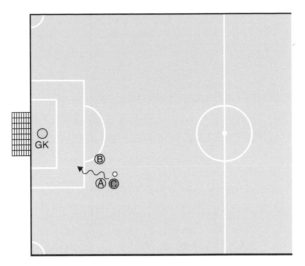

Figure 11.11   The second defender should not position square to the first defender.

Setting the Offside Trap

Knowing how and when to catch opponents offside is an ability all players must acquire. Providing it is not overused (becoming a dangerous tactic for the defense to use and simultaneously destroying the character of a game), it is a legitimate and important part of defensive play. To use this technique safely, your players must be taught the following fundamental tactical aspects of this maneuver:

- A knowledge of the rules governing offside play.
- The ability to simultaneously observe the player with the ball and the tactical situation that is developing. Such vision often begins with the simple instruction to players to keep their heads up.
- The recognition by all defenders that only the player at the very back of the defense—usually called the rearmost defender—should execute or spring the offside trap. The rearmost defender is the key player in executing the move personally and in controlling the actions of other defenders.

The following figures show how the offside trap can be used to stop an attack. To successfully employ the offside trap, there is a clear sequence of decisions which you must emphasize with your players. The most important of these is that only the rearmost defender can "spring the trap."

1. *Identify the Rearmost, and Key, Defender*

   In figure 11.12, the defenders (players X and Y) are outnumbered by four attackers; player B has the ball. Player Y goes forward to contain player B. The nearest defender going to meet the ball is a good play. Player X is now the rearmost, and therefore the key, defender. Player X must first give cover to player Y. (If player B dribbles past player Y, then player X is the only defender who can prevent a direct attack on goal). However, while giving support, player X must also recognize the possibility of playing the offside trap.

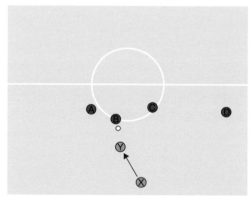

Figure 11.12   Identifying player X as the rearmost, and key, defender.

2. *Prepare but Don't Act*

   While supporting player Y, player X must also watch the movements of all the attackers, including player A, who may be hoping to make a blindside, or backdoor, run, as shown in figure 11.13. This is the essential skill of the good defender—being able to watch the ball and the developing situation at the same time.

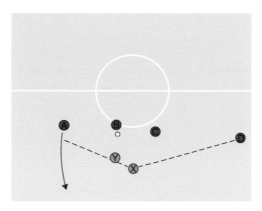

Figure 11.13 A defender must be able to watch the ball and the field at the same time.

3. *Spring the Trap*

The defenders hope that the attackers, in their haste to take advantage of the situation and before player B releases the pass, will continue running forward and move goalside of player X. Once they move goalside of player X, they become offside, and the trap has worked. In this situation, player X simply stands still and lets the attackers put themselves offside, as shown in figure 11.14.

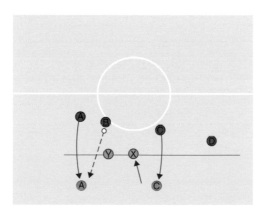

Figure 11.14 Springing the trap.

Against more experienced attackers, player X can actually produce the off-side situation by moving quickly upfield just before player B releases the pass forward. This is a critical moment, and the decision and timing must be exact; if player X makes the move too late, not only are the attackers not offside but they are in an even better position. Judging when to move requires practice in attack versus defense. The defender must watch both the player with the ball and the movements of the other attackers. One useful signal of when to move comes when player B, with the ball, looks down at the ball to kick it. At this moment, player X can often outwit the attackers by pushing forward very quickly to leave opponents offside.

Only the rearmost defender can set the offside trap. Because the second defender will often also be the rearmost defender, he must always be alert to the possibility of catching the attackers in an offside position. To set an effective offside trap, the rearmost defender must do the following:

- Make sure he is the rearmost defender by looking both ways across the field
- Identify the attacker who is most easily caught
- Split his attention between this attacker and the attacker who has the ball and who will usually be covered by the first defender, and be patient, watching and waiting until he anticipates that the attacker with the ball will actually make a pass forward

Remember, the attacker must pass because dribbling does not breach the offside rules. Just the pass, the defender should move quickly upfield leaving the chosen attacker as the only player between the ball and the goalkeeper at the moment the ball is played. This is the critical move. Offside rules have changed considerably over the past few years, and a thorough understanding of the rules is essential for both you and your players before implementing such tactics, as attackers and defenders.

Defensive Drills

This section contains a number of drills that show how a defender can be really effective in preventing, or at least slowing down, attackers by skillful positioning and intercepting. As you will see, it is not always necessary to physically tackle an attacker to defend a position successfully. These skills require a higher level of experience and ability. Drills for beginners, featuring the basic tackles, are covered later (page 223).

Drills for Intermediate Players

The following drills are appropriate to use when coaching intermediate defensive skills. In addition to these drills, you can also use London Bridge on page 106 of chapter 6 to help your players improve their defensive positioning skills, in particular the ability to jockey, which is a key defensive skill.

Defensive 1v1

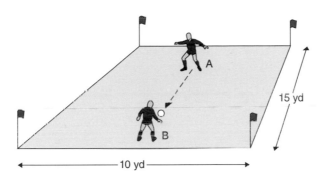

Equipment   One ball for every two players; four flags or cones

Organization   Players are in pairs of equal ability (one attacker, one defender), and each pair is in a 15- ×10-yard playing area marked by flags or cones.

Instructions   The defender (player A) plays the ball to the attacker (player B), moves toward the attacker, and tries to prevent the attacker from getting over the line behind the defender but without executing a tackle (i.e., jockey only).

Coaching Points

- The defender should keep her body crouched, in a sideways position, with one foot forward and her weight on her toes.
- The defender should look at the midline of the ball.
- The defender should threaten to tackle and strike with the leading foot to steal the ball. By threatening to tackle, the defender may cause the attacker to move the ball quickly and carelessly, offering the defender the opportunity to steal the ball without having to tackle.
- The defender should back off slowly if the attacker carries the ball forward.

Coaching Progressions

1. Players observe normal rules for tackling.
2. The defender identifies the weaker kicking foot of the attacker and forces her to attack that way.
3. Introduce a second attacker. Player A now plays the ball to either player B or player C and has to stop either of them from getting behind the line. (Players B and C may interpass, and the offside rule applies.) ∎

Intercepting the Pass

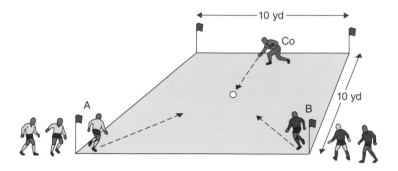

Equipment   A supply of soccer balls; four flags or cones

Organization   Players are in two lines of equal number, and each line is positioned in a corner of a 10- × 10-yard square marked by flags or cones.

Instructions   You serve the ball toward the players. Players A and B must both try to win the ball and play it back to you. After the play, the next players in line take a turn.

Coaching Points

*   The moment you serve the ball, players must make instant judgments about whether they can get to the ball first. Some decisions are easy, such as when the ball is directed in favor of a player. But sometimes players have an equal chance. In this situation, players should always go for the interception and hope they are quicker off the mark or a faster runner to the ball than the other player.

*   Players who quit in 50/50 situations will never win the ball.

Coaching Progressions

1.   Serve passes in a way that is absolutely clear which player will get to the ball first. This develops the confidence of the players to move forward and make successful, if easy, interceptions.

2.   As the players gain confidence, serve the ball slightly in favor of one player, using odds such as 60/40. Players have to develop much finer judgment, make their decisions early, be quick off the mark, and be determined to win possession.

3.   The player who wins the ball becomes the attacker and has to turn with the ball and dribble it across the target line behind the defending player.

4.   The player who does not win the ball becomes the defender and must either stop the attacker from turning with the ball or jockey the attacker and force him sideways. When the player wins possession of the ball, he returns it to you. ■

Equipment   One ball for every two players

Organization   Players are in pairs of equal ability, moving in free space.

Instructions   The attacker tries to turn with the ball and beat the defender. The defender tries to stop the turn. Players change roles after three or four attempts.

Coaching Points

- The defender positions about 1 yard behind the attacker (arm's length is a good guideline).
- The defender's position should be sideways to the attacker and the body lowered by bending the knees in an attempt to see the ball through or around the attacker's legs.
- The defender should stay on her toes and be patient.
- The defender should take great care and be certain of contacting the ball cleanly if challenging for the ball through the attacker's legs. Any miscalculation may result in conceding an unnecessary free kick.
- The defender should be prepared to challenge for the ball when the attacker tries to turn.

Coaching Progressions

1. The defender attempts to contain an opponent in a corner of the field of play.
2. The defender tries to force the attacker into a less penetrating direction and away from the defender.
3. Practice takes place in the penalty area, and the attacker has a target to shoot at or pass to, if she is able to turn with the ball.   ■

Purpose   To force the attacker to move in a direction that reduces the danger of an attack or gives the defender an advantage (e.g., moves the attacker toward a second defender or the touchline where there is less room for a move).

Equipment   One ball for every two players

Organization   Players are in evenly matched pairs, facing each other 5 yards apart near any straight line on the soccer field. The defender positions with his back to the line.

Instructions   The attacker has the ball and tries to beat the defender by getting the ball onto the line behind the defender.

Coaching Points

- The defender uses a technique similar to jockeying but with a much more definite body position that directs the attacker to one side.

- The defender positively "invites" the attacker to go one way by offering additional open space on that side. He can even point with his arm in the direction he wants the attacker to move.

Coaching Progressions

1. The defender forces the attacker in the direction the defender selects.

2. The defender identifies the weaker kicking foot of the attacker and forces the player to attack that way. Players may also use this technique in the Defensive 1v1 drill on page 213. ■

Drills for Advanced Players

The following drills are appropriate to use when coaching advanced defensive skills. For these drills, the tempo of the play is increased by adding realism and urgency to the attackers' role, by allowing attackers to start their runs at the defenders from approximately 5 to 6 yards away, and by giving them the support of a second attacker.

Teamwork in Defense

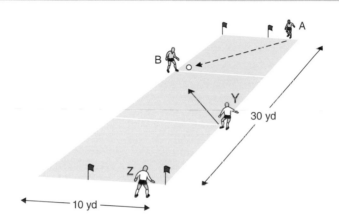

Purpose   To teach two defenders how to combine against an attacker

Equipment   One ball for every four players; four flags

Organization   Players are in groups of four, an attacking team of two and a defending team of two, and each group is on a 30- × 10-yard mini-field divided into three squares. Goals are marked by flags and are 6 yards wide.

Instructions   Player Z acts as goalkeeper. Player A plays the ball to player B, who controls the ball, turns, and tries to get past player Y and score past player Z in the goal. Player Y cannot start to defend until player A actually passes the ball to player B. This is a physically demanding activity, and each drill should take no more than 2 minutes if the attacker is not successful. Teammates change places after two attempts.

Coaching Points

- Emphasize any of the coaching points covered in this chapter as they arise.
- Encourage inventiveness and positive, aggressive play from the attackers, but disciplined and watchful play by the defenders.

Coaching Progressions

1. Player A helps player B to eliminate player Y before scoring past player Z.
2. Introduce the offside rule to help player Y in his defending.
3. Reverse the direction of play with player Y receiving the service from player Z, and player B becoming the defender. ■

Advanced Intercepting the Pass

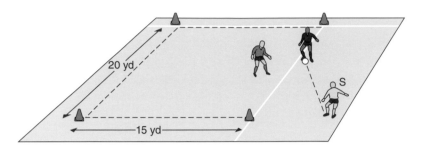

20 yd

15 yd

S

Equipment   One ball for every three players; cones

Organization   Players are in a group of three (one attacker, one defender, one server).

Instructions   The server plays a variety of balls to the attacker. The attacker tries to gain possession and beat the defender to a line of cones 10 to 15 yards behind the defender and stretching 20 yards infield from the touchline. The attacker should keep moving to off-balance the defender.

While the server has the ball, the defender positions himself to see the attacker and the server but on a line between the attacker and the goal that the defender is defending (this is known as being goalside of the opponent). The defender intercepts the pass if it is safe to do so. If not, the defender defends as appropriate.

Coaching Points

- Remind the defender that good positioning is a continuous process of decision making.

- The defender should always be in a position to see the ball and the attacker, and between the attacker and the defender's goal at a distance that gives the defender an opportunity to intercept any passes to the attacker's feet.

- If the defender positions himself too close to the attacker before the pass is made, then he leaves himself exposed to a pass behind into which the attacker can run. The defender should position himself so that he will win any race to the ball played toward his goal.

- The defender should observe the play as it develops and continually adjust and readjust his marking position in relation to the attacker's movements. The best defenders do not allow attackers to receive the ball behind them—they allow passes to feet in front but not passes to space behind!

Coaching Progressions

1. The server may dribble the ball in various directions before making the pass. This changes the picture for the defender and alters the angles of passes.

2. Develop the practice into a small-team game or a functional practice in which players adhere to specific roles or functions. ■

Basic Tackles

This section examines the techniques of the three basic tackles in soccer: the block tackle, the side block tackle, and the sliding tackle.

Coaching the block tackle first introduces the idea of hard but safe body contact, which can help some beginners overcome a natural aversion to that feature of defensive play. Take great care when coaching this tackle; a player who becomes overcompetitive can cause an accident. For this reason, we recommend strict discipline and matching players for weight, as well as for height and ability, whenever possible.

Determination When Tackling

Determination is the key to successful tackling. A player who is hesitant when going into a tackle is much more likely to be injured—and not win the ball. Positioning correctly and being patient before being quick and aggressive toward the ball are all integral to winning the ball. Good defenders dispossess opponents fairly using a variety of strategies and techniques, but no chapter on tackling is complete without a word about determination. Without a wholehearted, fearless commitment to a well-timed tackle, a player is likely to be beaten and is also likely to get hurt. There is no substitute for a hard but fairly executed tackle. Be sure to make it very clear to your players that determination is essential for success. Following are the attributes of a good tackler:

- *Good positioning.* Players must be aware of the overall tactical situation that is developing in addition to the individual players they might be marking.

- *Anticipation.* Players must think ahead. If they can anticipate what is going to happen, they are already planning their moves.

- *Speed and acceleration.* Players have to be quick, both in outsprinting their opponent and in getting to the ball first.

- *Timing.* Only experience will help players here, but the timing of their moves is crucial.

- *Striking at and through the ball.* Players must always follow through the tackle; they should not stop at the ball.

- *Recovering quickly if the first tackle is unsuccessful.* Players must be prepared to get up quickly and back into the game if their first tackle is unsuccessful. They must use their recovery lines.

- *Determination.* Above all, players must be determined. Those who go into a tackle in a halfhearted manner seldom win the ball, but often get injured.

- *Tackling in a fair and sporting manner.* There is no place in the game for players who deliberately kick, hold, push, or pull an opponent or exhibit any form of violent behavior.

Block Tackle

This tackle is very effective when the attacker comes directly toward the defender, especially when space is limited as in a crowded penalty area. This tackle is a powerful movement, and when done well, not only stops the attacker but gives the defender a reasonable chance of winning possession. To generate sufficient force to overcome the momentum of the attacker, the defender's body has to be crouched to lower the center of gravity, the instep of the striking foot has to move as if to go through the ball rather than stop it, and the leading shoulder has to move powerfully forward as the foot strikes the ball (see figure 11.15a). A player whose body position is similar to that shown in figure 11.15b will never win a tackle because he is pulling away from the situation and is off balance.

Figure 11.15   Block tackle: (a) correct and (b) incorrect.

Side Block Tackle

Using the front block tackle is one way to deal with an attacker who brings the ball directly toward a defender. To stop the player who is moving past the defender diagonally or who is already past, there are two main techniques—the sliding tackle, which will be discussed in the next section, and the side block tackle. Teaching the side block tackle first allows the defender to stay upright and also provides a very useful introduction to the sliding tackle.

The side block tackle is best considered in four stages. First, the defender runs hard, possibly on a recovery run to move to a position alongside the attacker (see figure 11.16a). Next, the defender turns inward toward the attacker using the foot nearer the attacker and turning the hips and shoulders in that direction (see figure 11.16b). The defender then crouches down and hooks the inside of the tackling foot around the ball (see figure 11.16c) and completes the turn while hooking the ball until it breaks clear from the attacker's foot (see figure 11.16d). Ideally, the defender gains possession of the ball; in reality, the defender often stops the attacker while the ball bounces free. With beginners, it is important that the defender be still standing upright after the tackle and can attempt to continue to pressure the attacker.

Figure 11.16 Side block tackle.

Sliding Tackle

A good defender stays on his feet as long as possible and only uses the sliding tackle as a last resort. If it fails, that defender is temporarily out of the game. Nevertheless, on many occasions the sliding tackle is the only way to stop an attacker who has broken through; for this reason it is an essential skill for every player. Moreover, because this tackle is a spectacular and exciting achievement when executed successfully, all players enjoy practicing it, provided the ground is soft and the players wear protective clothing. Never allow your players to practice sliding tackles on hard, dry ground without protection; more harm than good will result.

The sliding tackle contains three stages: the chase, the slide, and the sweep. The tackling player chases the ball (see figure 11.17a) until confident that his lead foot will overtake the ball. The near leg (which is the left leg in figure 11.17a) leads, allowing the player to sink down onto the left leg, which curls beneath the seat of the defender. The far leg (the right leg in the figure) swings around in a wide sweep, with the foot hooked, toward the ball (see figure 11.17b). The tackling leg sweeps through the ball and either traps it with the hooked foot or, more usually, plays the ball away (see figure 11.17c). Most defenders love the sliding tackle, especially when the surface is soft and they come out with the ball!

Figure 11.17   Sliding tackle.

Tackling Drills

Tackling often requires body contact, and players can and do fall over and get hurt. Indeed, a sliding tackle requires the defender to make contact with the ground. It follows that, in addition to adhering to strict rules of safety, you should require players to wear protective clothing and knee pads. In addition, tackling drills should, whenever possible, take place on soft, grassy, well-watered playing areas; avoid hard, bumpy, dry surfaces.

Drill for Beginners

The block tackle is the first tackle to teach to beginners. Because the block tackle can be dangerous if taught poorly, you should use a series of progressions into the full action, as described in the following drill.

Block Tackle

Figure 1   **Figure 2**   **Figure 3**

Equipment   One ball for every two players

Organization   Players are in pairs of equal size, weight, and ability, and each pair has a ball. Players begin by standing 1 yard apart with the ball in the middle.

Instructions   Players place their hands on each other's shoulders, keeping their arms straight (see figure 1). Both players tackle gently so that the inside of both players' feet come into simultaneous contact with the ball (see figure 2). Next, players drop their arms. This is the same tackle, but the shoulders now come into play. Players increase force and realism, but the ball should not move (see figure 3). After this, players take one short step backward. On command, they step in with the left foot and tackle with the right. Both players should tackle simultaneously; this is most important. Players move from two or three steps' distance from each other, but do not tackle with 100 percent effort. They now progress to a full challenge for the ball, but you should limit the number of attempts to five.

Coaching Points

- Players should keep their bodies crouched with a low center of gravity.
- Players should use the inside of the foot and keep their knee over the ball.
- The tackling foot should be turned out about 45 degrees, and the knee and ankle should be locked on impact with the ball.
- Players should put their weight into the tackle, shoulder forward.
- Players should strike through the ball, not at it.

Drills for Intermediate Players

For intermediate players, we introduce active competition. In these drills, we give the defender a small target or line to defend and allow the defender to move backward or channel the attacker to one side before making the tackle.

Corner and Line Attack

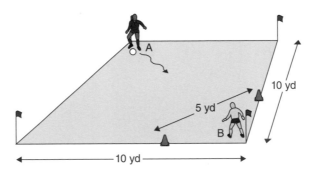

Figure 1

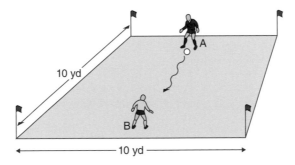

Figure 2

Equipment   One ball for every two players; four flags; two cones

Organization   Players are in pairs (one attacker and one defender), and each pair is in a 10- × 10-yard square marked by flags or cones.

Instructions   The attacker (player A) has the ball and tries to attack the defender's (player B's) corner by running with the ball through the small goal positioned at the corner of the square, which is 5 yards wide (see figure 1). Next, player A tries to attack player B's line (see figure 2), which is harder to defend because the area is wider. In both scenarios, player B tries to win the ball. Player B must stay on her feet, using no sliding tackles.

Coaching Points

- The defending player should be in a low, balanced position, and the feet should not be square to the line of attack.
- The defender should make a firm positive move with a follow-through. ■

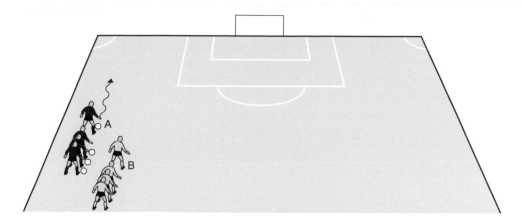

Equipment   One ball for every two players

Organization   Players are in pairs of equal ability, size, and weight (one attacker, one defender). Both players stand facing the same direction along the sideline, but player B (the defender) is about 10 yards behind player A (the attacker).

Instructions   The attacker (player A) has the ball and, on your command, dribbles it forward at a steady pace and in a straight line inside the sideline. The defender (player B) chases player A from the side and executes the tackle. Players switch roles after each attempt.

Coaching Points

- The defender should run hard to get level, turn on the nearside foot, and crouch down as he turns to achieve a lower center of gravity.
- The defender should hook the tackling foot around the ball and complete the turn, hooking the ball hard until it breaks clear.

Coaching Progressions

1. The attacker increases the pace of the dribble.
2. The defender tries to actually win possession of the ball rather than just force it away from the attacker and possibly over the sideline. ■

Drills for Advanced Players

Again, for advanced players, the secret of coaching tackling successfully is to create realistic drills but also ensure the safety of the players by requiring that they wear protective clothing and practice on soft ground, as described for players at the intermediate level. The emphasis on determination, indeed courage, becomes increasingly important as the realism of the drills increases for advanced players.

Tackling Pen

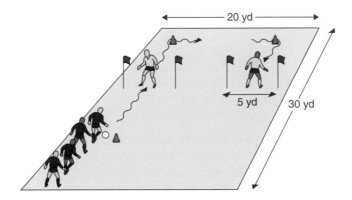

Equipment   One ball for each attacking player; four cones; four flags

Organization   Players are in a group of unlimited number (two defenders, the rest attackers) in a 30- × 20-yard mini-field marked by cones, with 5-yard-wide goals marked by flags.

Instructions   Defenders remain between their goals and do not move more than 2 yards from this area. Defenders try to stop the attackers from dribbling the ball through the small goals. Attackers use a continuous, single-file approach, giving the defenders time to recover their positions between tackles. Attackers score a point every time they are successful dribbling through the goals.

Coaching Points

- Defenders should keep their bodies crouched with a low center of gravity.
- Defenders should use their instep and keep their knee over the ball.
- Defenders should put their weight into the tackle, shoulder forward.
- Defenders should strike through the ball, not at it.

Coaching Progressions

1. Players compete to see how many attackers beat the defenders and vice versa.
2. The defenders change at regular intervals, because this is a very demanding drill. ■

Equipment   One ball for every three players

Organization   Players are in groups of equal ability, size, and weight (two attackers, one defender). Players line up as shown in the diagram for the Side Block Tackle drill on page 225, but in three lines instead of two (two lines of attackers with one line of defenders between them).

Instructions   The attacker in the first line (player A) has the ball and, on your command, dribbles it forward at a steady pace and in a straight line inside the sideline. The defender (player B) runs alongside player A and then executes the tackle. The defender, after completing the first tackle, turns and then immediately chases and tackles a second attacker (player C), who waits for the first challenge to finish and then moves off in the opposite direction. By doing this, the defender is required to challenge for the ball using both the left and the right foot as she chases both attackers one after the other. Being able to challenge successfully with both the left and right foot is an essential skill for all defenders.

Coaching Points

- The defender should run hard to get level, turn on the nearside foot, and crouch down as she turns to get a lower center of gravity.
- The defender should hook the tackling foot around the ball and complete the turn, hooking the ball hard until it breaks clear.

Coaching Progressions

1. The attackers increase the pace of the dribble.
2. The defender tries to actually win possession of the ball rather than just force it away from the attackers and possibly over the sideline. ▪

Sliding Tackle

Equipment   One ball for every two players; defenders wear sweatpants

Organization   Players are in pairs of equal ability and speed (one attacker, one defender). Both players stand facing the same direction along the sideline with player B positioned 10 yards behind player A (the setup is similar to that in the figure for the Side Block Tackle Drill on page 225, but with the recommended equipment change).

Instructions   The attacker (player A) has the ball and dribbles it forward at a steady pace and in a straight line. The defender (player B) runs alongside player A and executes the tackle.

Coaching Points

- The defender should not jump in—this is a foul.
- The defender should watch the ball and strike through it.
- The defender should always tackle with the outside leg, the one farther from the attacker at the start of the tackle.
- The defender should use the nearside hand to cushion the fall and make sure she can reach the ball before attempting the tackle.
- The defender should sprint hard to catch up with the attacker, but should not get too close behind the attacker. The defender will need room to execute the slide.

Coaching Progressions

1. The tackling player sits on the ground in the correct position while you explain the position.
2. Players practice gently lowering down into this sitting position, learning how to take the weight on the nearside hand.
3. Players practice moving and tackling a stationary ball, emphasizing playing through the ball.
4. The player with the ball dribbles in a straight line at an easy pace to invite the tackle and keeps going until tackled. The speed increases as the players progress.
5. You roll the ball for the two players to chase. The tackle must be made within 20 yards by the designated tackler. ◼

Drills for All-Star Players

For all-star players, the skills of being the first or second defender, intercepting or stopping an opponent from turning, and tackling and recovering if beaten have to be put into the context of realistic game situations. Players in these roles have to use the techniques covered in this chapter in the following drill, but the essentials of being the first, second, or third defender must be the foundation for using these techniques.

Competitive Defense

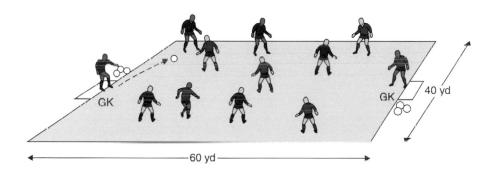

Equipment   Twelve soccer balls; two goals; cones to outline the playing area; two sets of different-colored bibs

Organization   Each team has six players, including the goalkeeper, two defenders, one midfield player, and two forwards. However, the teams may also be organized into a 2-2-1 formation. The playing area is 60 × 40 yards with balls positioned around the area and to the side of the goals. The game is played according to the rules of soccer.

Instructions   Teams play according to the rules of the game with throw-ins, corner kicks, free kicks, and goal kicks being taken.

Coaching Points

- When the goalkeeper throws the ball to a teammate or when passes occur as play develops, you can help the defending players decide who is the first defender, who is the second defender (at what angle and distance), and who and how the other defenders mark opponents or space.

- When the ball is to the sides of the pitch, defenders who are neither the first nor second defender but are marking opponents within passing distance on the ball side of the pitch should mark closer than those defenders who are on the far side of the field, away from the ball. All defenders who are responsible for marking opponents must remember the golden rules of marking:

  ○ Be goalside of your opponent.

  ○ Be ballside of your opponent (i.e., slightly nearer the sideline than her) unless the ball is in a central location, in which case the defender should be inside the opponent (i.e., nearer a midline drawn down the center of the pitch from penalty spot to penalty spot).

» continued

○ Be at a distance that allows you the chance to intercept any pass made to the opponent, but not so tight that the opponent is encouraged to run behind to receive passes.

○ Your feet and shoulders should be "sideways-on" to allow you to move quickly, both forward and backward. as required by good defending.

○ As the ball is moved around the pitch, the responsibilities of the defenders change from being the first, second, or third defender (i.e., the player marking players or spaces).

Coaching Progression

1. Defending team regains possession before opponents have made four successful passes to teammates.

2. After possession is regained, the other team drops deep to the half-way line and commences pressing and marking tactics. ■

PART III

Tactics and Teamwork

IN PART III we present our ideas on coaching tactics and teamwork in five chapters. Chapter 12 introduces the work of Allen Wade, who first identified the nine general principles applicable to team games. By using these principles, you can determine how well, or how badly, you team is performing—and the opposition!

In chapter 13 we provide a brief history of the way early systems of play developed. This leads to an explanation and analysis of the modern systems of play together with an analysis of their strengths and weaknesses and the duties of individuals within these systems.

Chapter 14 contains a detailed discussion of the methods and practices we recommend when you are coaching your whole team. This chapter also builds on the individual and group coaching principles introduced in chapters 2 and 3.

Chapter 15 is at an advanced level and is new. It explains how players using modern tactical formations and movements can both react to, and initiate, successful team plays. Because these tactics are advanced, not all coaches will have players of sufficient maturity to play at these levels. Nevertheless, for those of you who do have such players, are seeking to advance or confirm your own knowledge, or both, this chapter is essential reading.

Chapter 16 deals with restarts—throw-ins, corner kicks, free kicks, and penalty kicks. Here we introduce and develop a series of tactical moves. We start with basic moves for beginners and develop these, step by step, into moves that players can use in match situations. Again, by employing some of the methods outlined in chapters 2 and 3, the players themselves can become involved in designing their own plays. This is a very important section of book, which we believe will benefit coaches at all levels.

Principles
of Play

• • • • • •

ONE OF YOUR main objectives as a coach is to improve team play—but how do you know when your team is playing effectively—what are the criteria? You can't judge simply by the result, because opponents may have been strong or weak; and you can't judge simply by the score, because at any moment in the game the score might not be a true reflection of how well the teams are playing. A measure is needed, a set of permanent criteria against which you can analyze how well or how badly your team is playing. You must know what to look for and be able to recognize good team play.

This chapter introduces the concepts and nine principles of team play that were first identified by Allen Wade in 1967 and are still in use.

Three Principles Common to Attack and Defense

The first three principles that Wade identified are common to both attack and defense. They are possession, support, and communication. These concepts are very closely related, but team analysis always starts with the same question: Which team has the ball?

Possession

If a team has possession of the ball, observe how well the players keep possession as they progress toward the opponents' goal. A team that continually gives the ball away or makes haphazard passes is not playing well. Keeping possession is very important, and players should only lose possession when they take a shot on goal, attempt a killer pass in the appropriate situations, or dribble. Players should never lose possession in the defending or middle thirds of the field, unless it is a matter of safety.

If the team does not have possession of the ball, observe how effectively the players, both individually and collectively, work to regain possession. If players rush wildly into tackles or do not know how to support and cover each other, then they are defending poorly. When defending, a team should put pressure on its opponents by denying them time and space to play the ball and marking and covering efficiently.

The first judgment about successful team play is based on an analysis of how well players keep or regain possession in their bid to score or prevent goals. A look at support and communication may identify why players are or are not successful.

Support

Are the players making the right decisions and running intelligently into good supporting positions when their team has possession? This feature of good team play is closely associated with the willingness of players to make unself-ish runs. Any team in which players stand and watch each other is playing poorly. See figure 12.1 for an example of poor support. In this figure, player A has no support in attack, and player Z has no support in defense.

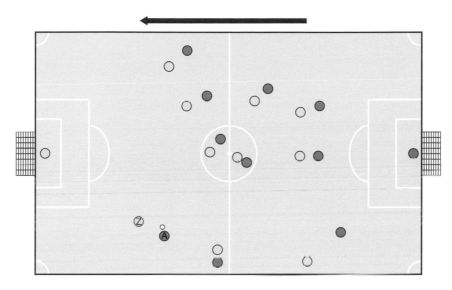

Figure 12.1   Poor support in attack and defense.

Now take a look at figure 12.2. In this figure, players B, C, and D are all supporting player A, which is an example of good support in attack. The principle of support also operates in defense, as shown in figure 12.3. When a player goes to challenge for the ball (we call this player the first defender),

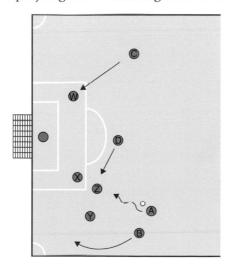

Figure 12.2   Good support in attack.

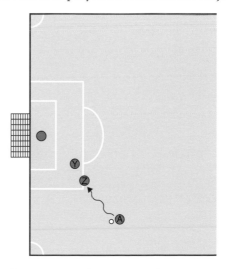

Figure 12.3   Good support in defense.

he should always be supported by a second player (the second defender). In general, the second defender supports at an angle of 45 degrees, protects the most direct pathway to goal, and is never more than 10 yards behind the first defender. Often, he is much closer to the first defender than 10 yards, depending on the circumstances.

Communication

The final concept common to attack and defense is communication, which we introduced in chapter 2. On a soccer field, good communication is achieved by looking, calling, and signaling. Good communication involves talking and calling informatively, not shouting; for this reason, it is an advanced aspect of team play. Watch your players carefully to determine the quality of communication between them during play. Also notice how well team members encourage each other, especially when things are going poorly and mistakes are being made. Even young players can be quite cruel to each other, so encourage positive communication.

An American psychologist, A.T. Welford, showed that the human ear normally can get the brain to deal with only one message at a time. If several messages or sounds arrive simultaneously, they have to wait in line. Consider how this law affects a soccer player in possession of the ball. If the inexperienced player is inundated with shouts from six teammates, he processes only the first call; the remaining five are just background noise adding to the confusion. Worse, the six players may all be shouting different advice (see figure 12.4). The player can deal only with the first call, so the first call must be the correct one. You can prompt this by encouraging players to look and think more and to shout less. This will help provide good communication.

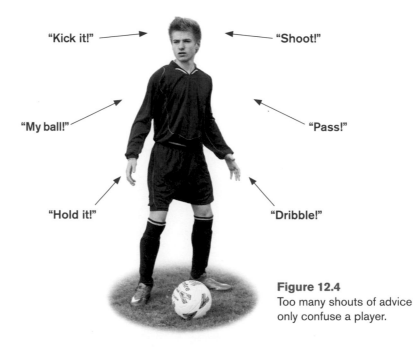

"Kick it!"   "Shoot!"

"My ball!"   "Pass!"

"Hold it!"   "Dribble!"

Figure 12.4
Too many shouts of advice only confuse a player.

Six Principles of Attack and Defense

We now consider the six principles used to analyze team play: delay, concentration, and balance in defense; and penetration, width, and mobility in attack. However, we always analyze them in pairs because every attacking strategy corresponds to a defensive strategy. It is not unlike chess—every move has a countermove. The principles are combined as follows:

- Delay in defense versus penetration in attack
- Concentration in defense versus width in attack
- Mobility in attack versus balance in defense

Delay in Defense

Delay is important in defense. Slowing the opposition and interrupting the chosen path to goal gains valuable time for your team to recover to protect its own goal. This holds true on both an individual and a team basis.

Individually, players must not rush wildly into tackles. They should remain calm and composed, jockey slowly yet positively, watch the ball, and try not to be beaten by the opponent. If a defender remains goalside of an attacker at the correct distance and thus prevents a direct shot on goal, that defender is playing well.

Collectively, two or more players can combine very effectively to prevent the direct progress of opponents toward goal. If they cannot regain possession, they must try to delay the attack by forcing the attackers to play the ball sideways or backward away from the danger area. Defenders should follow two rules of defense:

1. The nearest defender to the ball (the first defender) usually meets the player with the ball and delays his immediate progress.

2. The supporting defender (the second defender) must cover the first defender. As noted previously, the second defender usually stands at an angle of about 45 degrees, never more than 10 yards from the first defender depending on the circumstance, and supports the first defender in preventing the attacker's preferred path to the goal.

Penetration in Attack

To counter a delaying tactic, an attacker tries to penetrate the defense with passes, runs, and dribbles with the ball and, of course, shots at goal. Penetration involves players looking forward, past opponents and, whenever possible, delivering accurate passes beyond them toward the opponents' prime defending areas and into the goal-scoring zones. Penetration usually requires fast, direct play resulting in shots at goal. Again, this can be achieved both individually and collectively.

First Attacker

The attacker who receives the ball in and around the penalty box (the first attacker) should be prepared to turn toward the goal (if possible), take the ball directly toward the defender, try to outmaneuver the defender, and look for a chance to either shoot at goal or make a pass to a teammate in a goal-scoring position.

Second Attacker

The second attacker should be prepared to support the first attacker by running past defenders into a goalside position (while watching out for being caught offside), perhaps moving out wide to create more space for the first attacker, and trying to take out defenders by running at them (being careful not to obstruct).

If a team is exhibiting good penetration, players move the ball swiftly and positively toward the opponents' goal and are prepared to shoot, dribble past defenders, make killer or lead passes, and move forward into strike positions. Encourage all of these qualities and attitudes in your players.

Concentration in Defense

A team may, as a defensive tactic, recover to place 11 players between the player in possession of the ball and its own goal. By doing this, it is exhibiting a defensive principle of play known as concentration. An attacking team moving forward toward a crowded defending half, or even a penalty area, is faced with no room to move forward and not enough space between defenders. Concentration can also take place on a smaller scale; three or four defenders may move to areas adjacent to the player with the ball and the offensive support players to outnumber them and close off the attacking team's preferred attacking angles and passes.

Defenders who want to make plays difficult for the attackers can simply crowd the danger area, as shown in figure 12.5. However, good defending is still required; defenders must still press the ball, mark opponents and spaces, and challenge intelligently and fairly. Simply having numbers in and around the defending area does not guarantee defensive success.

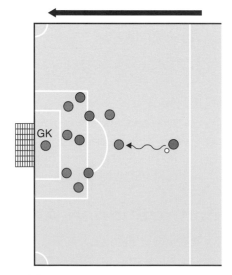

Figure 12.5
Good concentration in defense.

Width in Attack

To overcome concentration, attacking teams may use a further principle of attacking play, that of width. If a team attacks on a wide front, that team automatically stretches the defense across the field and opens up spaces between defenders, which attackers can then exploit (see figure 12.6). Width can be established by using wingers, by overlapping play, or by having midfield players make runs beyond the wingers in the middle third of the field toward the flanks to receive passes. Once width has been established, the team must use this advantage to enter the penalty box with passes, crosses, or dribbles.

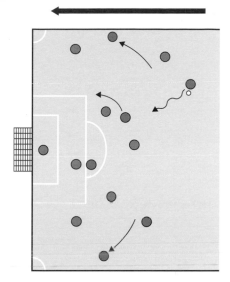

Figure 12.6 Attacking with a wide front to stretch the defense.

The concepts of concentration and width provide two more permanent features of team play to develop. Does your team concentrate its defense in times of need, and do you have sufficient width in attack to improve your chances of success?

Mobility in Attack

Perhaps the worst example of team play is when two fullbacks stand rigidly in their own half of the field when everyone else is attacking the other goal, as shown in figure 12.7. Such a team formation is seldom the fault of the players, who have probably been told to stay back.

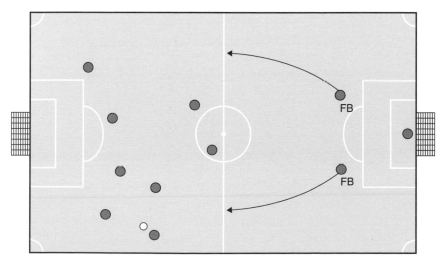

Figure 12.7 Poor tactics by two fullbacks, who lack mobility and should have moved forward.

Honey Pot Soccer

Let us consider concentration and width in relation to one problem that all coaches of young players experience—the overcrowding of players around the ball, as shown in figure 12.8. This phenomenon of players converging on the ball like flies around a honey pot, making good play impossible, is common in junior soccer.

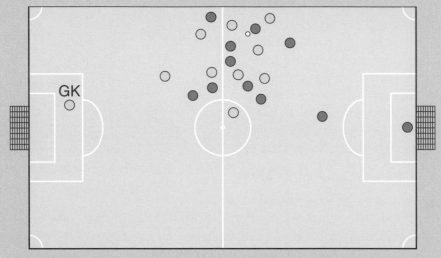

Figure 12.8 Honey pot soccer lacks basic principles of width and concentration.

The solution lies partly in the concepts of making space and going wide, which are best taught with the small-team games and practices described in chapters 3 and 5 and the game of Silent Soccer shown on page 268. By using 4v4 games and gradually increasing both the numbers playing and the area being used as players age, you can introduce all the principles of play to younger players gradually to enhance their understanding of these vital principles.

Even the most game-intelligent of players between the ages of 6 and 11 have a hard time making sense of the bigger game (i.e., 11v11). Many adult players have little grasp of the fundamentals of these principles of the game!

You can draw increasingly on your knowledge of the game principles outlined here to judge the quality of your team's performance both in practice and during match play.

This strategy is wrong on two counts. It is wrong in practice because these defenders are too far back to support the attacking play. The fullbacks can only wait for the ball or for the opposition to arrive, and meanwhile they may also lose the possible tactical advantage of catching the opposition in the offside trap. Second, this strategy is wrong in principle. Soccer is a fluid, moving game and can only be played skillfully when all players exercise mobility. They must be allowed the freedom to move anywhere at any time in accordance with their own judgment of the situation. Certainly, young players must be taught to make correct judgments about when, where, and how to move; as we have seen, teaching this is not an easy task. Nevertheless, you must undertake this task, because if individual players cannot make good judgments, the team will never play well.

Good mobility in attack is demonstrated by players who change positions skillfully and run off the ball to draw defenders out of position and open up passing or shooting opportunities. Mobility is also demonstrated by fullbacks who overlap by moving around and in front of the player with the ball and by midfield players who run forward into the penalty area (from which over 90 percent of all goals are scored). These are all examples of the successful execution of mobility in attack. The counterstrategy in defense is balance.

Balance in Defense

Balance is easy to understand by considering a child's seesaw. For example, if a winger beats her fullback and all the remaining defenders immediately rush over to this side of the field, then the defense is clearly off balance because nobody is left in the penalty area, as shown in figure 12.9. When the ball and players are located on one side of the field, the defending team must be aware of any threats that may arise on the opposite side and position sufficient defenders to cope with the problem should it arise.

A well-balanced defense should position a sufficient numbers of defenders on the ball side of the field to counter any

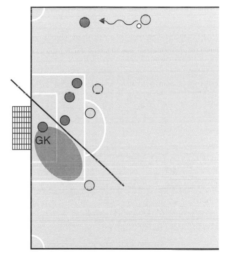

Figure 12.9   Lack of balance resulting from defenders moving over too far.

attacking threats there. Then, defenders on the other side will give appropriate support to each other, can cover against any central threat to the penalty box, and are also able to move quickly to manage the defending circumstance on their own side of the field should the play be switched. They can move from a central cover to a pressing and marking position quickly and efficiently while other supporting defenders can readjust their positions according to the changing movement of the ball.

Team Formations and Systems of Play

TO ORGANIZE YOUR players to the best advantage, you must understand the workings of the various team playing systems. Keep in mind, though, that a system of play is only as good as the players within it. Players, not team formations, win games. If this were not true, two opposing teams using the same system would always tie!

Systems of play refers to 11v11 games and the deployment of players in certain roles within a team, often performed in designated areas of the field. These systems are designed to capitalize on the strengths of both individuals and groups of players and to minimize weaknesses that may be detrimental to the team's performance. This poses a problem when coaching youngsters, who cannot be expected to play a system successfully until they are mature enough to see what is happening in the entire game and to anticipate how plays are going to develop. Further, they must also be able to kick the ball at least 30 yards. In the absence of these abilities, the 11v11 game is inevitably reduced to 20 youngsters all swarming like bees around the ball, as we discussed on page 240. However, you can introduce mini-systems of play using 6v6 or 7v7 games. With youngsters, don't expect too much too soon, but do use the coaching methods set out in this chapter and in chapter 14.

Development of Systems of Play

Before 1870, when the rules of soccer were first standardized, teams played in a 1-2-8 formation, as shown in figure 13.1. There was no passing and no heading, and players dribbled and hacked (tackled) and occasionally shot for goal. Dribbling was the primary skill. In 1867, the Queens Park team from Scotland introduced the concept of passing and, because of the way long through passes began to penetrate the defense, the system changed to 1-2-2-6, as shown in figure 13.2. Incidentally, the Queens Park team played from 1867 to 1874 without having a single goal scored against them!

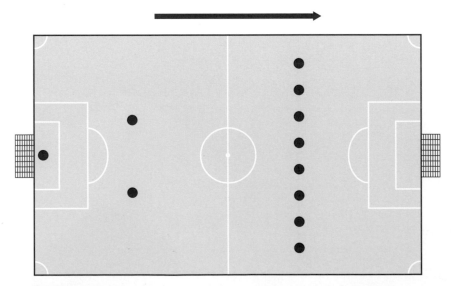

Figure 13.1   The 1-2-8 formation used before soccer rules were standardized.

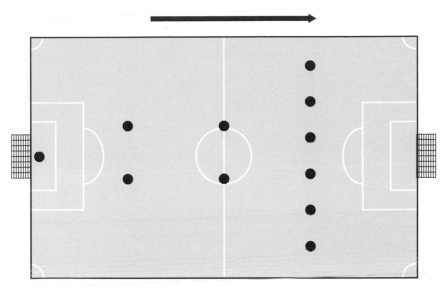

Figure 13.2   The 1-2-2-6 formation used after passing was introduced.

Increasingly, soccer became a game in which team effort was more important than individual talent. As a result, the next system to develop was one that used an attacking center half. This player was the best on the team, and his main duty was to link attack and defense (see figure 13.3).

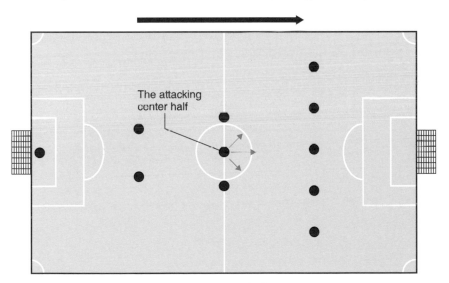

The attacking center half

Figure 13.3   Formation using the attacking center half.

In 1925, the new offside rule reduced the number of players who had to be between the ball and the goals from three to two. This gave immediate impetus to the attacking game. To counter the attacking game, Herbert Chapman of the Arsenal Team in England introduced the stopper center-halfback system (see figure 13.4).

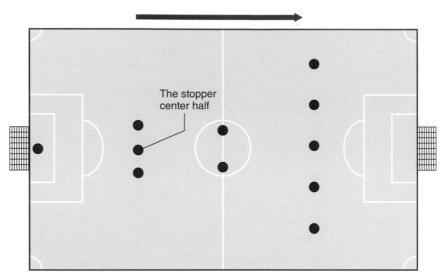

Figure 13.4 Formation using the stopper center half.

The stopper center-halfback system soon led to the invention of the famous WM formation, which reigned supreme for 30 years until Hungary introduced the deep-lying center forward system in 1953. In this system, the deep-lying center forward remained behind the attackers but played forward passes to them and then followed up. The WM formation was the forerunner of modern systems and is still an effective system to use. Although this system is outdated nowadays, it had an excellent balance between attack and defense, provides for good support, maintains depth, and allows players to attack on a wider front. The system is so named because the distribution of players on the field forms a pattern that looks like the letters W and M (see figure 13.5).

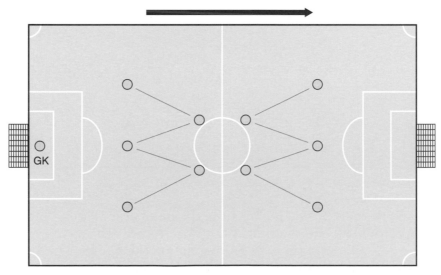

Figure 13.5 WM formation.

Although several modern systems are now available and more popular, the WM system is still an effective attacking formation, especially if a team has a powerful center forward or striker, two fast wingers, and clever inside forwards and halfbacks. A team must also have a tall, commanding central defender and two mobile fullbacks. If you play this system, don't let your two wingers become isolated and just stand and watch. If the ball is not reaching them, they must be prepared to leave their positions and look for the ball, usually infield or deeper toward their own goal.

Four Modern Systems of Play

As explained earlier, modern systems are structured around the deployment of the players and the performance of their roles and responsibilities on the field of play (which are often easier to recognize in the early stages of the game). Thus, for example, the 4-2-4 system basically has four defenders, two midfield players, and four attackers. Similarly, the 4-3-3 system has four defenders, three midfield players, and three attackers.

4-3-3 System

The 4-3-3 system, as shown in figure 13.6, employs a four player zonal defense while maintaining a balance of players in both midfield and attacking roles ahead of the back four. It is a popular system throughout the world in both domestic and international competition. The numbers referred to only indicate the players' general operational areas on the field—they do not explain the tactical movements, interchanges, and cohesive interplay among the players or units in a team.

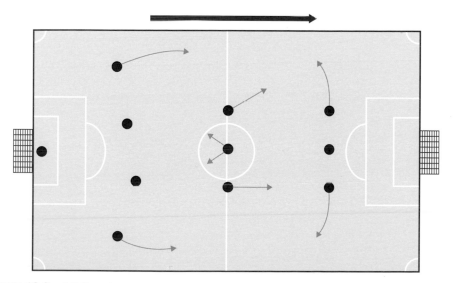

Figure 13.6   4-3-3 system.

The 4-3-3 system usually ensures that the team has the number of players in midfield needed to defensively oppose other systems of play without being outnumbered. If the two wider attackers also drop into the wider midfield areas when possession is lost, then the team is able to operate with five

Basic Components of Modern Systems

Modern systems are determined by the abilities of the players, the preferred playing style of the coach, and often the strength of the opposition and the state of the game. If a team is losing 0-1 with 2 minutes to go, it is unlikely to employ a defensive system and indirect style of play unless a professional team is playing.

Fundamentally, all modern systems are based on the dimensions of the field, the phases of the game (attack, defense, and midfield play), the strengths and weaknesses of the players of both teams, sometimes the system of play adopted by opponents, and of course, the preferences of coaches for one system of play over another.

Because 90 percent of goals are scored from inside the shooting zone (within 18 yards of the goal), it follows that players must both attack and defend these zones effectively. The rules of the game state that every team must have a goalkeeper. Therefore, all modern systems are designed around the distribution of all other players with primary tasks to either defend, operate in midfield, or score or create goals (assist) for teammates in the attacking third of the field (see figure 13.7). As the coach, you decide the numbers of players with defending, midfield, and attacking roles based on the major factors explained in the previous paragraph.

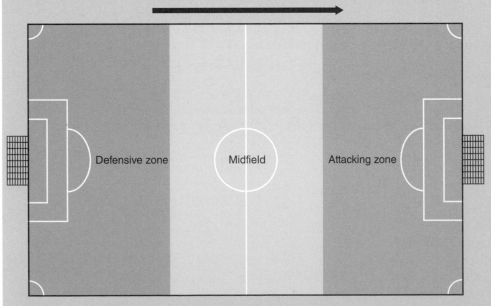

Figure 13.7   Areas on the field of play.

midfield defenders. From an attacking viewpoint, there are sufficient players in the midfield area to build attacks through this part of the field, although it is not only the midfield players who will create goal-scoring opportunities here. Defenders may also move forward to support those in possession of

To determine how to position your players, you must analyze the three phases of the game: attack, midfield, and defense. The players can be located to increase the effectiveness of any of the three phases, but you are always faced with a choice: If your intention is to strengthen the defense by allocating extra players to it, then to some extent attacking effectiveness may suffer adversely. Basically, the same principle applies if you allocate more to the other two phases of play. The differences can be explained by analyzing four of the most common modern systems of play: the 4-3-3, the 4-2-4, the 3-3-4, and the 4-4-2. Fundamentally, these systems are all based on the arrangement of the seven players as shown in figure 13.8.

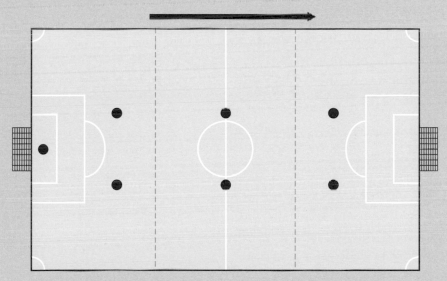

Figure 13.8   Modern systems achieve balance between attack and defense by organizing the field with two attackers, two midfielders, two defenders, and a goalkeeper.

the ball. For instance, you may teach the two wing fullbacks how to overlap the wide attackers. In figure 13.9, the fullback makes a long, forward overlapping run to meet the ball coming from the middle of the field.

You are also well advised to teach the three strikers how to work as a unit. For example, if player C, as shown in figure 13.10, goes wide with the ball, players A and B make near- and far-post runs into the penalty box, respectively. Player B might move toward player C to support if needed, and midfield player E may then make runs into the penalty box to contact any crosses delivered by either player B or player C.

In a 4-3-3 system of play, you must work with the midfield players on supporting the attacking players in possession of the ball and going beyond the strikers when necessary to receive passes behind the defense. In fact, some coaches encourage two of the three midfield players to attack and score goals while the other gives support to the attack from the rear as it develops into the attacking third of the field. In a 4-3-3 system, midfield players are expected to score goals from either outside or inside the penalty box as appropriate.

Another issue to clarify is the roles of the three attacking players. Many coaches operate with two wide forwards/wingers who position as wide outlets and also supply players in the penalty box with

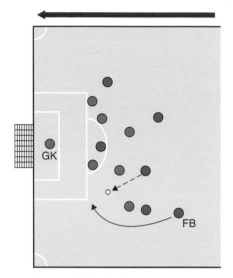

Figure 13.9 Fullback overlapping in the 4-3-3 system.

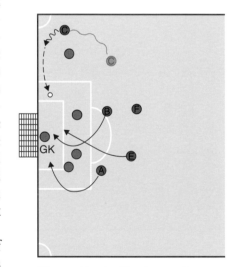

Figure 13.10 The three strikers must play as a unit in the 4-3-3 system.

passes and crosses from the flanks, and one central forward. Other coaches operate with three forwards/strikers who interchange positions and roles in the forward line, becoming the wide outlet when necessary and also functioning centrally as needed.

So, as with all systems of play, players in the 4-3-3 system operate from designated areas of the field but interchange both positions and roles as the game unfolds. To be successfully employed, systems need a degree of flexibility built into their functioning, so you must teach your players their tactical responsibilities as their roles change.

4-2-4 System

The 4-2-4 system, as shown in figure 13.11, is designed to use four players in clear attacking roles and four defenders. This gives both good attacking and good defensive coverage, but places great demands on the two central midfield players. To play this system, a team must have two fit, clever midfield players who generally function between the forward and back units of the team. On occasion they may break beyond the forward players, but their major role is to be available for passes from the back players and to feed and support the forward players.

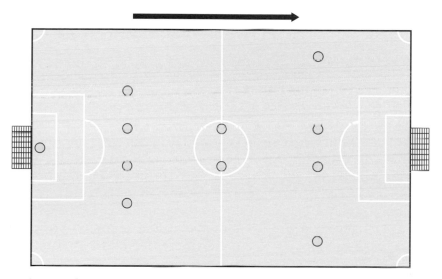

Figure 13.11   4-2-4 system.

When in possession, midfield players need immediate support; figure 13.12 shows how the wide players in the team can provide that support. Both the winger and the fullback move into positions to receive the ball, the winger in front of the opposing fullback to receive the ball to the feet, and the fullback moving forward to receive the ball to the space ahead. The midfield player in possession now has two early pass outlets to supply and must choose the most appropriate pass based on the pressure from the opposition. If one of the two central midfield players does break forward, then the other will hold his position in the center of the field.

Coaches often select the 4-2-4 system of play when they have two quick or clever wide players. The wide players' major task in possession is to attack the opposition fullback and to produce crosses or passes to players in goal-scoring positions. The wide players produce these crosses and passes either by beating the opposition fullback in a 1v1 situation or, by combining their play with that of others to deliver the cross. For instance, the fullback on the same side as the receiving wide player may overlap to receive the ball from the winger.

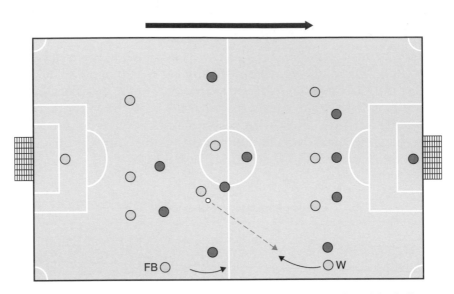

Figure 13.12 Supporting the midfield when your team is in possession of the ball.

Whenever the wide player is in a position to deliver a cross into the box, the winger on the opposite side should move infield inside the penalty area into a goal-scoring position around the far-post area. The incoming wide player joins the two strikers in a central goal-scoring position in the penalty box, ready to receive a cross from the winger or the overlapping fullback. The two strikers can operate in tandem with their movements and actions complementing each other in the buildup play as the team moves forward and in and around the penalty box in anticipation of crosses and passes.

In the 4-2-4 system, teams must also avoid becoming overstretched as they both attack and defend. When attackers stay up and defenders stay back, midfield players become isolated, often outnumbered and with too much ground to cover without support from others, as shown in figure 13.13. Regardless of the chosen system of play, successful teams must attempt to be compact when defending, as well as providing both close and distant support when attacking. When attacking, the defensive unit should move forward to compress the play and offer close support to midfield players especially, who will also move forward in support of the attacking players. On a loss of possession, attacking players are expected to defend by pressing the ball, meaning that they will move to meet the opponent with the ball, or by dropping deeper toward their own goal, maintaining team compactness by doing so. Remaining compact reduces the likelihood that the team will become stretched and midfield players will become isolated, as mentioned earlier.

Finally, if the opposition begins to dominate the midfield areas of play because of numerical advantage, you may need to change either your tactics or your system of play.

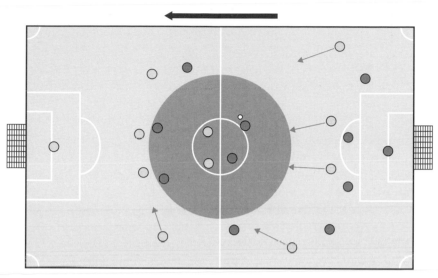

Figure 13.13   Attackers and defenders must work to close the midfield gap.

3-3-4 System

The 3-3-4 system, as shown in figure 13.14, keeps a strong attack by having two wingers, two strikers, and a numerically adequate midfield of three players at the expense of one defender. If you play on a narrow field, this system may be very suitable. The system requires quick and adaptable defenders who can read the play as it develops and move into wide defensive areas to contain the play as a wide back in a back four would be expected to do. The

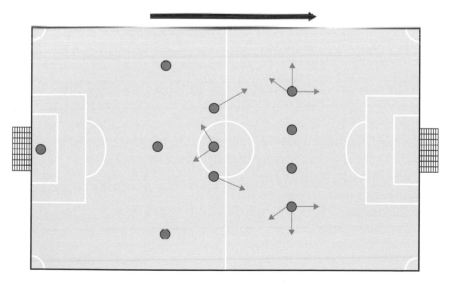

Figure 13.14   3-3-4 system.

system offers early width to the attacking team, but expecting the wide back to overlap in the attacking third of the field on a regular basis is unrealistic given his defensive role and responsibilities.

The basic requirements of the four front players are similar to those outlined in the 4-2-4 system of play, and the forward and support roles of the midfield players are much the same as those in the 4-3-3 system. In the 3-3-4 system, one of the midfield players should be of a defensive nature, usually the central of the three, and she may at times drop into the central positions in the back three as others move to defend in the wider areas. If the opponents play with four forwards, then the defensive midfield player may drop to become one of the back four as the team readjusts its system of play accordingly.

The 3-3-4 system can be quickly converted to a 3-5-2 system of play when the team defends by deploying the wide attackers into the midfield areas to assist the three midfield players. The two forwards would then be expected to delay the opponents' attacks being built up in their defending half of the field by pressuring sensibly or giving ground slowly ahead of the back four as they bring the ball forward.

4-4-2 System

In the 4-4-2 system, as shown in figure 13.15, players are arranged into a strong, compact defense and midfield unit of eight players, with two mobile forwards in attack, who are supported by the two wide midfield players as frequently as possible. Clearly, the arrangement of the players into a block of eight means that both defending and midfield units can offer early and quick support to each other and provide defensive security as a priority. This system is often used by professional teams playing away from home and seeking a tie rather than a win.

From the attacking viewpoint, the two wide attackers may not be wingers as such in that they have the capability to eliminate opponents in a 1v1 situation. However, they may be efficient receivers and distributors of the ball in and from those wider positions. They generally adopt deeper support positions to receive the ball on regains of possession than the archetypal winger because of their deeper defensive role. This system may need the fullbacks to overlap regularly to make quick forward progress down the flanks.

Central midfield players largely offer support and are playmakers in the central areas, but one may break forward as the other holds a securing midfield position. As the two wide players join the central midfield players in defense, opponents may push more players forward as they attack, particularly

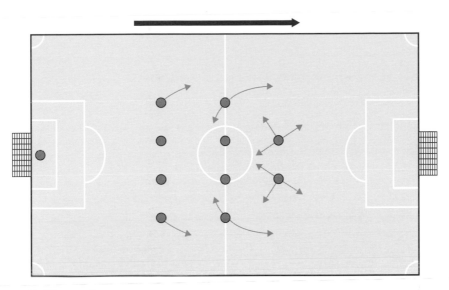

Figure 13.15 4-4-2 system.

down the flanks. On regaining possession with numbers behind the ball, the team could benefit from fast breakouts or counterattacks. The movements of the two strikers can help a team counterattack quickly, especially if they can make well-timed runs into spaces behind the defensive line that has pushed forward to support the attack or can make runs into the spaces vacated by fullbacks pushing forward. Counterattacks must be quickly supported by players breaking from deep, particularly the midfield unit of four, but not all at the same time!

As with all systems, the types of players on your team largely dictate the tactical possibilities you can use within the basic system of play. It is possible to play a 4-3-3 system of play without wingers and a 4-4-2 system with wingers, just as the capabilities of the strikers will dictate whether the counterattacks you require are possible. The systems examined in this section are probably the most commonly used throughout the world, but you must slightly adjust the tactics within the system to produce an efficient way of operating for your team. The system is really the framework, or the most effective locating of players, to enable a team to use the players' personal attributes in conjunction with those of their teammates. It outlines the basic areas of operation, defines the roles the players will play (to a large degree), and brings some order and understanding to a team's play.

Variations of the Basic Systems

We now examine two of the most popular variations of the basic systems: the sweeper system of defense and the target player system of attack.

Sweeper System of Defense

Some European teams play one defender behind two, three, or four defenders. This defender is called the sweeper, or free back, as he has no specific marking duties. Those defenders around and ahead of this player mark opposing players, leaving the sweeper free to read the game, communicate with and direct the defenders, and cover important areas behind the marking defenders. If a team has quick, disciplined, and tenacious defenders, with an intelligent reader of the game playing behind them, then this system can be highly effective.

The sweeper system is often thought of as a defensive system, but this is not always the case. It depends on the instructions given to those players ahead of the sweeper and markers. If they are instructed to drop deep and defend only in the defending half of the field, then some believe that this is defensive soccer. However, if the team does drop deep in this way, presumably it will do so because it believes it is likely to be outgunned by the opponent or it believes it can regain possession of the ball in deeper positions and quickly counterattack when the opposition has been drawn forward and has left space behind its defense.

Any system of play can be adapted to this tactical thinking. For example, a 4-4-2 system can be adapted for a team to defend deep in its own half of the field with the expectation that opportunities for rapid counterattacking will arise. Two popular sweeper systems are shown in figure 13.16, *a* and *b*. In figure 13.16*a*, the sweeper (S) plays behind three defenders. In figure 13.16*b*, the sweeper (S) plays behind four defenders.

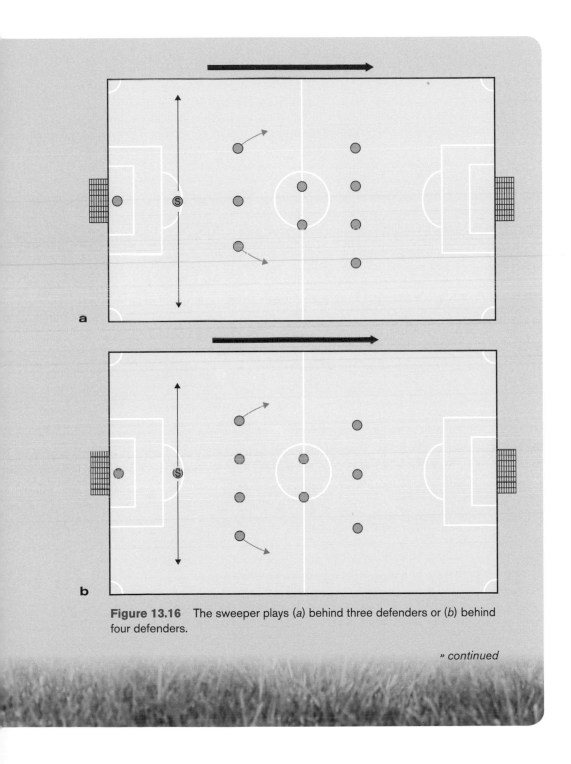

Figure 13.16 The sweeper plays (*a*) behind three defenders or (*b*) behind four defenders.

» *continued*

The sweeper, or free player, is in fact in a prime position to create the play from a position deep in her own half of the field and also to continue to contribute to creative play as it progresses toward the opponents' goal. The master sweeper will initiate attacking play on receiving the ball from either the goalkeeper or other back players. She should possess excellent passing skills over a variety of distances and should also be confident enough to carry the ball forward into the midfield area and create from there also. Many of the great sweepers originally played as midfield players; the qualities of a good midfield player are necessary for the creative sweeper to influence her team's attacking play.

Target Player

The target player is the player who operates against the opponents' rearmost defenders and gets as close as possible to the opponents' goal without moving offside. The target player often plays directly in front of the rearmost defender and, by facing his own players, presents a target for them to pass to (see figure 13.17).

Because the target player plays in front of the rearmost defender (just like postplay in basketball), he is obviously in a dangerous striking position. If the ball comes to the target player, it means that most defenders have already been bypassed and the attacking team may have achieved a 1v1 situation in a potential scoring area. If a player

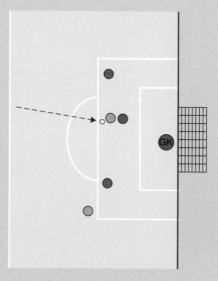

Figure 13.17 A player stands in front of the rearmost defender and presents a target for his teammate.

in such a position can turn with the ball and attack the only remaining defender, then clearly this is good attacking play and offers the opportunity to strike at goal. It follows that the best tactical advice to give to a target player is, Turn if you can. If he cannot turn, and this is often the case because the ball comes at a very fast pace, the target player should try to lay off the ball to a supporting player (see figure 13.18).

If an attacking team uses the target player against your defense, your own players must move forward quickly toward the opponents' goal just before the ball is played to the target player. In this way your defense can either intercept the pass or play the target player offside.

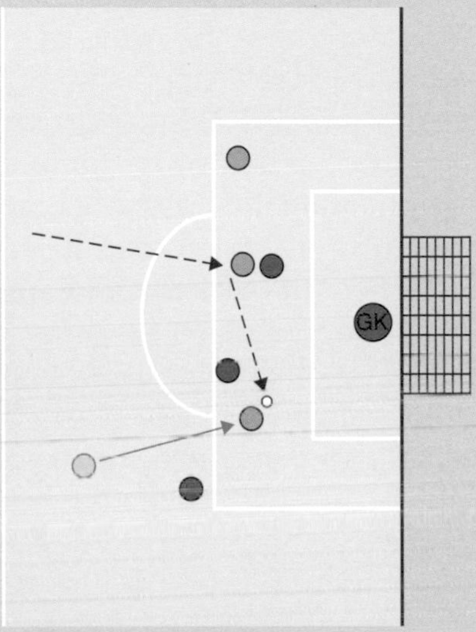

Figure 13.18 The target player passes the ball behind the defense to a supporting player.

If the ball reaches the target player, your defender must do everything possible to stop the turn—that is, to keep the target player with his back to the goal to prevent the shot and mark any likely receiver of his passes.

Selecting a System

One of the most frequently asked questions is, Which system should I use? Only you can answer this question. You must determine how to best accommodate the strengths and weaknesses of individual players and design or modify a system to suit the needs of your team. These are the key factors to have in mind when selecting a system.

The second most frequent question is, Where shall I play my least able players? First, notice that we talk about *least able players,* not *weak or poor players.* Accommodating the least able players is an important coaching strategy, particularly in youth soccer organizations, where everyone gets a chance to play. Quite often, the questions to answer are, "To what degree can the less able player be supported by the other players?" or "Where would this player cause the most problems for the opposition?" Some professional teams who have to play a slightly injured player because they have made all their substitutions put that player in a striker role, knowing that an opponent cannot afford to ignore his presence in the buildup or finish of an attacking move.

Playing the less able player in a defensive position is a risk that may be punished, although this may not be the case if your less able player is up against an equally less able player in the opposition! So there can be no definitive answer. You may well have to make a quick decision to reorganize your team if the less able player is being exposed by an opponent. Part of your role is to identify the threats from the opposition once the game has begun and adjust your team accordingly, or even change the system of play, to meet the situation created by the opposition.

A word of caution: Don't try to fit players into set positions until they have tried to play several positions. Players should be given the opportunity to try a variety of positions as part of their general education.

Individual Duties and Responsibilities

Because the success of any system depends on the way the players make it work, each player must have specific roles and duties. This final section analyzes the fundamental duties that players occupying each position should understand and try to incorporate into their game. First, we address three basic rules that all players should observe, regardless of their position or the system.

1. When in the defensive zone, players should think safety first—that is, preventing a goal rather than stealing the ball. Mistakes here can be costly, and it is always better to give away a throw-in or a corner kick rather than a goal-scoring opportunity. Giving away possession of the ball to the opposition in the defending half of the field is a major source of goals for the opponents, so defenders must be sure on the ball or safe—both would be ideal!

2. When in the midfield, players must keep possession of the ball whether developing attacks are fast or slower buildups. If the opposition is well organized, midfield players may have to be patient, retain possession, and play the ball around; if the opposition is disorganized and can be exposed, play has to be quick and direct. But above all, midfielders must keep possession.

3. When in the attacking zone, players must be aggressive and prepared to take risks; they should try to beat the defenders and shoot whenever possible. They don't score unless they shoot!

We now consider the specific duties and responsibilities of each position. The following sections describe the basic but important playing strategies that each player should learn.

Goalkeeper

After gathering the ball safely, the goalkeeper should either look for a quick throw to an unmarked colleague to gain an immediate advantage and counter-attack, or wait temporarily until his team has dispersed and feed a free player who intends to build up an attacking move. Additionally, the goalkeeper may delay distributing the ball until teammates have moved forward and are organized and ready to receive a long pass with a kick either from the hands or the ground.

No matter where the opponents are building up their attack, the goalkeeper should always stay in line with the ball and with the center of her goal and be in a position to support the back line of defenders if the ball is played in behind them.

Rather than standing rigidly on the goal line, the goalkeeper should move forward to the edge of the penalty area when the ball is in the opponents' half and retreat slowly as the opponents attack (see chapter 10).

Fullbacks

Fullbacks should be adept in their marking and interception skills, attempting to gain possession of the ball before it reaches their opposing winger. If the opposing winger does receive the ball, the fullback must try to jockey him and force him into a position from which crossing the ball would be very difficult. Patience and an aggressive attitude will be needed to do this, and all fullbacks must be dominant in 1v1 situations. Fullbacks should always position themselves so that if the ball is played over their heads or past them, they can always win the race to the ball that is moving toward their own goal.

When the attack is on the other side of the field, the fullbacks' first duty is to cover the spaces behind the central defenders by moving closer to them, which means leaving their own winger to cover the middle of the field.

Central Defenders

Central defenders play in either a sweeper and man-to-man marking system or a zone defense system as designated by you. Central defenders must be good readers of the game. They must also know who and how to mark as the central attackers change positions, and they are also largely responsible for covering each other in the central areas of the field.

The defenders should always try to keep attackers who receive the ball facing away from the defenders' goal (i.e., stop the turn), but if attackers do turn, defenders should jockey them away from the goal by being patient, staying on their feet, and preventing shots at goal or passes into the penalty area. It is also vital that central defenders in any team combine together, know whether they are using a man-to-man or zone marking system, and be first to the ball when crosses are delivered into the penalty box.

Midfield Players

Midfield players should link the play between defenders and attackers. This requires an understanding of good support positions through 360 degrees and all the skills needed to retain possession of the ball. Midfield players should attempt to play accurate forward or diagonal passes through or between opponents if possible and not give square passes unless forced to. A square pass across the field that is intercepted by the opposition may eliminate two or more of the defending players. This is often the case because defenders generally move up the field with the expectation that the player with the ball will play it forward toward the opponent's goal, not across the field. All great midfield players place primary importance on retaining the ball when building attacks from the midfield areas. Making timely forward runs into goal-scoring positions is a further important skill for any midfield player.

When the opposition runs or passes the ball past them, midfield players must run quickly along their recovery line toward their own goal to position themselves goalside of the ball once again if they are unable to press the ball and force errors from their opponents.

Wingers

A winger's first duty is to be available to receive passes in flank/wide positions and to attack either alone or in combination with others so as to cross the ball into the penalty box. When the attack is on the other wing in advanced attacking areas, wingers should move into the shooting zone, often into a position adjacent to the post nearest to them without being offside.

Defensively, a winger must, whenever possible, apply pressure on the opposition fullback in possession of the ball and stay with that fullback if she makes forward runs toward the goal. The winger must also move centrally toward her own central midfield players if the opponents attack on the other side of the pitch and be able to support and cover those midfield players when necessary.

Strikers

Strikers should always be available for the ball in advanced positions. Their willingness to support and move into positions where they can be seen and receive the ball is a great help to those in possession and the sign of players who play for the team, not just their own goal-scoring statistics!

However, the prime role and function of a striker is to score goals and provide for others in goal-scoring positions. They must possess an insatiable desire to score goals as well as pace, cleverness both with and without the ball, and excellent finishing techniques. Also, the ability to turn and attack defenders in a 1v1 situation is a further asset possessed by the very best of strikers.

Although this chapter is about team formations and systems of play, it is true that systems are only as good as the players involved. Systems and tactics are important, but it is the players who, collectively, win or lose matches. Your principal role as a coach is to isolate the skills and techniques that individual members of your team need to develop—and spend most of your time helping them to do so.

Coaching Teamwork

• • • • • •
YOUR ROLE AND responsibilities as a coach extend far beyond coaching your team on game days, important though this is. Coaching during an 11v11 competitive game is not easy because so much is going on and the players do not really want to be shouted at and told what to do, especially while they are playing—they just want to get on with the game. It follows that your lasting influence on your players takes place during practice sessions. For this reason, the importance of preplanning these sessions cannot be overestimated. In this chapter we introduce some of the techniques and strategies we have found helpful when planning practice sessions, not only for small groups, but for when you are working with your complete squad.

We have found that the most effective way to approach any coaching session is to ask questions, such as: What do I want to coach? What is the aim of the session? In which part of the field is it appropriate to site the practice? How many players should be involved in the practice and what equipment is needed to conduct the session? What methods should I use to deliver the session (i.e., practice types and coaching styles)? In this chapter we attempt to answer the what, where, and how of planning coaching sessions and show how planning well will result in a more effective and more enjoyable session for all concerned.

What Do I Coach?

Before your session, you should have a theme in mind. You may base this theme on how your team played in the last game, preparation to play in the next game, or your long-term development curriculum.

Following are typical session themes that you can choose from (these sessions may be conducted with individual players, groups or units of teams, or the team as a whole):

- How to play when your team has possession of the ball
- How to play when the opposition has the ball
- What to do at the moment the ball changes possession—the breakdown point
- What to do at restarts and set plays
- How to encourage players to help each other

Where Do I Coach?

Whenever possible, always set up the coaching practice in the area of the field where such play normally takes place (e.g., coach the goalkeeper in the goal, the winger on the flanks).

To observe the practice, position yourself either to the side of the practice area or on the field of play. Never be in a position that interferes with the action. Your position from which to observe the practice is vital because, unless you can identify the challenges and difficulties for the players, you will be in no position to rectify or advise players on alternative courses of action and therefore will not be able to do your job!

You should vary your position according to the progress and changes in the structure of the practice. Stay aware so you will know when to change your location according to those changes.

How Do I Coach?

The answer to the question of how to coach is: with flexibility! Each session, each group, and each occasion is unique, and you must meet the challenge of being effective in every coaching situation.

Because sessions will differ in themes, the number of players, and conditions, you must always be prepared to challenge and support your players. Therefore, you must be a master of the teaching arts. Organizational skills, communication skills, observational skills, and teaching skills must always be of the highest order regardless of the circumstances—hence the requirement for flexibility.

Following are some methods you may want to use when conducting sessions with your team.

Game Conditioning

The first method, game conditioning, can improve both individual skills and teamwork. For example, if you are unhappy about the way your players ran to support each other in the last game, you may design and conduct possession practices that focus on two-touch soccer. This will require that players move to support positions both early and quickly to provide outlets for the player on the ball who has restricted touches. If you find that your defenders watch where the ball goes rather than where their opponents move, you can use man-to-man marking games to encourage them and instill a discipline to mark and track opponents and deny them possession especially in the important goal-scoring areas.

You may also decide to invent special rules. For example, blowing the whistle twice in succession might mean that the team in possession has given away an indirect free kick. This will show you how quickly players react at the breakdown point when the ball changes hands. Similarly, three quick blasts on your whistle might indicate a direct free kick against a team within 30 yards of the goal, enabling you to observe how effectively the team organizes itself to defend, perhaps forming a defensive wall.

You may also choose to impose conditions on the whole team or even individual players according to the needs of those players or the team. Do not, however, condition players without a good reason. Introduce a condition only for the purpose of enhancing the development of the player and the group. Merely imposing a condition for no particular reason can be more for your benefit than that of your players.

Silent Soccer

One of the best conditioned games for encouraging good team play is Silent Soccer. In this game, players play a standard soccer game, but no player is allowed to call out or even whisper for any reason. The penalty for doing so is a direct free kick. Players quickly realize that they have to think and act for themselves. The benefit of this is that players have to observe the play as it is developing and act accordingly. They must look off the ball when their team is both in and out of possession. Discerning players will quickly learn to constantly look and adjust their performances based on what is happening. Because no one tells them what to do or how to play, their actions are entirely the result of their own thoughts. This can give you an insight into what they are thinking. Further, because the players are quiet, it is much easier to communicate with them, and you will not finish the session with a headache or a sore throat!

You may stop the play from time to time and bring the group together for a short period of time (e.g., 2 minutes). In this time you can ask questions about the players' individual and group performances, offer alternatives, and indicate aspects of play that they should pay attention to in the next period of play.

Use Silent Soccer for limited periods, and hear and see the difference. This is a boon for coaches of the noisy young, and it is much enjoyed by the more sensitive players who, for once, are not continually shouted at by teammates. Silent Soccer is a thinking and acting game—the essence of good soccer.

Attack Versus Defense Practice

Attack versus defense practices are the easiest to explain and probably the most enjoyable of all practice situations for both the players and the coach. In this type of practice, the players get to enjoy the nearest thing to a competitive game against another team and you, the coach, can emphasize whichever and whatever skills and tactics you choose. You can highlight team plays and individual strengths and weaknesses, all during developing, realistic situations.

Arranging an attack versus defense practice is easy. Using half of a full-size soccer field, you simply divide your players into their normal team positions, either attackers or defenders (midfield players can be either), and have your attacking players try to score against your defending players (if you have a large number of players, simply arrange your attackers into two or three groups that take turns attacking the defense; this is commonly called "wave attacks"). During play, you can highlight whatever aspects of the game you choose (team plays, restarts, individual positional play, etc.). You can concentrate on specific themes, such as the back for defenders, beating the offside trap, attacking free kicks, and, of course, the situations of the game that arise naturally.

There are only three instructions to remember when using attack versus defense practice. These are:

1. The attackers must keep attacking until they either score or lose possession.

2. The defenders, if and when they gain possession, must try to pass the ball amongst themselves until they succeed in getting a player, in possession of the ball, over the center line. The center line is considered their "goal." The attackers, of course, do their best to regain possession from the defenders to restart their attack. In many ways the game is continuous.

3. And, finally, each time the drill is restarted after a goal has been scored or the ball has gone out of play over the goal line, it is best done with a long kick upfield by the goalkeeper or the coach. The reason for this is that it gives the defenders time to move forward out of the penalty area and get close to the center line before the start of the next attack.

Advance Calling

In the advance calling method, you think ahead for the players, calling, for example, "Kelly, make a through pass to Chris." Because you are not playing, you can more easily think ahead; by talking to your players, you can help them develop tactical appreciation. This method keeps the game flowing, and the players learn while playing. It is most important when introducing new players to plays, especially set plays such as free kicks.

Playback System

The playback system is probably the most important of all coaching methods. Here you stop the play and recreate it by reconstructing what happened. You can then, if necessary, discuss the situation with the players, offer more positive options, or ask the players for their opinions as to how best to handle the circumstance. If necessary, you can not only demonstrate what happened and why, but also show players what is required, which is a very effective way of communicating good tactical play.

Following are the stages of the playback system:

1. Arrange and start the practice.
2. Observe the practice and identify the deficiency (e.g., making the wrong decisions or performing poorly).
3. Stop the practice and move to the focal point.
4. Rearrange the players accurately.
5. Replay the move correctly and rectify the error.
6. Restart the play and observe the modified actions.

Stage 1—Arrange and Start the Practice

Imagine that a team was using a 4-2-4 system in a previous game, and the four defenders did not cover each other very well. The coach might choose an attack practice and position himself behind and to the side of the defenders, as shown in figure 14.1. To begin the practice, the coach or the goalkeeper kicks the ball forward to an attacking player, probably C or D, who are the midfield players who feed and support the forwards as they attack.

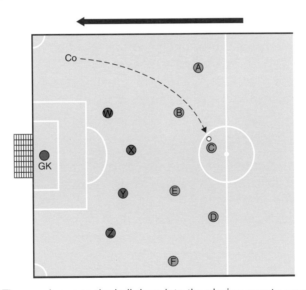

Figure 14.1   The coach serves the ball deep into the playing area to create a realistic start.

Stage 2—Observe the Practice and Identify the Deficiency

From a selected coaching position, after checking the practice organization and the attitude and understanding of the players, the coach simply observes the performance of the defenders until one of them either covers a teammate particularly well or makes an error in positioning or defensive decision making. Selecting a good example, as discussed in chapter 2, will give a double positive effect. For example, in figure 14.2, player F cannot outmaneuver player Z in a 1v1 situation, so player F passes to player E. Player Y fails to react to this pass.

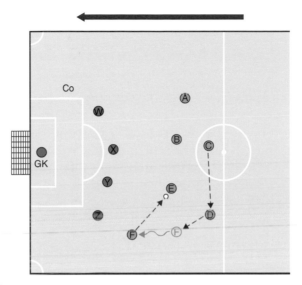

Figure 14.2   The coach identifies that player Y failed to react to player F's pass.

Stage 3—Stop the Practice and Move to the Focal Point

The coach stops the play using a clear command such as "Freeze" or "Stop," or blows a whistle. Then he moves quickly to the key player, or focal point (player Y as shown in figure 14.3). That player may, however, already understand his error!

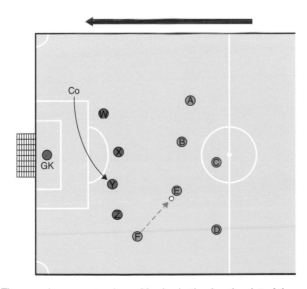

Figure 14.3   The coach moves to player Y, who is the focal point of the coach's input.

Stage 4—Rearrange the Players Accurately

The coach then stands by the key player and rearranges the other players into the positions they held just prior to the situation that needs attention. The coach should ensure that all players can both see and hear him as he does this.

Stage 5—Replay the Move Correctly and Rectify the Error

The coach then replays the move to show the players what happened before offering an alternative.

The coach should be precise and concise and speak and act with clarity. When appropriate, the coach can use the question-and-answer technique or ask the player to demonstrate a better alternative. This includes the player in the decision-making process, although the coach at times should have the final decision especially when constructing a unified approach and team understanding. Replaying the move after the alternative has been agreed on cements the strategy in the player's mind and gives the coach an opportunity to observe and confirm the understanding and skill of the player. Once player Y makes the required response, as shown in figure 14.4, the coach can support the action by reciting the rule, "Nearest defender goes to meet the ball." The coach should also make sure players W and X know how they should react.

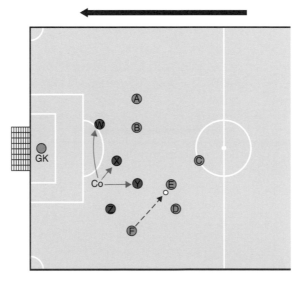

Figure 14.4 Defenders react correctly, and player Y meets the player with the ball, while players X and W move across the field to cover.

Stage 6—Restart Play and Observe the Modified Actions

The coach then recreates the original situation accurately by replacing everyone in their initial positions. When the coach calls "Play on," player F passes once again to player E. The defenders should now react correctly. If all is well, the practice can continue. If all is not well, then the coach stops the practice once again, recreates, teaches, and then restarts the practice with the correct alternative once more.

Once the coach achieves the correct reaction from the players, he moves to the side and watches for the next point. The game now continues until the coach is ready to move forward toward the next coaching point.

Using Video Effectively

Video is valuable for analyzing almost any aspect of technical or tactical play and is very useful for examining individual player and unit performance. For example, you may want to observe the play of your back four defenders during a competitive game. By focusing exclusively on their movements and what is happening immediately ahead or behind them, a video can give you an opportunity to examine, in depth, the individual actions and responses in the actual game situations. In this way the video of the game becomes your reference. It provides the focus for the design of future coaching sessions. It also has another very valuable advantage—it is highly motivational for the players because they can see themselves in action and begin to appreciate their performances, which is always a wonderful way to start a practice.

If you have the time or a parent can help, video is an excellent teaching aid. Editing the video to create a definite focus is the most efficient and effective way of presenting learning material to players. Lengthy stretches of irrelevant video are tedious to watch, but showing extracts from a competitive game in which some players may not be involved is still relevant to the improvement of team performance and should be part of the learning process. If you have the time, it can be very beneficial to give individual players copies of videos of their performances and go through them with the individual players, explaining the details of their performances.

Do not, however, allow the viewing of videos to replace regular field practice. Have players arrive early to practice to watch videos. In this way a wealth of visual material can reinforce the field practice.

Tactics in Defense, Midfield, and Attack

• • • • • • •

THIS CHAPTER HAS been included for coaches who want to take their knowledge of team tactics to a higher level. Not all teams have players who are mature enough to absorb and execute these ideas, but those of you who do will find in this chapter the beginning, or the confirmation, of a deeper understanding of tactics in defense, midfield, and attack.

What does *tactics* mean in soccer language? Basically, tactics are the individual, group, or team maneuvers or moves used during a game to gain an advantage or deny the same to an opponent. Tactics form a major part of an overall game plan and are largely planned by the coach, although clever players can adjust their tactical play according to their opponents or the game's events.

Intelligent tactical play involves the use of technical, physical, and even mental factors in the quest to disadvantage an opponent. A player who understands the game, can read events as they unfold, has a wide range of techniques, and knows his own attributes can be flexible with the tactics he employs. The more a player has "game intelligence"—the ability to make accurate and critical decisions under match play conditions—the more he can be involved in the tactics of the game and continue to be effective as the necessity for tactical change becomes apparent.

As well as the basic game plan, tactics are also derived from the team's style of play—how a team is encouraged to play the game—their way of playing. For example, an energetic, high-intensity, direct soccer team employs different tactics from those of a team that plays at a slower, more controlled speed and uses technical ability to retain possession.

Tactics are both planned by the coach and practiced in pregame training or are intuitively implemented by quick-thinking players during the game. They are primarily designed and used to take advantage of a weakness in the opposition, to negate a strength in the opposition, to employ a perceived strength of one's own team, to minimize a weakness in one's own team, or to achieve a required position on the field of play.

As indicated earlier, tactics may be used by the team, a group within the team, or individual players. What is vital is that all players understand how the team intends to achieve the result and their tactical role in that process; your role is to make sure they do. Whereas strategy is the *end*, tactics are the *means* of achieving that end. Put simply, team tactics are founded on the careful planning of how you intend to create and score goals and how you intend to prevent goals from being scored against you.

Defensive Tactics

Teams need to understand how they can defend successfully in a variety of circumstances. Some teams, as a mainstay of their defensive tactics, defend early (i.e., as soon as they concede possession to their opponents). Others may choose to recover, regroup, and prepare themselves to defend later. In this section we examine the basic principles of these two approaches.

Team Defensive Tactics

Initially we look at the tactics involved in defending late and then counterattacking. We then examine how teams can initially defend deep to concentrate their resources.

Late Team Defending

Defensive team tactics may be as straightforward as deciding where to first engage and pressure the opponents' buildup play. If you decide that your opponents are highly skillful in possession of the ball and can play cleverly and quickly through a team that lacks compactness, you may decide to defend deeper with the first serious defense against the player on the ball taking place around the halfway line and with your strikers exerting that pressure. The midfield line will organize itself behind this first pressing line, and the back line will likely be positioned on or around the edge of the penalty area, as shown in figure 15.1. This would give your team 11 players between the ball and its goal and would, providing your team is defending well, produce a problem for the attacking team in penetrating your defense. The teams that use this tactic often employ a counterattacking play upon gaining possession of the ball as space is available behind the opponents' defense. In addition, space is often created between the defensive back players through which attacking passes and runs can be made.

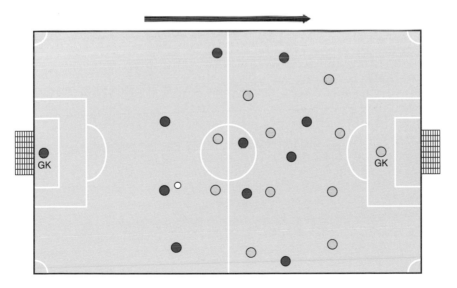

Figure 15.1 Defense positioning to defend deep.

Early Team Defending

Alternatively, a team may decide to pressure the opponents as early and consistently as possible when they are in possession of the ball (see figure 15.2). The attacking team has possession in its own defending third of the field and is immediately pressured by your forward players. With the midfield and defending lines pushing forward onto opponents to support the forwards who

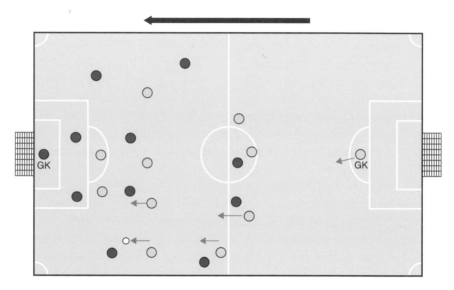

Figure 15.2 Defense pressing early.

Implementing Defending Tactics

The best teams can use both early and late team defensive tactics depending on what the coach or the circumstances require. Of course, one of your major coaching responsibilities is to teach your players in training to recognize why, when, and how to implement these two differing tactics so they can transfer their training groundwork into game play. Again, the better teams can execute the range of defending tactics knowing that they must adhere to defending principles of play and incorporate good individual defending skills.

You must decide how your team should defend based on your players' attributes and level of understanding, and also after an assessment of the opposition, if possible. You may have to change those tactical options if the game proves different than expected, including players changing positions and therefore their roles and responsibilities, changing the personnel on the pitch, or changing the tactics your team is using.

are pressing, your team retains defensive compactness, but in a higher position on the field of play. You may choose to employ this tactic if your team is losing the game and needs to regain possession of the ball, or if you believe the opponents will surrender possession if your players sustain pressure for long periods of the game.

Group Defensive Tactics

Although teams may adopt different defending strategies and tactics, within the team organization, units may operate differently, yet still achieve a successful result and defend effectively. In the following sections we give some examples of how this may function.

Man-to-Man Marking

A group or unit in the team may use specific tactics to gain or take away an advantage. For instance, players in the central midfield unit may mark their immediate opponents on a man-to-man basis. Opposing midfield players find receiving possession of the ball and operating when in possession of the ball difficult under the tight marking circumstances. By applying this tactic, a team may reduce the number of times a very skillful opposition "creator" in midfield both receives the ball and creates problems. First, because other players are reluctant to pass to a teammate who is tightly marked for fear of losing possession, and second, because if the teammate does receive the ball, he is immediately restricted in his options because of the man-to-man marking. Some teams that play with a sweeper and man-to-man defense also mark on a man-to-man basis ahead of the rear defenders and sweeper and so mark midfield opponents individually.

Zone Defense

Alternatively, a central midfield unit may be organized to defend on a zonal basis. This means that, largely, players in this unit defend against opponents that come into their personal zones in the midfield areas of the field and pass on opponents who move their position across the field of play to the next midfield player in the zone. They may still be required to run with opponents who make forward runs toward their goal, but generally they attempt to defend in the left, center, and right midfield areas of the field.

Although it seems that a zone defense may give opponents more time and space in which to receive and distribute the ball, if employed correctly, the receiver of the ball will be under immediate and intense pressure by the midfield player defending in that zone. The other midfield players in the unit will slide across the field according to the movement and location of the ball and will not mark as tightly on their immediate midfield opponents (see figure 15.3).

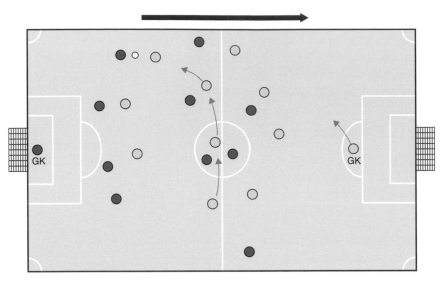

Figure 15.3 A sliding, midfield zone defense.

Individual Defensive Tactics

Individual defensive tactics are based on players' skills in reading the game, positioning, marking, and challenging for the ball. For example, if a very quick and left-footed opponent operates on the left flank, a right fullback may, by his positioning, prevent the winger from progressing with the ball between the defender and the touchline. He directs the winger infield to prevent him from immediately using his left foot to cross the ball. The positioning of the fullback's feet and body when the winger receives the ball will largely influence the direction in which the winger moves. With a right-footed winger on the left flank, the same principles apply, but the intention of the fullback is now to prevent the opponent from coming infield and perhaps attacking the central areas of the defense. The fullback will push the winger outside so he has to operate near to the touchline in a reduced space. This simple individual defending tactic can reduce the winger's effectiveness. The negation of the winger's contribution can constitute part of an overall team defending tactic of reducing the number of crosses delivered into the defending team's penalty box.

Central defenders can also use individual tactics against the strikers. If a central defender learns, or already knows, that the striker tends to spin very late and quickly, then, when that striker attempts to run behind the defense to receive a pass, the center back will mark behind the striker at a distance (perhaps 2 to 3 yards) from which he will not be beaten to a ball passed behind him toward the goal. If the ball is played to the striker's feet, the center back can, of course, move as the pass is in transit to a tight marking position and attempt to intercept or prevent the striker from turning with the ball. However, if the striker has very little pace and consistently requires that the ball be played into his feet or chest area, the central defender can mark tight and so increase his chances of intercepting the ball or challenging for it knowing that he is unlikely to be exposed with a pass behind the defense.

Attacking Tactics

As with defending tactics, numerous attacking options are available based on the individual abilities of your players. Also, you have your own preferences for how you want your team to play. In this section we give examples of how some teams operate at the team, unit, and individual levels—but there are many others!

Team Attacking Tactics

A team's attacking identity is based on how it uses possession in a game. Some teams attack as quickly as possible along the most direct route to goal and do so by making the fewest passes necessary. Other teams are less direct in their play and refuse to put possession at risk until they reach the attacking third of the field. Such teams make as many passes as necessary to reach the goal-scoring areas, through 360 degrees if necessary.

At different stages and for different reasons during a game, a team may deliberately retain possession to compel the opponents to take a risk in trying to regain possession. The rear defenders may choose to pass the ball across the field to each other in a controlled, contrived, but calculated manner to attract the strikers to chase the ball to regain possession. If the strikers make an error of judgment when chasing and are eliminated (for example, by approaching too quickly, challenging for the ball at the wrong time, or being exposed to a wall pass), a back player can move forward with the ball into midfield and create an overload of attacking players in that area. Additionally, if the strikers are energetically committed to regaining the ball, after a time they may become fatigued; their state of exhaustion will then render them less effective in their attacking obligations. The art of diligently waiting and enticing opponents to make errors is a tactic used by many teams at the highest levels of modern soccer.

Additionally, a team that is winning a game by 2-0 with 10 minutes to go may deliberately retain possession of the ball to run the clock down. Players do this by making square and back passes unless there is an obvious and safe forward option that does not put possession at risk. This tactical use of possession again may draw the defending team forward to try to regain the ball, leaving exploitable space behind the defense or between defenders.

A team that has a quick and effective wide player who is capable of beating a fullback in a 1v1 situation in the attacking third of the field may regularly supply this player with the ball both early and quickly, especially from midfield areas of the field. The wide player is then likely to receive the ball when the opposing fullback is isolated without any defensive support.

A team that has a wide player who has good ball control skills but may not be an effective dribbler may need to assist the wide player with an overlapping player, usually a fullback breaking forward (see figure 15.4). In this way the team can still produce crosses and passes into the penalty box and expose the opponents' fullbacks.

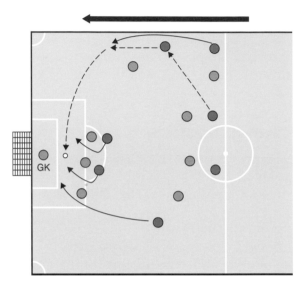

Figure 15.4   Overlapping play on flank positions.

You will craft your team's tactical use of possession according to the capabilities of your players and those of your opponent. An analysis of your players' technical competence, tactical intelligence, and psychological and physiological capabilities should be the basis of your overall game plan and team attacking tactics for the forthcoming opponents.

Group Attacking Tactics

When we discuss group tactics, we are referring to a unit in the team (e.g., a back four or a midfield three) or players who regularly play adjacent to each other (e.g., a winger and a fullback). Many player associations throughout the team involve combined thought and movements.

How a team operates with its strikers significantly influences the tactics it adopts as part of the playing tactics and strategy for both attackers and defenders. For example, many teams function with two strikers playing up against the opponents' two central defenders almost alongside each other, creating what is virtually a 2v2 scenario. Central defenders often prefer this tactical arrangement because their roles and responsibilities are quite clear as to who marks, who covers, and when (see figure 15.5). Much of the movement of the strikers is lateral and toward the ball, and the central defenders are rarely distant from either of the two strikers as they make their movements. Because

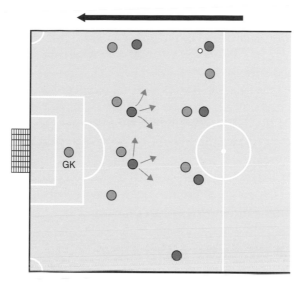

Figure 15.5   Two strikers playing up against two central defenders.

both strikers perform much of their work from starting positions relatively close to the center backs, the defenders react positively and assuredly knowing which striker is the responsibility of which center back. A center back can deal with the lateral movement of the strikers by passing on a striker to a fellow center back, if appropriate, with the defenders supporting and covering each other as necessary. The center back can track any movement toward the ball knowing that he has cover from the other center back and fullbacks.

If one of the strikers functions "off the front" in the area between the back and midfield lines of the opponent, a different set of issues confronts the central defenders (see figure 15.6). When the other central striker is not

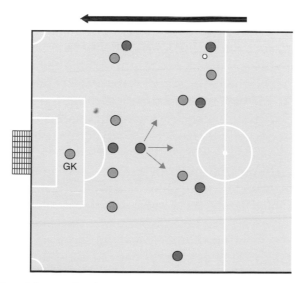

Figure 15.6   Two strikers split roles.

playing up against one central defender, but between the two, then the center backs have awkward decisions to make. Which center back marks this striker? And when do the central defenders counter any movement made by the top striker, as he is often called?

Because center backs in a zonal back line are expected to cover and support each other, they frequently elect to stay and play alongside each other, leaving the responsibility of the deeper-playing striker to someone else. If unattended, the deeper striker can attract the ball in a central attacking area often under little pressure if he positions intelligently and can distribute the ball calmly and precisely. Many teams play with one striker between the central defenders and one deep, whereas others alternate those responsibilities according to the demands of the game—either striker can take on either role.

Individual Attacking Tactics

As with all tactical choices, the tactics used by individuals in the attacking team can be preplanned based on knowledge about the opponent or can be spontaneous, instinctive reactions to events that unfold in the course of the game. An understanding of a player's or team's significant attributes against an opponent is the key to effective preplanned tactics.

If a slow-turning fullback is selected to oppose a quick wide player, the wide player can use certain tactics to increase his chances of success. Simply playing the ball behind the fullback and chasing after it may not produce the results required. The fullback or his coach will surely have recognized his deficiencies and adjusted his defensive play accordingly. The fullback may have learned that he must jockey the quicker players from a more distant position; he may also have learned to adjust his feet and body position to maximize his limited turning speed when chasing faster players.

Tactically, the slower, but intelligent fullback will have discovered survival techniques in coping with players who attack him at speed. This presents a challenge to the attacker. One tactic for the attacker would be to get close to the defender before playing the ball past him. Also, if the attacker can cause the defender to turn and change direction as the attacker plays the ball behind him, that is likely to increase the difficulties for him.

Let us suppose that the defender is jockeying the attacker outside and toward the sideline. By attacking the defender at a quick but controlled speed and actually threatening to drive infield with the ball, the attacker can cause the defender to turn to counter this movement. If the attacker can take the ball to within 1 yard of the defender's inside foot before playing the ball outside him, then the time that the defender has to react to this move is severely reduced.

This action of attacking the defender's inside line and playing the ball outside and past him from a position close to his feet is an effective tactic for a wide player to use to eliminate the fullback in a 1v1 situation (see figure 15.7). The thought process usually precedes the tactic, but the best players

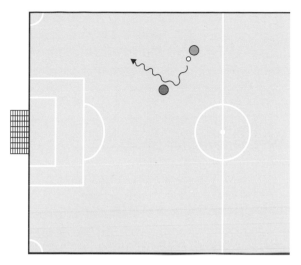

Figure 15.7 Wide player attacking the defender's inside line.

have the mental flexibility and technical and tactical ability to change their minds and actions at the last second to respond to the situation as it unfolds.

In the early stages of the game, midfield players under severe pressure as they receive the ball may simply but carefully pass with one touch to other support players positioned around them with the simple thought of retaining possession. Often, these simple passes are directed square or backward and are easy to read and predict. As the game develops and midfield players continue to play simple one-touch soccer successfully, opponents may reduce their commitment to exerting quick and aggressive pressure and allow the midfield players a yard or two of space on receiving the ball. Now the intelligent midfield player will change his tactics and begin to be more destructive in his passing, taking the opportunity to turn and play past the pressing opponents. If a midfield opponent then returns to his pressing tactic on the ball receiver, the midfield player can begin to pass the ball past the defender to a teammate, perhaps with the outside of his foot, and move quickly for the return pass—often known as a wall pass or a one-two. The midfield player has now mixed up his individual tactics when in possession of the ball and demonstrated to his opponent that no matter the circumstance, he can and will play with tactical intelligence, which is supported by the necessary technical ability—a difficult challenge for any defender!

Individual attacking tactics abound all over the pitch during the game. Strikers may spin behind opponents for passes in behind the defense or move to go behind the defense but instead come to receive the ball in front of the defense. Fullbacks may deliberately take their time on the ball to attract opponents before playing wall passes as their opponents overcommit in an attempt to gain possession. Center backs may mostly pass the ball simply and short, but then surprisingly drive forward into midfield with the ball, moving beyond the first defending group of players, the strikers. A striker, on receiving the ball to his feet against a tight marker, may move backward to feel the contact from that marker. From this position he may turn quickly knowing that the center back is too tight for his own good. An alternative would be for the striker to screen the ball and supply passes to others knowing exactly where the center back is positioned. Endless small battles are enacted throughout the game as each team seeks to win the proverbial war.

You have the vital role, along with your players, of analyzing your players' qualities and extending their range, while teaching them how to best implement those effective qualities for their own good and that of the team. Individual player, unit or group, and team tactics are the ingredients of your game plan. You will be worth your weight in gold if you can develop players who play the game with intelligence and craft—who have "old heads on young shoulders."

Some young players appear to have an advanced game understanding at an early age—they appear to be aware of their own abilities and how best to apply them in their and the team's best interests. It is to your advantage to invest much time in the development of tactical acumen. Knowing how to teach the techniques and skills of the game is vital; teaching players how to use tactics is essential in the development of effective players and will eventually produce good team results.

16

Set Pieces

SET PIECES, ALSO called set plays, are a vital phase of the game whether attacking or defending. As much as 40 percent of a team's goals may result from set pieces. For very young players, set pieces are not a priority in their development process, but for teams that play in competitive leagues, they should be an integral part of team preparation. One of the hallmarks of a well-coached team is that its players know how to organize themselves quickly and efficiently for corner kicks, free kicks, and throw-ins and have a good understanding of how to execute both attacking and defending tactics.

This chapter examines a series of moves and strategies for all three kinds of set plays and explains how to teach these moves and build them up from basic principles. In addition to knowing these moves and strategies, your players should know that restarting the game as quickly as possible might be the best way to catch the opposition unaware.

Throw-Ins

Every player must be able to execute a good throw-in. This is the most common way of restarting the game because the ball is continually going out of play over the touchline (incidentally, the reason the sidelines are called touchlines may be because restarting the game at the touchline is the only time outfield players may touch the ball with their hands). When executed well, the throw-in has great tactical value. Unfortunately, many young players find it a difficult skill to learn, and even professional players make mistakes.

Basic Throw-In Technique

To execute the throw-in, the player must face the field of play, throw the ball with both hands from behind the head, and keep both feet on or behind the touchline and in contact with the ground throughout the throw. Facing the field and staying behind the line are easily done; releasing a balanced two-handed throw while keeping the feet on the ground is more difficult, especially when trying to achieve a long throw (as discussed in Tactical Advantages of the Long Throw on page 294). The following sections outline the basic technique for a throw-in and include suggestions for helping your players avoid the common pitfalls associated with this.

Holding the Ball

Facing the field of play and the intended direction of the throw, the player holds the ball behind the head with the ends of the fingers and with the hands behind the ball in the W formation (see figure 16.1).

Throwing Action

When making the throw, the player arches the body backward and then releases forward in a natural sequence (or in technical terms, a kinetic chain): first the upper body, then the arms, and finally the fingers with an important snap-down action at the moment of release, which helps to generate power (see figure 16.2).

To ensure that the ball is released from above the head and not in front of the head, which is a foul throw, the beginner should concentrate on releasing the ball with a high trajectory; aiming at the feet of a receiver comes later. As with all throwing actions, a good follow-though is important to achieve accuracy and distance.

Figure 16.1
Proper body positioning for a throw-in.

Figure 16.2   Complete throwing action for a throw-in.

Where to Position at Throw-Ins

Players who crowd around the thrower, as shown in figure 16.3a, deny themselves the space, and therefore the time, to play the ball. Overcrowding around the thrower is all too often a feature of poor team coaching of throw-ins; players cannot be taught too soon how to adopt the much wider, open positions shown in figure 16.3b.

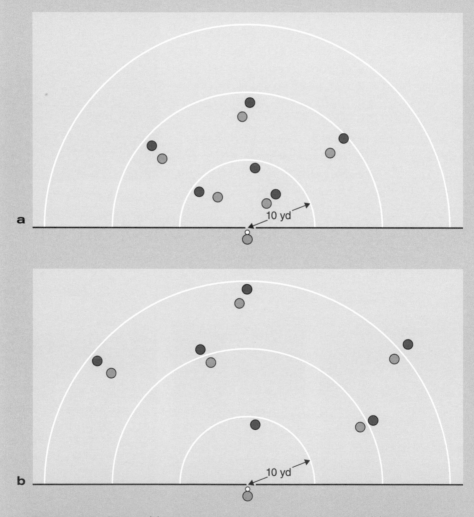

Figure 16.3 Players (a) positioned too close to the thrower and (b) well positioned for the throw-in.

If a receiver does happen to incorrectly position himself too close to the thrower (within 10 yards) and a quick throw to a player further away is not possible, the thrower can still use this receiver if both of them combine to execute a basic move. In this move, the thrower throws directly to the feet or the head of the receiver (see figure 16.4a). The receiver must return the ball to the thrower in such a gentle, accurate, and controlled manner that the thrower can move onto the field and play the ball to a better-positioned teammate with a first-time kick or can dribble the ball away safely. The receiver can return the ball accurately by using either a push pass or side-volley (see figure 16.4b) or by gently heading the ball back. Either way, the ball must be returned in such a manner that it does not cause issues with control for the thrower, who might be under pressure from an incoming defender.

Figure 16.4 Basic move for the throw-in.

Footwork for the Running Throw

For a throw-in, players often use a running approach to gain momentum and increase the distance of the throw, releasing the ball with one foot forward and one backward. However, keeping both feet on the ground, which the rules require, when attempting a long throw can be difficult even for experienced players. The momentum gained by running a few steps may cause the back foot to lift off the ground. To prevent this, we advise that beginners use a square, two-footed stance (see London Bridge on page 106), as shown in figure 16.5. They can run as fast as they like, but by split-stepping into a square, two-footed stance, they will keep both feet on the ground. However hard players may throw, their feet will not leave the ground until they have released the ball.

The two most common errors with the throw-in, after the foot fault, are throwing the ball with one hand too dominant and releasing the ball too late and thus not from behind the head. We recommend a useful method for overcoming both problems simultaneously. Stand with your player as shown in figure 16.6. One of your hands covers the ball once the player has adopted the ready position. Now, as the player attempts to throw, gently resist the movement at the correct point of release. This gives the player the kinesthetic feel for the correct action (for more information about kinesthetics, see chapter 2).

Figure 16.5 Correct foot position for the throw-in.

Figure 16.6 Resisting movement to help a player achieve the correct feel for releasing a throw-in.

Responsibilities of the Thrower and Receiver

A quickly taken throw-in can catch the defending team unaware and can result in attacking moves against an unprepared defense. Remember that at the throw-in, your team has complete control of the ball and can dictate play. All players must therefore be coached in the basic responsibilities of being a thrower and receiver and be encouraged to develop tactical moves in both attack and defense.

Thrower Responsibilities

- The thrower must face the field of play and look for the player who is in the best position (i.e., closest to the opponents' goal or not covered) and must catch the attention of that player, either by calling the player's name or by establishing eye contact.
- The thrower must direct the throw to either the head or the feet but never the body of the receiver, so the receiver can play the ball immediately without having to control it first.
- The thrower then must move onto the field and be ready to kick any return pass, ideally directly toward the opponents' goal.

Receiver Responsibilities

- The receiver must take up a position at least 10 yards from the thrower.
- The receiver must take note of the nearest defender and decide exactly how much time and space she has to work within.
- The receiver must either control the ball and turn toward the goal (if she is not closely covered) or play the ball back immediately to the thrower with the foot or the head (very seldom in junior soccer is the thrower covered by a defender).
- Finally, and most important, the receiver must accept the responsibility to trigger the throw. The thrower may have the ball, but the quick, signaled reaction of the receiver actually starts the move. Receivers can, and must, make decoy runs and moves to create opportunities for the thrower.

Tactical Moves at Throw-Ins

Before we introduce actual tactical moves at throw-ins, it is useful to establish some basic thoughts in the minds of your players. First, you need to continually emphasize with all your players the importance of reacting quickly, whether they are in an attacking or defensive situation. Second, you need to ensure that your players are aware of how the offside rule affects play. A player cannot be penalized for being offside directly following a throw-in.

Attacking Tactics at Throw-Ins

The faster a player thinks, the more likely he will be to gain a tactical advantage. This advice is especially true with free kicks and throw-ins. Some players do not naturally respond quickly and need to work to develop this skill. You cannot stress too often the number one basic tactic for throw-ins—to take the throw quickly whenever possible.

Players should also remember to throw the ball forward. The rules of the game state that a player cannot be given offside (penalized for infringing the offside rule) directly from a throw-in. Throwing the ball forward toward the opponents' goal keeps the attacking momentum going and often results in getting a player deep into the opponents' defense.

The no-offside rule at throw-ins is a tremendous advantage if used correctly, but this advantage is lost if the ball is thrown in square or even backward. Balls are thrown square or backward in professional soccer and used to good advantage, but this is seldom the case with young players. A ball thrown backward to an inexperienced player can be disastrous. Nothing is worse for a defender receiving such a throw than the feeling of insecurity that occurs when an attacker rushes in to charge down (bodily block) the kick.

Tactical Advantages of the Long Throw

The long throw is a very useful tactic and, when executed near the opponents' goal line, can be almost as good as a corner kick because of the greater accuracy of the throw. This play, which is very successful in games, requires a deep-lying player (usually a central defender) to make a forward run behind those apparently engaged in the throw-in. The thrower simply uses a long throw over the heads of the players to land the ball at the feet of the running player. As shown in figure 16.7, players A and B move in close to the thrower as player C runs down the field behind them.

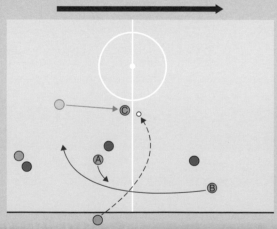

Figure 16.7 Players A and B move in to the thrower so that player C can move down the field behind them.

Defensive Tactics at Throw-Ins

Organizing defense for throw-ins requires four essential tactics, as described in the following sections. Time and circumstances may prevent players from achieving all four safeguards on every occasion, but players should aim to achieve them.

A good example of defensive cover at a throw-in that achieves all four safeguards is provided in figure 16.8. However, a system of defense is never infallible; it depends on the defensive skills of the players concerned.

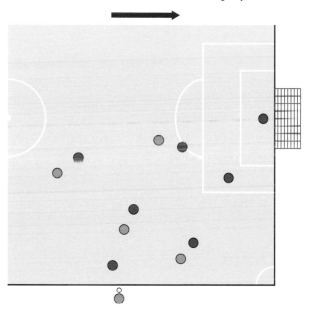

Figure 16.8   Defensive cover in which all four safeguards are achieved.

1. *One-on-one marking.* Every potential receiver should be covered on a one-on-one basis. This means that sufficient players must run hard to cover each attacker. This usually involves forwards helping the defense.

2. *Getting goalside.* All defenders should position themselves goalside of the attacker they are marking so that each defender can always see the attacker she is covering as well as the thrower. This means that defenders must move when the attacker moves to avoid being caught out of position.

3. *Covering the thrower.* We have already discussed how attackers can play the ball back to an unmarked thrower, who can then play the ball forward. Accordingly, defensive players must cover the thrower so that the opposition cannot use this move. The best player to cover the thrower is the winger who plays on the same side of the field, especially because he can also position himself halfway between the thrower and the opponents' fullback, who may come forward in support.

4. *Keeping a spare defender.* A well-organized defense always retains a spare defender behind the area in which the throw-in is taking place. Ideally, this is the fullback on whose side the throw is taken.

Watch your players in competitive games and observe how many times, if at all, they achieve the four safeguards when it is possible for them to do so. After observing their play, you may need to show them how and where to position themselves to defend at throw-ins. This can be done during "chalk-and-talk" sessions, but is more effective on the field in live situations (as discussed in more detail in chapter 14). In addition to these methods and practices, we suggest two other approaches as follows:

- Divide your team into two groups of four or five players and let each group, independently of you and other groups, design its own attacking moves from a throw-in. Now simply play one group against another and see how well they defend.
- Have your players both attack and defend in full-game situations and coach during play.

You need realistic situations when coaching defense at throw-ins. By observing what players do when they are tired or have to think for themselves, you will be able to make the changes that can result in a successful team.

Throw-In Drills

In this section we introduce a number of drills recommended for players at various levels of ability from learning the basic throw to developing that skill and moving on to the long throw. We then offer realistic, gamelike situations in which players both cooperate and compete.

Drills for Beginners

We have found a very simple method of introducing the basic throw to beginners. All you have to do is set up partners facing each other and separated by a regular set of goals, as shown in Over the Goal. We then introduce a slightly more difficult drill (Basic Throw-In Drill on page 298) with three players (two attackers and one defender) to try to establish the basic move of simply playing the ball back to the thrower. If the ball is well played to the thrower, she has the time and space to play the ball forward or to another, better placed player.

Over the Goal

Equipment   One ball for every two players; goals or other barriers

Organization   Players are in pairs on each side of a barrier, ideally the goals, over which the players can throw.

Instructions   We recommend teaching beginners to throw the ball to each other over the top of the goals. In this way, players concentrate on height rather than distance, and a foul throw becomes almost impossible. By concentrating on height rather than distance and by using a square, two-foot placement, beginners soon learn the correct throwing action and are not likely to foul.

Coaching Points
- Players should face forward with their feet-shoulder-width apart.
- Players should hold the ball in the W formation.
- Players should arch back, uncoil, and release the ball above the head on a high trajectory.
- The fingers should snap down as they release the ball.

Coaching Progressions
1. The distance from the goals increases.
2. Players try to throw the ball over the goals from the penalty spot and the penalty area line.

Basic Throw-In

Equipment   One ball for every three players

Organization   Players are in groups of three (two attackers, one defender), standing near a line that represents a sideline.

Instructions   The receiver (player B) triggers the practice by moving. The thrower (player A) aims at player B's head or feet. Player B plays the ball back using the head or feet. The defender (player Z) tries to stop the move.

Coaching Points

- Player B should be at least 10 yards from player A.
- Player A must throw to player B's feet and then move forward onto the field.
- Player B should try to make an effective and well-timed move to slip away from the defender and should give a quality return pass to player A.

Drills for Intermediate Players

To practice throw-ins with intermediate players, we move on to two drills—one for improving distance and accuracy and one for introducing a slightly more complicated competitive situation.

Target Throw-In

Equipment   One ball for every two players; three or four flags

Organization   Players are in pairs, standing near flags at various distances.

Instructions   Players can now add accuracy to distance by trying to hit each flag with the ball, using the correct throw-in technique.

Coaching Points

- Reinforce the concept of aiming at a target.
- Be on the watch for a foul throw; ensure that one hand is dominant in the throw and that both feet remain on the ground throughout the action.

Coaching Progressions

1. Players throw from the sideline into the penalty area and then into the goal area.
2. The receiver moves into the "dropping zone" to get to the ball. This makes it a realistic challenge for both the thrower and the receiver. ■

3v2 Throw-In

Equipment   One ball for every five players

Organization   Players are in groups of five (three attackers, two defenders) standing near a line that represents a sideline.

Instructions   The attackers (players A, B, and C) try to keep possession away from the defenders (players Y and Z) and make three successful passes to each other.

Coaching Points

- Players B and C should move in relation to each other and player A.
- Players B and C should try to lose their defender by making false moves. ■

Drills for Advanced Players

With advanced players, we introduce realistic drills that are easily transferred to actual game situations. For even more realism, you can work with players in their actual team positions. Thus, the attackers form a unit down one side of the field, and the defenders play in their usual roles (e.g., fullback marking the winger).

Crossover Play

Equipment   One ball for every five players

Organization   Players in groups of five (three attackers, two defenders) positioned alongside a touchline or sideline.

Instructions   Player A triggers the move by running directly toward player B. Player B reacts by sprinting past player A and through the vacated space to receive a forward throw from player C. The defenders (Y and Z) mark behind players B and C. Because they do not know when and how attackers A and B are going to move, they are temporarily disadvantaged.

Coaching Points

- Player A should call and move in a sufficiently convincing manner to deceive player Y into moving with player A and thus out of position.
- Player B should wait a second before reacting (giving player Y time to be deceived) and should always run forward on the outside of player A.
- Player C should pretend to throw to player A but actually delay throwing until player B is well forward. Player C should then throw the ball beyond player B for him to move toward. ■

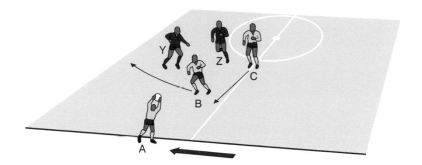

Equipment   One ball for every five players

Organization   Players are groups of five (three attackers, two defenders) positioned along the touchline.

Instructions   Player B triggers the move by moving upfield, taking player Y out of position. If player Y fails to react, then player B will obviously be ideally placed to receive the throw. If player Y does react, player C moves into the space left by player B and executes the basic move. Once one of the attackers, or the thrower, has managed to get into an open position from which he can play the ball forward or to another part of the field, the objective has been achieved. The drill is over and you restart the drill.

Coaching Points

- Player B should make the first positive move, because either outcome is successful. And because there is no offside from a throw-in, the move gives an additional advantage of creating depth in attack.
- Player C should wait a second before reacting.
- Player C can also decoy player Y by pretending to move away from the thrower before actually moving toward him.
- Player A should watch what is happening and make the most effective response. ▪

Penalty Kicks

The penalty shoot-out has become an exciting climax to some World Cup matches; millions of spectators watch in awe as the drama unfolds and intensifies if a sudden death situation arises. Many fans do not like this conclusion, but it is probably the only resolution when extra time has expired and the score is still tied.

Fortunately, younger players are seldom involved in such dramatic situations. In youth play, penalty kicks usually just arise as part of the normal game and not as a means of breaking a tie and determining the final score. Nevertheless, penalty kicks, either saved or scored, can and do win games. Every coach must spend time selecting and coaching penalty takers and, equally important, teaching goalkeepers and other players how to position themselves for and react to penalty kicks.

Penalty Takers

When selecting penalty takers (you should always have two or three potential players in mind because the state of the game or player availability may not allow you to go with your first choice), a coach should identify players who can remain calm under pressure and who have a powerful, accurate kick. We recommend having occasional penalty competitions at the end of practice sessions to allow you to watch and select your most suitable players.

Penalty-taking strategies vary considerably, but all penalty takers should be encouraged to concentrate on the four most vulnerable targets—the upper and lower corners of the goal (see figure 8.1 on page 142). Thus, the kicker usually attempts a low instep drive into one of the bottom corners or a more lofted kick into the top corners. Obviously, the power and direction of the kick must be sufficient to beat a goalkeeper's diving reaction.

After practicing, penalty takers usually select two of the four targets to use in game situations should the opportunity arise. In the actual game, the kicker is more likely to be successful if she selects one target and one kick and sticks to that decision. Changing one's mind during the approach to the ball is seldom a good idea, unless the goalkeeper moves too early in one direction or another.

The following points outline the basic process for a penalty kick:

1. Place the ball carefully on the penalty spot so that it may be struck cleanly.

2. Take up a starting position at a side angle of about 20 to 30 degrees from the direct line to goal. (This means that the goalkeeper will not know which side of the goal the kicker is aiming at).

3. Observe the position of and any movements made by the goalkeeper.

4. Decide which scoring technique to use and select the intended target before approaching the ball.

5. Approach the ball with a controlled and fluent run-up.

6. Concentrate on striking the ball accurately and forcefully with the chosen technique at the chosen target.

7. Follow up the shot in the event of any rebounds from the goalkeeper.

Professional players, of course, use several variations of penalty kicks, including feinting one way and kicking the other; split-stepping, or halting, in the approach run in the hope that the goalkeeper will commit to one direction so they can place the ball in the opposite corner; or simply blasting the ball as hard as possible and hoping for the best. Our advice? Stick to the basic moves outlined above unless you have an exceptional player.

Goalkeeper

During penalty kicks, the goalkeeper must stay on the goal line (the basic goal-keeper's stance is shown in figure 10.1 on page 177). He can move his arms and body once the kicker has started her run and can move along the goal line but not ahead of it. If his feet move ahead of the goal line and the kick fails, the referee will order the kick to be retaken.

The goalkeeper usually positions in the center of the goal. However, some keepers prefer to position slightly to one side and invite the kicker to aim into the larger space that they feel more confident in defending; they may find it easier to dive in that direction.

Other Defenders and Other Attackers

Other defenders and other attackers also have roles to play during a penalty kick. They must take up positions outside the penalty box and the penalty arc (located 10 yards from the penalty spot). They too must keep their feet outside the line and must not enter the penalty area or the arc until the kick has been taken. Entering the prohibited areas will result in either a successful kick being retaken (if an attacker encroaches) or an unsuccessful kick being retaken (if a defender encroaches).

Either way, there is no point in contravening the rule. What these players can and should do is react as quickly as possible if the ball rebounds into play off the goalposts or the goalkeeper, who might stop but not hold the shot. In both cases the ball is live, and whoever reacts first can either score or prevent a goal.

Corner Kicks

Whenever a team wins a corner kick in the game, it has an excellent opportunity to go one step further and convert a corner into a goal. For this reason, your players must know how to organize themselves quickly and efficiently. Also, because many goals are scored directly from set plays such as these, time spent coaching your players in these situations is time well spent. In this section we cover two types of corner kicks—short and long corners—and in both cases consider both attacking and defensive tactics.

Short Corner Kick

Every player should know how to use a short corner kick to restart the game quickly and perhaps gain a surprise tactical advantage. The short corner, performed quickly as opponents are still organizing themselves defensively, often enables an attacker to move into the penalty area before delivering the ball. This can result in a more dangerous cross or pass when the ball is played, especially on wet ground. The short corner often draws defenders away from the goal-scoring areas and can frequently cause panic in the defense. In addition, for short corners, you must be sure that your players know how the offside rule affects their positioning.

Basic Short Corner Move

The only way to take a short corner and not be offside is shown in figure 16.9. This is referred to as the basic move in some of the more advanced plays. In the basic move, player B must stand on the goal line about 6 yards from player A. (This ensures that player A is not caught offside.) Player A plays the ball firmly to player B after ensuring that the opponents are playing according to the rules and standing at least 10 yards away.

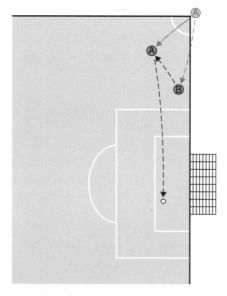

Player B plays the ball gently back to player A, as shown, so that player A can take two or three strides and deliver the moving ball into the goal area from a changed angle of delivery. The short pass also helps the attackers in the box to time their movements into preorganized delivery areas. Both players A and B have to practice to ensure that they pass and

Figure 16.9　Taking a short corner using the basic move.

move accurately. Alternatively, on receiving the ball, player A may decide to run with the ball toward the near-post area of the goal, thus attracting defenders from the vital and central goal-scoring area in front of goal.

If players stand as shown in figure 16.10, they may get caught offside. The reason is that once player A has played the ball to player B, player A is technically standing in an offside position (i.e., in front of the player with the ball).

Short Corner Variations

Many variations can be played at a short corner. Two very effective moves involve a third player who moves up from a deep-lying position to cross the ball. In the first variation, this third player can be brought into play by an extension of the basic move; instead of crossing the ball after the first pass, the kicker plays the ball back to the deep supporting player, who crosses the ball from a different angle (see figure 16.11). In a second variation, the third

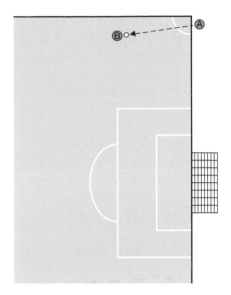

Figure 16.10   Improper setup for the short corner.

player can be brought into play when the kicker ignores the basic move and plays the ball directly back to the third player (after the fullback has moved forward unnoticed), as shown in figure 16.12.

In figure 16.11, player B comes from the near-post area to receive the first pass; player A plays the ball into the path of player C, who moves from a deep

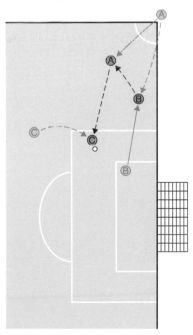

Figure 16.11
Variation 1 on the short corner kick.

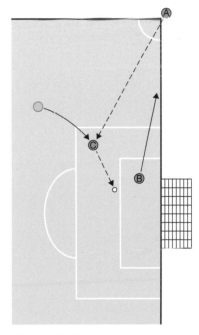

Figure 16.12
Variation 2 on the short corner kick.

position to deliver the ball into the penalty area. In figure 16.12, player B comes from the near post, but player A passes the ball to player C to cross. Player C may also run with the ball into the penalty area if defenders do not react quickly enough to the move.

Another very effective move is to have the player who always supports the kicker for the basic move come to the corner to prepare for the kick but be sent back by the kicker, who pretends to elect to take a long corner kick. As the decoy player turns his back on the kicker and begins to walk along the goal line back toward the goal, the kicker rolls the ball forward along the goal line to the decoy player, who turns, receives the ball, and then possibly turns once again to face the penalty area. This move has the advantage of getting a player with the ball into the penalty area at a position ideal for a pass back to an incoming shooter. Of course, this move can be negated if the defenders react quickly by following the decoy player as he moves away from the kicker. If a defender follows the decoy player toward the ball, the short corner can still be passed to him, but he simply returns the ball to the kicker using one touch. The kicker's pass must be made to the decoy player's feet when he is about 10 to 15 yards away.

Long Corner Kick

Only the most accurate kickers should be allowed to take long corner kicks. Hold elimination competitions during practice to select those who can deliver the ball into chosen target areas consistently well. Ideally, you should have a specialist long corner kicker on each side of the field. Inswinging corner kicks (figure 16.13a), in which the ball spins toward the goal, are always more effective than outswinging kicks (figure 16.13b), which are usually less

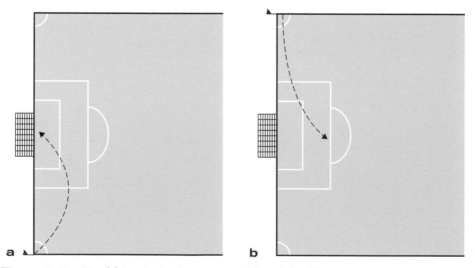

Figure 16.13 The (a) inswinging long corner kick and the (b) outswinging long corner kick.

dangerous because the ball spins away from the goal. For this reason it pays to cultivate a left-footed kicker to take corner kicks from the right-hand side of the field, and vice versa.

There are many variations of the long corner kick, and you should choose and practice those that are most effective with your players and use their talents. However, one variation of this kick has been, and will continue to be, productive for many teams. Arrange seven attacking players (plus one kicker and two players back behind the action) as shown in figure 16.14. Each should have a landmark starting position and should memorize it, keeping in mind that it is purely a starting position from which to operate. The landmark starting positions are as follows (place players in the exact spots at which they should start and give them the following directions):

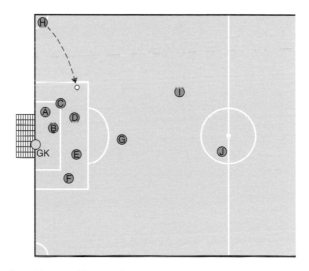

Figure 16.14 Attacking positions at long corners.

- Player A is in front of the goalpost nearest the kicker 2 yards forward of the post and 2 yards from the goal line.

- Player B is just in front of the goalkeeper between the goalkeeper and the ball (this player must not touch or try to interfere with the goalkeeper at any time during the corner).

- Player C is at the corner of the 6-yard area nearest the kicker.

- Players D and E are in line with the penalty spot and level with the left and right goalposts, respectively.

- Player F is at the corner of the 6-yard area farthest from the kicker but moves in as the kick is taken.

- Player G is on the edge of the restraining arc as shown in figure 16.14. This player's major role is to collect any clearances that reach the edge of the penalty box and to initiate a further attack or even shoot if the opportunity arises. Should the opponents secure possession from a clearance from the corner kick around the edge of the penalty box, then player G is probably the first defender to oppose the attacker with the ball or to recover to assist any players stationed around the halfway line who are under the threat of a counterattack.

In this formation, players can attack the goal and the shaded goal-scoring area, take advantage of any rebounds or knockdowns, collect any semi-cleared corners, and take possession of any corner kick that a teammate kicks

Tactical Variations for Long Corners

Tactical variations for long corners are of two types: near-post plays (in which the target is the area around the goalpost nearer the kicker) and far-post plays (in which the target is the area around the goalpost farther from the kicker).

Near-Post Plays

Near-post plays have two main variations. The target player (player A in figure 16.15), who is positioned in or moves into the near-post area, (1) attempts a direct strike on goal, usually by heading the ball, or (2) back-heads the ball into the area in front of goal, hopefully into the path of the three converging attackers or to the player in front of the goalkeeper or any attacker who positions in front of the goalkeeper.

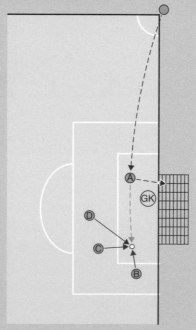

Figure 16.15 Player A heads the ball directly into the goal or tries to flick the ball to the far post for players B, C, and D coming in.

inaccurately. The kicker, player H, after delivering the ball, should, if it is delivered toward the near-post area, expect a defender or the goalkeeper to clear the ball back into the area or adjacent to the area from where the ball was delivered.

Consequently, the kicker can collect the defensive clearances and initiate a further attack. If the ball travels beyond the near post toward the far-post area, then the kicker should make his way toward the central areas outside the penalty box and be prepared to collect any clearances or recover toward the halfway line if the opposition launches a counterattack from its possession.

Far-Post Plays

In figure 16.16, the kicker aims to deliver the ball to the area at the far side of the goal. Ideally, this target area is outside the reach of the goalkeeper (at least 6 yards from the goal) but close enough to the goal to enable an incoming player to achieve a direct strike on goal, usually by heading the ball. A target landing area 8 to 10 yards from the goal line is ideal. In this figure, player A runs forward to draw opponents to the near post, but the corner is played long for other forwards coming in.

Note that attackers can confuse defenders by making decoy runs and executing tactics from either the long or the short corner moves. Such moves, of course, must be rehearsed and signaled for maximum benefit. All players should understand that the player taking the kick can signal the move, or a designated player by his movement can trigger a delivery from the kicker.

When using the far-post corner, you may have noticed that one player (player A in figures 16.15 and 16.16) makes the same starting move regardless of whether it is a

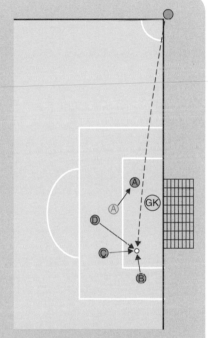

Figure 16.16 Player A runs forward to draw opponents to the near post, but the corner is played long for other forwards coming in.

near-post or a far-post move. This kind of consistency is an important advantage to your team, because players gain confidence by rehearsing and executing tactical moves. This run may also drag defenders away from the target area. Now, because the ball has traveled over the decoy runner's head, this player, if he stops and turns to face the goal area where the ball will land, can reenter the attack. He can lose his marker and might even score from a goalkeeping error or rebounding shot.

Players I and J stay back as shown to defend against a fast break and will have to mark any attacker that is placed by the opponents around the halfway line. The question for you is: How many players, and which ones, should you hold back if the opponents leave two or three players around the halfway line?

Defending Corner Kicks

Professional teams typically use a combination of two defensive marking systems, zone and man-to-man, to cover the danger areas and individual players. For younger players, this combination can be too complicated. A simpler method involves simply assigning each player to a zone with instructions to be the first to the ball if it comes into that zone (i.e., zonal marking).

Figure 16.17 shows a defensive organization of eight players plus one goalkeeper. During critical moments in the game (e.g., you are winning 1-0 with a minute to play), bring all 11 players back into defense. Note that players I and J, the two forwards, can stay upfield in wide positions and try to attract at least three defenders by moving about.

Again, you should give each player a starting position, as follows (from which the defender will attack the ball or adjust her position and role as the corner play develops):

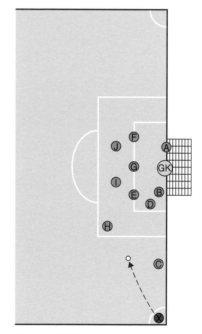

Figure 16.17
Defensive positions at corners.

- The goalkeeper is in the center of the goal line, at a 45-degree angle to the field.

- Player A is on the goal line behind the goalkeeper.

- Player B is just outside and just ahead (half a yard) of the post nearer the kicker.

- Player C is 10 yards from the kicker and in line with the intended line of the kick.

- Player D occupies and defends the area in front of the near post and starts 2 yards from the goal line and between the near post and the sideline of the 6-yard box as shown in figure 16.17.

- Player E is on the 6-yard line opposite the near post.

- Player F is on the 6-yard line opposite the far post.

- Player G is between players E and F in a central position along the 6-yard box.

Player H is in the corner of the penalty area on the same side as the corner. From here, he can prevent a short corner by joining player C to make 2v2 if needed. This player is also in a position to receive a throw from the goalkeeper and break away, and he may also collect any clearances in that area of the field. It is surprising just how many inswinging corner kicks are cleared by the defense into the area around player H.

What you do with players I and J is at your discretion. Some coaches leave players I and J up the field to attract opponents away from the penalty area and lessen the threats at goal. Others position I and J almost level with the near and far posts and also level with the penalty spot but "pinching" in toward the penalty spot by 2 yards.

The danger with zonal marking is that players start in their allocated positions and may fail to attack the ball when necessary, leaving it to others. Each player is responsible for attacking the ball between herself and the next defender, and in front of herself if she is the first defender. The flight will dictate whose responsibility it is to make the first contact with the ball, and that first contact may be from the goalkeeper if it is within her range. Note that if not involved in attacking the ball, a defender should constantly adjust her feet and position to react to any secondary defending situation that arises from others attacking the ball.

Free Kicks

Free kicks, especially those on the edge of the penalty area, create interesting and exciting situations; they also create vital coaching challenges. Players on a well-organized team know exactly how to respond in both attacking and defending situations because they have been well coached and well rehearsed in practice. In this section we first address three attacking plays and then show how these might be countered.

Attacking Free Kicks

The most effective of all free kicks is the direct shot at goal, especially the curved, or swerve, shot that can bend around the defensive wall and within the goal frame. The second most effective play involves two players. Three or more players who combine in a rehearsed move must spend a great deal of time in practice. Such moves are difficult for young players to master and are not recommended for them.

One-Player Moves

As mentioned, the most effective and spectacular free kick involves the best striker taking a direct shot (often a swerve, or banana, kick) at goal (see page 127). Such ploys can be enhanced if other players make decoy runs to distract the goalkeeper and other defenders, but success basically depends on the kicker's accuracy.

Select your best two or three players and have them practice shooting around a wall made up of two corner posts and perhaps a piece of rope or string positioned in various places in the penalty area. This simulates the defensive wall. (Players can use a kicking tee at first to encourage the swerve shot.)

Two-Player Moves

A player can play the ball either over the wall or around it. With two-player moves, the kicker passes the ball sideways for a colleague to shoot, or crosses the ball with a lofted kick over the wall for other attackers to head or shoot at goal.

Passing the Ball Sideways

Several moves are possible when the ball is simply played sideways with an inside of the foot pass. This opens up a space at the side of the wall through which the kicker can aim the ball. The kicker can play the ball either left or right, but it is usually better to play the ball centrally because this opens up the target (the goal).

Again, the kicker must signal his intention in some way, and the designated shooter should always allow a few yards to move forward to take the shot. Younger players especially need a few yards to prepare (balance) themselves for the instep drive. If the opponents place a player to the inside of their wall with the intention of pressuring the kicker, then the distance that the player has to move forward will be shorter.

In a useful variation of the sideways pass, two players face each other with their feet wide apart. From this position, either player can play the ball sideways through the legs of the other. As shown in figure 16.18, players A and B are on the ball and facing each other. Player A plays the ball through the legs of player B for player C to shoot. Note that player C remains a few yards behind the point at which the ball is actually kicked so that he can balance and time his approach run to the ball. For this reason the players concerned must practice.

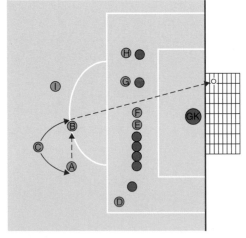

Figure 16.18
Variation of the sideways pass.

Crossing the Ball

This is a very simple idea to use at a free kick in a flank position. It is similar to a corner kick in that the ball can be played to the near or far post (usually the far-post area) or even the central goal-scoring areas. The kicker simply crosses the ball over the defensive wall into the path of designated attackers converging on goal. The delivery, as with a corner kick, can be either inswinging or outswinging. In figure 16.19, player A plays the ball over the wall to the near post so player B can head for goal. This is a simple move, but must be practiced to ensure that player B times the run correctly.

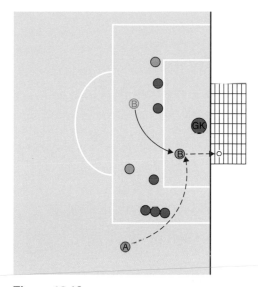

Figure 16.19
A technique for crossing the ball at a set free kick.

Players can make decoy movements and runs to open up better opportunities for chosen attackers to strike at goal. Against a man-to-man marking defense, attackers should know that they can create space for others to attack in preordained areas by moving their markers away from the intended target area before the delivery of the ball. Where those runs will take defenders should be designed and coordinated in practice sessions so that other players can enter the space created at the correct moment to contact the ball.

Tactical Variations for Central Free Kicks

Free kicks have many effective variations, and good coaches enjoy creating their own moves. When analyzing attacking free kicks, however, there are only three alternatives: (1) going around the wall (using swerve shots or passing movements), (2) going over the wall (chipping or playing the ball over the wall), and (3) going "through" the wall (players positioned in, in front, or at the end of the defensive wall can move out of their position at the last moment to create a gap). We consider this third alternative, called "attacker in the wall," first.

Attacker in the Wall

Among the standard moves are those that involve placing one of your own players at the end of the defensive wall; at the last moment, that player moves out and away from the wall, leaving a space through which the shooter aims. Such a tactic is unlikely to be effective against a well-organized defense, however, because defenders will simply form behind the player who is on the end of the wall. However, even if the opponents take that option, the view of the goalkeeper as the ball is struck will be impaired by the extension of the wall.

The attacker-in-the-wall tactic has two effective variations. The attacker in the defensive wall can move forward to the kicker and play the ball sideways for the shooter, or that player can turn behind the wall and strike at goal from a chipped pass over the wall. In the first variation, as shown in figure 16.20, player A stands in the wall. As player B kicks, player A moves forward and passes to player C, who shoots. In the second variation, as shown in figure 16.21, player B stands in the wall. As player A chips, player B turns, collects the chip, and shoots.

Any intelligent player vested with the responsibility of taking free kicks should be able to read the positioning of defenders and ascertain the option that will be most likely to produce success. Quite often, a free kick taken quickly as the goalkeeper is organizing the wall and defenders are still taking up their positions can result in a goal either from a direct strike at goal or a pass to an unmarked or loosely marked player able to strike at goal.

Some of the free kick ploys recommended here

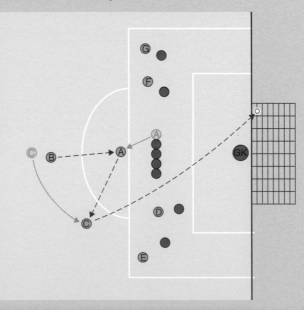

Figure 16.20 Variation 1 of attacker in the wall.

may not be possible because of the defensive organization. You and your players will need to devise alternatives (not so many as to be confusing) to your favored free kick.

Ignoring the Wall

A very effective scoring alternative is to ignore the wall altogether and attempt to feed a player in a position from which he can strike at goal, usually on the opposite side of the penalty box from the wall. As shown in figure 16.22, player A runs behind the wall, making sure he is not offside, in order to take player X out of position. Player B runs from the rear into the space behind the defender. He can now shoot or cross the ball. Some players will have to play unselfishly and make runs and movements that shift opponents to allow teammates to take advantage of the space created and provide the opportunity for a strike at goal. Every run must be convincing and purposeful. A halfhearted and slow run gives defenders time to read the intended ploy and react to the real threat.

Defenders who are required to mark players rather than spaces can move either toward the ball, away from the ball, or across the ball's line of flight. Players moving into central and therefore goal-scoring positions are usually marked tighter than those moving away from the ball and the goal. Practicing the runs and deliveries at free kicks

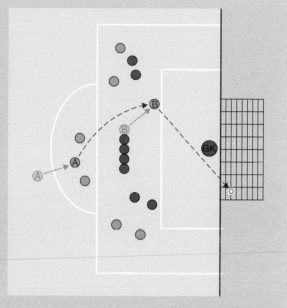

Figure 16.21 Variation 2 of attacker in the wall.

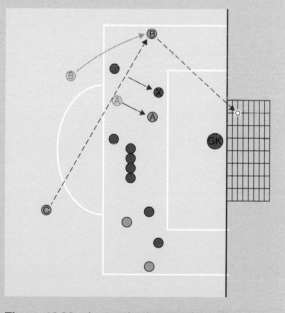

Figure 16.22 An attacker ignores the wall.

» continued

and corners is time well spent. Most important, the delivery must be accurate! If you have a specialist kicker, so much the better—even international teams often depend on such a player!

Playing the Ball Behind the Wall

The farther the free kick is from the goal, the more the space behind the wall can be exploited. As shown in figure 16.23, player B positions behind and to the side of the wall. She is likely to be tightly marked by an opponent and may have to lose the marker with a quick, short movement (a fake move) before receiving the pass from player A. Player A plays the ball to player B so player B can play the ball behind the line to player C, who runs from a deep position to shoot. Note that in this move, player A has to play the ball to player B's left foot so that player B can make an accurate, flowing pass. If the move is on the other side of the penalty

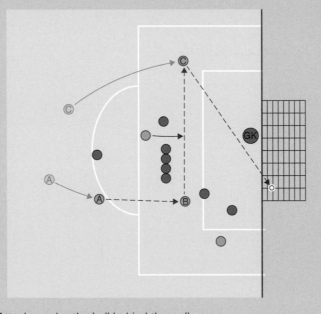

Figure 16.23 Attackers play the ball behind the wall.

area, player B will have to pass with the right foot. The pass to player B must be quick and, if possible, disguised.

Although in figure 16.23 the pass from player B is to player C running from deep, other players, perhaps spinning off the inside of the wall or coming across the face of the wall, could receive the pass from player B. Remember that defenders will always try to see the ball and are particularly susceptible to intelligent movement when they turn their heads to locate any ball played past or behind them. Attackers will gain an advantage if they watch both the ball and the heads of their respective defenders as they make their moves.

Defending Free Kicks

All 10 outfield players must be prepared to defend at free kicks in and around the penalty area, either by joining the defensive wall or by occupying key positions around it.

Number of Players in the Wall

The first decision—how many players to have in the wall—should be made by the goalkeeper according to the position of the kick. The number of players is generally determined by the position of the ball (see figure 16.24). In area 2, two players can be positioned, although many teams now operate with only one defender depending on the number of attackers on or around the ball because of the acute angle. In area 3, three players are the usual requirement. Areas 4 and 5 are the most critical areas to defend because of the likelihood of direct shots on goal. For this reason, four or five players usually form the line, taking

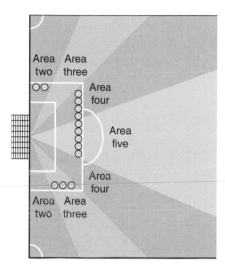

Figure 16.24 The number of players needed in the defensive wall is determined by the area of the field where the ball is.

the positioning of the end player as directed by the goalkeeper. Note that in extreme cases of an indirect free kick inside the goal area, all 10 players would be positioned in the wall.

Positioning the Wall

The key player in positioning the wall is the second player (player 2). The goalkeeper, having established how many players he wants in the wall, now concentrates on defending his goal against a quickly-taken free kick. It is important to position the wall so that an attacker cannot shoot directly at goal, especially if such an attacker is capable of striking a curve or banana kick. This is achieved by positioning the second player in the line so that near goalpost and the ball are in an imaginary straight line. Since the position of the ball is fixed, the defenders are positioned so that the near goalpost appears "as if it is arising out of the second player's head." Another player stands alongside player 2 on the outside of the wall, and two or more defenders stand inside player 2 covering the near half of the goal. When players are in this position, the goalkeeper takes responsibility for defending the exposed far half of the goal.

Many teams nowadays have at least one player who is capable of bending a ball around a defensive wall. If so, this is not easy to counter. However, players in the wall must be tightly adjacent to each other so as not to allow any direct strike at goal to penetrate (see figure 16.25). Attackers may beat the wall by directing the ball around it—but never through it! After the kick, the players in the wall should turn to help defend against any shots that travel behind them and are parried by the goalkeeper or rebounded into play from the goal frame.

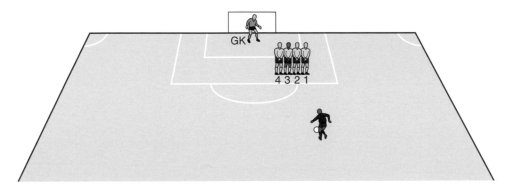

Figure 16.25   Strong defensive wall forcing the attacker to kick around it.

Anticipating the Type of Free Kick

Another consideration is the type of kick the opponents are likely to use. It is also possible for the defenders to anticipate which type of free kick the attackers will select from the position at which the free kick will be taken. The greater the angle and distance of the free kick from the center of the penalty area, the more likely the attackers will attempt to cross the ball to the far post like a corner kick. In this event, your tallest and best defensive heading players should be strategically positioned in the wall to counter this play. If the kick is taken from the front of the goal, the opponents are more likely to either shoot at goal directly or use a two- or three-player combination. In this situation, the taller players should be positioned in the wall. So, the location of the free kick, the quality of the opponent likely to strike the ball at goal, and the physical and defensive attributes of the defending players are all factors that contribute to the decision of how to defend at free kicks.

How to Stand in the Wall

Male players should stand tall and face the kicker shoulder to shoulder with their hands held in front of the groin area. Female players should do the same now that protective equipment is available for the upper body. If your team does not have such equipment, consider having your female players adopt the following positioning:

- stand sideways to the kick, looking over their shoulder at the ball but tightly close with each other;
- put one leg forward and one leg back;

- hold the arm nearest to the kick straight and well in front of the body to protect the breast; and

- the outside end player on the wall should face the sideline and look over her shoulder so that she can move quickly to any two- or three-pass move on her side of the penalty area.

Of course, to cover the same area as males who stand square, females may need to place an additional player in the wall.

Positioning Around the Wall

The players who remain after the wall has been formed must be positioned to stop or reduce the success of the opposition's attacking moves. In particular, the remaining players must cover the area into which a sideways pass might penetrate and the area into which a lofted kick might be directed.

Figure 16.26 shows a typical way defending players might be positioned against a free kick requiring four players in the wall. Players A, B, C, and D are the wall. Player E is the player who, if the opponents move the ball sideways to engineer a direct strike at goal, presses (goes to meet) the ball immediately. His role is to prevent the shot or pressure the striker who is in the act of shooting at goal; his starting position is a yard inside the end player in the wall (player D). He must be quick in getting to the ball but balanced and in control as he arrives to exert the pressure.

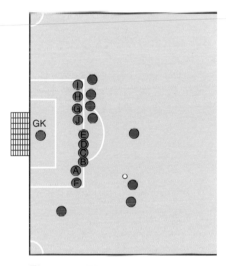

Figure 16.26 A typical defense for free kicks.

Player F positions himself 2 to 3 yards outside the wall and protects the space between the wall and the touchline. Opponents may not position a player in this area but may at the last moment try to move a player quickly and late into this area to produce a strike at goal or receive a pass. Players G, H, I, and J mark opponents according to the positions they take up and the movements the opponents make.

In addition, the goalkeeper's position is determined by two priorities: (1) being able to see the ball and (2) being on the most vulnerable side, which is the one not covered by the wall. However, the goalkeeper must not stand too far from the center of the goal line because of the danger of the swerve shot into the unguarded side of the goal. The best compromise is to stand where he can see the ball and as near to the center of the goal line as possible. He may be positioned a yard or two forward of the goal line, depending on the location of the free kick. In a sense, he is narrowing the angle (a tactic referred to in chapter 10) as he would do on any strike or intended strike at goal.

Because of their importance, tactical moves from corner kicks, throw-ins, and free kicks (and penalty kicks) have to be rehearsed many times. During the heat of the moment even experienced players can forget what they have practiced. Appointing a player to mastermind the set plays and advise the other players about which move to use is a good idea. More than one player may be capable of fulfilling this role, and a good team may designate different players to organize different plays.

Setting aside practice time for coaching and rehearsing set plays is vital. Because some set plays involve small numbers of players, you can often work with just these units before or after regular practice so that the players not involved in the play will not be inactive. If an assistant coach is available, you can divide the team into attacking and defensive units for practice and then bring them together in attack versus defense situations directed toward creating and rehearsing set play situations.

One of the hallmarks of good coaches is that their players know exactly how to organize themselves for set plays and how to use these plays successfully in games. Set plays represent the only time in the game when your team has possession of the ball and the opposition must allow 10 yards of space to execute the move and does not know what to expect. You must take advantage of these conditions by being well prepared. Never forget that as many as 40 percent of a team's goals will arise from set play situations.

PART IV
· · · · · · · · · · · · ·

Team Management

IN PART IV we present three chapters on team management. Chapter 17 deals with the preparation of your team, both physically and mentally. We include warm-up and cool-down exercises and ball skills preparation activities. We also address the issue of how to speak to your players before, during, and after the game. We discuss what to say and how to say it. Most important, perhaps, is what you say to them after the game, which should depend not only on who won or lost but on how they played.

We appreciate that not all players are easy to work with, and indeed, even parents can be difficult at times! In chapter 18 we identify the types of players that can be difficult and cause problems, not just for you but for other members of the team as well. We then present our ideas on how to work with these players and, if the need arises, parents.

Chapter 19 is one of the most detailed in the book. It breaks down the various fitness elements that collectively produce the well-conditioned player who can sprint, accelerate, jump, turn, and keep on running for up to 90 minutes and longer if necessary. We examine each component of fitness in detail, recommend tests, and identify training schedules that allow players of differing conditioning levels to exercise at the same time. All of the activities described in this chapter can take place outside on the soccer field with your players wearing boots (cleats), which is a great advantage. Finally, and importantly, we have added a new section on diet and nutrition. Although the emphasis is on soccer, the dietary guidelines offered here can help all of us eat more healthfully on and beyond the playing field.

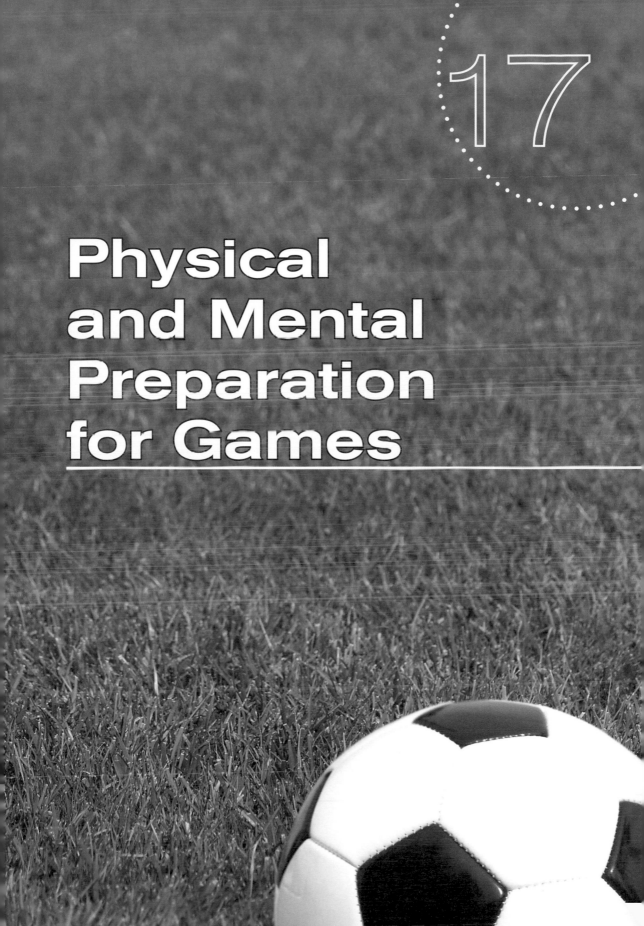

Physical and Mental Preparation for Games

17

YOU WILL NEED to prepare your players, both physically and mentally, for competition. However, do not think that because we present the information on physical and mental preparation separately, we believe that they are separate things, that there is a simple distinction between mind and body. Nothing could be further from the truth. Throughout this book we have tried to promote a holistic approach to dealing with your players.

Physical Preparation

Proper physical preparation for competition is essential if your players are to perform at their best. It also reduces the chances of players being injured while playing.

Warm-Up

In soccer, most injuries occur during the first 15 minutes of the game, because of insufficient warm-up, and during the last 15 minutes, because of fatigue. Thus, you should try to get your players as fit as possible and always give them a thorough warm-up before play starts. For young players, who seldom pull muscles, warm-up activities may include some drills with the ball, but for older players, especially adults, we recommend a set program as described in Warm-Up Sequence for Soccer.

Many players start their warm-up by stretching; this is wrong. Muscles respond best when they are warm, so the correct way to start a warm-up is with general body exercises that gradually increase the heart rate and the breathing rate. For safety, these general body movements must also be low-impact activities; that is, they must not expose the muscles to violent or sudden stretching to the full extent of their range.

Ideal starting exercises include running in place or skipping; the best practice is to gently run backward and forward across the field six times. The first two runs should be gentle and loose, the movements free and relaxed. The third and fourth runs can include sideways and backward movements. The final two runs should be at increased tempo and should consist of four phases—jogging, striding, accelerating, and slowing down—each phase covering about 15 yards. In cold or inclement weather, players should wear warm-up suits.

After the starting exercise, players are ready to begin progressive stretching (note that a stretching session is also an ideal time for a final tactics talk and mental preparation). The stretches must concentrate on the front, back, and insides of the thighs, and on the spine. Goalkeepers must also include gentle rolling and springing movements as well as shoulder mobility exercises. All stretches should be static stretches; that is, the muscles should be gently extended into a stretch position and held for 10 seconds. Don't let your players bounce up and down using ballistic movements, because such actions are dangerous. When static stretching is over, the players should then move into ball drills.

Warm-Up Sequence for Soccer

1. Engage in running activities as described in the Warm-Up section.

2. Stand, hold the ankle, and stretch the thigh backward; alternate legs (see figure 17.1a).

3. Cross feet. Static stretch the hamstrings by letting the body and arms hand down. Do not bounce up and down. Change feet and repeat (see figure 17.1b).

4. Shake and loosen arms and legs.

5. Open the groin muscles (adductors) by stretching the inside of the legs gently (see figure 17.1c).

6. Raise the knee and turn the leg 90 degrees sideways. This opens the groin in a second direction, or plane. Place a hand on the raised knee for balance (see figure 17.1d). Repeat on the other side of the body.

7. Shake and loosen arms and legs.

8. Stretch the arms above the head. Bend slowly backward as if preparing to throw the ball. Gently simulate the throwing action a few times (see figure 17.1e).

9. Finish with a 5-second run in place or short sprints across the field; then move into ball skills preparation.

Figure 17.1
Warm-up exercises for soccer.

Ball Skills Preparation

All players need time to prepare their ball skills before the game. We always advise that they carry out a prearranged series of activities in small groups, as shown in figure 17.2. Some examples follow.

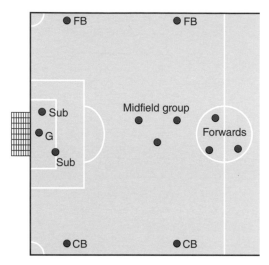

Figure 17.2 Pregame ball skills practice organization.

Goalkeeper

The substitutes prepare the goalkeeper by volleying balls to her from short range. This gives the goalkeeper the feel of the ball. The substitutes should then play a variety of balls from just inside the penalty area to give the goalkeeper practice at dealing with shots and crosses from both wings. Younger players should kick crosses form their hands to get height and accuracy. If the sun is out, the goalkeeper should practice while facing the sun to get used to this condition.

Defenders

The defenders work together in pairs (e.g., two fullbacks and two center backs). They should practice dealing with high dropping balls and, like the goalkeeper, must practice against weather elements such as the sun and wind. They must also practice long kicking, quick turning, and defensive heading.

Midfield Players

Midfield players should practice in their own group, using lots of short passing for accuracy. They must get the feel of the ball on the surface. Older players should practice chipping the ball, dribbling, and turning.

Forwards

Forwards do not go straight to the goal to practice shooting. They need to practice lots of short passing with each other, such as one-two passes and wall passes. They must also practice dribbling, attacking heading skills, and corner kicks. When the goalkeeper has finished his preparation, the forwards should practice shooting at the goal. When they shoot, they should build up the power of the shot—too hard too soon can be dangerous. The specialist penalty kicker should also have a few practice penalty kicks.

Substitutes

Keep your substitutes warm, and give them at least 5 minutes' notice before asking them to play. Warming up before the game does not keep them warmed up throughout! On the contrary, they cool off quite quickly and should keep active by running and stretching every 10 minutes or so and by doing ball work. They should also wear warm-up suits or something similar to keep them warm if necessary.

Cool-Down

If your players are in a tournament, they need at least 10 minutes of cool-down activities after the game. This helps to disperse lactic acid and clear the muscles. The ideal activities are the running and stretching activities you had the players perform before the game. The work should be moderate, starting with jogging and strides and gradually slowing to stretches. You will find that the best way to get players to cool down is to conduct a cool-down session yourself. The reason for this is that many players, tired after the game, think that cooling down is unnecessary.

Mental Preparation

In sports, mental preparation is just as important as physical preparation. You need to (carefully) prepare athletes mentally for competition. Poor mental readiness can be more detrimental to performance than poor physical readiness.

Pregame Talks

Overly dramatic talks in the locker room can be counterproductive. A well-known psychological law—the Yerkes Dodson Law—says that when performing skillful activities, players have an optimum level of arousal, or excitement. If you try to motivate some players too much, especially introverts, you can actually reduce their performance of skillful tasks because they become too emotional and excited. For example, you might make a sensitive goalkeeper too anxious to catch the ball properly or a young center forward unable to stay composed in the penalty area. Even an experienced player can have these problems, and you don't want to contribute to them.

To make players competitive, you have to get your psychology right. This means recognizing that any team contains a mixture of personalities. You must handle players individually and be careful when using pregame talks to psych up the whole team at the same time. Young players often need calming down more than psyching up. Emotions such as frustration, anger, fear, and jealousy usually interfere with performance. Successful players are competitive but not overanxious. They can retain their composure and stay cool under pressure. The following sections offer strategies we use to try to achieve and sustain this ideal.

Positive Approach

When we give pregame talks, we always try to use positive reinforcement. We continually reinforce the good, rather than the bad, by referring to movements, styles, or skills that have been successful. We do this so players will form mental images of the good plays they have made in the past. The following examples demonstrate this technique:

- "Sven [the goalkeeper], remember that quick throw to Mike last game? That was great—try for the same thing today."
- "Maya [a forward], remember last week how you avoided getting caught offside by looking both ways? Try to do the same again today."
- "Kai [a winger], when you centered that ball the other week from the goal line, you got the defense in all kinds of trouble because they were caught facing the wrong way. Keep looking for chances to get to the goal line before you center the ball."
- "Tania [a midfield player], that through pass inside the fullback against Simi was magic—try for the same today."

In all these examples, we remind the player of a successful play. In this way we hope to achieve a double positive effect: we make the tactical point (i.e., we remind the player of something they already know) and we create in the player's mind a good mental image that should be reassuring and build up his or her confidence.

High-Information Messages

Note that the previous examples are very high in what psychologists call information—that is, factual knowledge that helps players identify the kind of behavior expected from them in the coming game. In pregame talks we avoid making emotional appeals to players to try hard or do their best. Trying hard and doing one's best should be taken for granted; players need information about their own play, about how they should work as a team, and about what to remember about opposing players. Please review the examples in the previous section before you continue to our third recommendation about pregame talks: Use of the Voice.

Use of the Voice

You can achieve much by controlling your voice when you address your players. We believe that you can focus the attention of the players on important issues by adopting a quiet, calm, even conversational tone of voice. Certainly, a calm, confident voice reduces tension and anxiety and can help to steady young nerves. Our advice is to talk, not shout.

Soccer involves a high degree of skill, and excessive states of arousal are more likely to diminish performance than improve it. Also, when you use a loud voice infrequently, it has more effect when you do; save your loud voice for emergencies.

Also remember that coaching during play can be ruled excessive by the referee. Quite rightly, the referee can, and will, caution any coach or parent about excessive shouting—it is the players' game, not the spectators' or coach's! If you want to encourage your team during play, simply move around the side of the field giving quiet, calm encouragement where it is needed. Never use sarcasm or be overtly critical, and don't shout or scream, because this degrades both you and the players. Above all, try to encourage immediately any player who makes a serious error.

Keep It Short

Pregame speeches for young players should last no longer than 5 minutes. Young players have short attention spans, and a tactics talk to which no one listens is of no value! A pregame talk should be a summary of what you have covered in practice and what you want players to concentrate on during the game. It should not be a lecture about material you should have covered in practice.

Halftime Talks

Halftime provides an important opportunity to help your team, so be prepared. Players will listen to and be able to act on very few instructions at halftime. For this reason, we advise you to limit the key points you want to emphasize to three. After gathering your team, start by drawing attention to any good plays you observed. Then, mention your three areas for improvement, always using the double positive approach. At the end of your talk, summarize your advice by using key words or phrases (e.g., "Help each other with an early call, look for the through pass, and be first to the ball").

The messages you give should be factual, containing information and advice. Equally important is the need to be careful when speaking to individual players. You don't want to destroy a player's confidence by drawing attention to an error; who needs to be reminded that he shot wildly over the goal? A player who tried a shot and failed needs encouragement; he needs to be encouraged to keep taking the responsibility to shoot at goal. Here is a good approach: "Chris, don't worry about that miss, because if you don't shoot, you don't score; but do try to keep your composure when you shoot." This approach recognizes that a mistake was made but allows the player to retain his dignity and at the same time provides an instructional point for the player to assimilate. We have found this to be the best way to help players learn. Use the advice provided in chapter 2 to open the minds of your players.

Postgame Talks

After the game, thank the referee and the coach of the opposing team. They are (or should be) friendly colleagues with the same goals as you have, and the same emotions! When we talk to our players after the game, we use one of four strategies, depending on the result of the game and the way the team played. The latter point, the manner in which the game was played, is more important in determining what we say and how we say it.

1. The team played well but lost.

   Approach: "Well done! You played well today and should feel no disgrace in losing."

   Reason: A track and field athlete who achieves a personal best may not win the event but will gain satisfaction for having performed well. Similarly, if your team really did play well, players should not feel despondent because the result went against them. The best team doesn't always win.

2. The team played well and won.

   Approach: "Well done! You played well, and you deserved to win."

   Reason: Let your players enjoy victory, and enjoy it with them. At the same time, try to get your players to associate winning with playing well. The best team doesn't always win, but it usually does!

3. The team played badly and lost.

   Approach: "Well, we didn't play very well today, so we didn't win. We'll work it out in practice."

   Reason: If a team didn't play well, there is no point in disguising the fact, but remember that nobody plays badly on purpose. Don't dwell on failure, and don't criticize your players when they are down.

4. The team played badly but won.

   Approach: "We didn't play very well today, but at least we still won! See you at practice."

   Reason: You want your players to enjoy having won, but you know that it was a poor performance and that at the next coaching session you will be working hard to improve their play.

These four strategies provide the basis of what you need to say to the whole team after the game. Leave the "winning is everything" philosophy to others, and try not to overreact to either victory or defeat. As Rudyard Kipling advised, "Treat those two imposters [success and disaster] just the same!"

Finally, if you coach young players, you must always try to ensure that they love playing soccer regardless of the result. With young players, promote the importance of the intrinsic satisfaction of playing well over the extrinsic reward of winning. Throughout this book we have continually emphasized the importance of focusing on trying to play well and enjoying the game. By doing this, you help to ensure that your players look forward to their next game rather than worrying about the result of their last game.

18

Working With Problem Players and Parents

• • • • • •

EVERY COACH HAS to work with problem players, from violent or argumentative players to those who simply arrive late for practice every week. Coaches must deal with so many different kinds of problems that any solutions are at best little more than suggestions about how to approach a problem. Nevertheless, because many problems have familiar patterns or causes, it is worthwhile to identify these problems and to consider ways to resolve them.

This chapter begins with prevention, because we believe that many of the problems we have had to face could have been avoided with better management. Problems very often develop as a direct result of your own personality or the way you approach a situation.

In addition, you may have the additional, and perhaps more difficult, situation in which the personality of a parent, however well meaning, produces problems not only for the player but also for you! We discuss the role of parents in Dealing With Parents on page 335.

Aim for Prevention, Not a Cure

Have you ever considered that players only become difficult when they behave in a manner that conflicts with your personal views about what should be done, about what you think is right? Players who conform to your expectations rarely cause a problem; the nonconformists are more difficult! For this reason, we always make sure that players understand our general expectations. We also let them know that our expectations are accepted by parents and assistant coaches. We tell players our views about punctuality, about giving notice if they cannot attend practice or have to leave early, and about the attitudes we expect them to demonstrate toward officials, opponents, and teammates. In this way we try to make sure everyone knows what we expect.

Second, we try not to take good behavior for granted. We make a point of reinforcing the code of practice from time to time by rewarding behavior ranging from shaking hands after the game to never arguing with the referee.

Third, we try to be consistent. Consistency is one of the hallmarks of a good leader. Players should be able to anticipate how you will react in given situations, and they should be able to model their behavior after yours. For example, you cannot tell your players not to argue with the referee if you yourself enter into a public argument with the same official. Similarly, you must react consistently with all players and offer no special privileges to your best players.

Fourth, we always try to be optimistic that any problem can be resolved. This approach can be challenging, but it usually elicits a better response from players. Imagine the reaction of a player to a coach who said, "Oh, dear! I don't think I can help you improve."

Fifth, and perhaps most important, we have learned that it doesn't always pay to try to find an immediate solution. Certainly, some situations do require an immediate, almost instinctive reaction (e.g., a sharp word of caution to a player who is about to start an argument). Most of the problems examined in this chapter, however, are more deep-seated and will test both your knowledge and your management skills. With many of the more serious problems, the player must first accept that he really does have a problem, and finding out that you cause other people a problem can be an embarrassing or hurtful experience. Spending time preparing your strategy will often pay off in the long run.

Finally, please remember that the way to handle a problem player might be to enlist outside help—for example, another player, a friend, a parent, or a doctor. What matters most is that the problem is solved, not who solves it.

Types of Problem Players

We have identified seven types of problem players. Hopefully, you will never have to deal with any of them, but you would do well to be prepared. You will quickly realize that some problems are more deep-seated than others and more difficult to resolve. All coaches, for example, at some point have to deal with dropping a player from the team; knowing how to talk to a player in this situation can help soften the blow (see Dropping a Player on page 342). Finally, we all have to work with and consider the role of the parents, so, rather than leave this until later, we discuss it first.

Dealing With Parents

In an ideal world, parents would stand in one place, applaud good play by both teams, never criticize the referee, never argue with other spectators, never complain about your team selection or team tactics, never shout abuse at anyone at any time, and thank everyone concerned with running the game when it is over. In the real world, however, parents have been known, and will probably continue, to exhibit behavior that is less than ideal. As a coach, what can you do about it?

First, you can be a good role model (we talk about this in part I). Second, you can try to prevent undesirable behavior by ensuring that all parents know what is expected of them, perhaps at a preseason meeting or by letter when the children first join your team. If prevention doesn't work and the parent becomes an embarrassment, often not least to his or her own child, then the only thing left for you to do is to speak directly to the parent. This is best done after the game has finished, unless the behavior is so bad that it must be addressed during the game. If you have to do this, remember that a "soft word turneth away anger" (the parent is entitled to an opinion). If a calm discussion during or after the game doesn't work, the last resort is a separate meeting with the parent, yourself, and another person. Banning a parent from watching altogether is not really an alternative in a free society, and hopefully the situation won't require such drastic action.

Ball Hog

Ball hogs are usually skillful dribblers because they get so much practice with the ball, and they often mature into good adult players. Certainly, they believe that by keeping possession, they are acting in the best interest of the team because they will eventually produce a game-winning play. Generally, however, they hold the ball too long, lose possession, and frustrate teammates, especially those who have worked hard to get into good supporting positions. Worse still, other team members might even stop running to support them or be reluctant to pass the ball to them.

To solve the problem presented by this type of player, start with a question to the player: "Do you realize that on occasion you hold the ball too long and that this is hindering our team play?" Depending on the answer you receive, and given that the player cannot correct the problem alone, you can use any or all of the following strategies:

- During practices, explain to the player that for set periods of time, she will be conditioned to play two-touch (or even one-touch) soccer. This forces her to release the ball quickly and requires her to run hard to get into good supporting positions. This will demonstrate to her just how frustrating it is to run into good positions but not receive a pass. If the player shows improvement, you can begin to relax this condition (e.g., she can play normally when in the opponents' penalty area).

- During practices, supplement team drills with 1v1 dribbling competitions so that the ball hog and others can practice their dribbling skills. This is most important because it gives the ball hog a legitimate stage on which to demonstrate prowess.

- On game days, give special reminders to the players during pregame talks; for example, "Be content to beat one defender," or "Remember that it is dangerous to dribble in your own penalty area."

- On game days, set targets; for example, "Last week you were caught in possession of the ball four times. Can you improve on that today?"

- On game days, include in your game analysis a record of how many times a player destroyed your team play as a result of trying to dribble too much.

- On game days, give the ball hog special responsibilities during set plays to help encourage the spirit of unselfish teamwork. For example, put the ball hog in charge of set moves that require her to make the decoy run.

Violent Player

There are two kinds of violent players: the hothead who is guilty of frequent, short outbursts and the player who demonstrates a less frequent but more deep-seated problem.

Hothead

Hot-tempered outbursts can usually be traced to specific triggering moments such as a hard tackle or a bad call by an official. Here are some solutions:

- In your pregame talks, remind players that soccer is a body contact game that involves hard physical knocks.

- Remind players that officials will make mistakes and that reactions to such mistakes must always be tactical, not emotional. When a bad call is made, every player should concentrate on getting on with the game so that no one is surprised by a quick counterattack. The player who argues or reacts emotionally loses concentration on the game and temporarily becomes a liability.

- Reinforce your points by giving players a model to follow. For example, illustrate your pregame talk with a reference to a fine professional player, preferably a soccer player.

If preventive measures fail, you must employ correction or punishment of some kind. In order of severity, these include the following:

- Be prepared to substitute the player for a cooling-off period, even though the referee might let an incident pass. If short penalties fail to have an effect, substitute the player for the remaining period of the game.

- Do not include the player in your starting lineup. This will emphasize that playing on your team is a privilege too valuable to sacrifice for a momentary lapse of control.

- If the player does not respond to other measures, you will probably have to suspend the player for a set number of games. Hopefully, your hotheaded player will eventually realize that staying cool means staying in the game.

Players With Deep-Seated Problems

Players do exist who deliberately inflict pain and suffering on others. This kind of violence is characterized by deliberate kicking, late tackles, tackling over the ball, and fouling when the referee's line of sight is obstructed. Here are three solutions when you are dealing with such a player.

Expulsion

You can simply expel the player from your team. By doing so, you will undoubtedly earn the gratitude and respect of many of your players, who know that such behavior is degrading to them by association. Because they are members of the same team, such behavior reflects badly on them. Worse, if the behavior is tolerated other members may also resort to violence. If you expel a player, explain your reasons to him (even if you have to put them in writing) and offer your help if the player wants to try again. This gives the player the opportunity to reflect on his behavior and leaves the door open for a new start.

Reeducation

Alternatively, you can try to reeducate violent players. In effect, you will be using soccer as a vehicle for socializing the player, because this kind of problem is not caused by soccer but is brought to the game by the player. You can try the following strategies:

- In practice games, let the problem player referee; this may help to develop a soccer ethic.

- Talk to the player privately, pointing out that violence on the soccer field is just as bad as any other violence because it violates an important ethical principle—respect for other people.

- State your views on violence at team talks. You need not mention individuals by name, but you must make your views public and so reinforce your code of practice.

- In competitive games, substitute the player immediately after you see a violent act, especially if the referee fails to see the foul or take action. Or, suspend the player for a fixed number of games.

Outside Help

Seeking outside help is not an acknowledgment of failure on your part; on the contrary, it is an example of detached, objective thinking. Such help requires the knowledge and consent of parents or guardians, which reinforces the point that not all problems have an immediate or easy solution. Solving serious problems takes time and thought.

Timid or Frightened Player

The player who "chickens out" of a tackle or a 1v1 duel is in many ways more difficult to handle than the violent or aggressive player. You can always command a player to be less exuberant, but you cannot always command the timid player to be brave. A player must want to win the ball, and players who lack this inner drive are difficult to coach. Some young players, for example, will go to great lengths to avoid heading the ball. Even among professional players are those who can be intimidated. Such players develop a high degree of subterfuge and become adept at arriving at the ball a fraction too late, jumping out of the way to avoid a tackle, or kicking the ball away too hastily. Such avoidance tactics do not happen by chance; players employ these tactics out of fear of being injured.

One procedure for overcoming fear or anxiety that is very popular with swim instructors is called counterconditioning. The player is first removed from the stressful situation and then reintroduced to it in small stages. For example, the frightened nonswimmer is reintroduced to the water through an anxiety hierarchy of sitting by the pool followed by gentle, confidence-building activities. When applying this technique to soccer, you can approach the problem in several ways.

In practices, you can give the player special coaching in four key soccer skills, all of which involve a positive act by the player: moving to the ball, tackling, shooting, and heading. In each of these practices you should carefully explain the progressions, using the following procedure:

- Reintroduce the player to the anxiety-provoking skill in small stages.
- Make sure that at each stage you allow the player time to enjoy success and thus gain renewed confidence.
- Give the player your individual personal attention. If you cannot join in the practices as an active performer, choose your helpers wisely, and make sure that they are fully informed about what you are trying to do.
- Use positive reinforcement, and above all, be patient.

In competitive or even practice games, it is more difficult to give your problem player direct help because the other players control the situation. However, you can reward and reinforce successful actions and keep a game analysis. Use a pregame talk to remind the player to think and act positively and to avoid undue worry about the possibility of injury. Remind the player of successful practice experiences. Keep a record, and encourage the player to keep a personal diary of the number of successful plays during each game. Ideally, the number will increase during the season and thus encourage the player.

Positively reinforce every occasion during the game in which the player acts courageously, and use these as examples in future tactics talks. Finally, place your timid player in a position on the field that reduces the possibility of body contact and gives increased room to maneuver. For example, place the player first as a winger; then, as the player's confidence grows, put her into more physically demanding positions. You can also play the timid player for short periods of time and by careful substitution reward increasing determination with longer periods of play.

Above all, be patient. You might on occasion successfully elicit a positive response from a timid player by using loud verbal encouragement, perhaps even a mild rebuke such as "Come on. You can do much better than that!" But use this approach carefully with sensitive, possibly introverted players, because it may inhibit, not improve, performance.

Dictator

The dictator thinks and acts for everyone, gives a constant stream of commands, and dominates everyone around, including the weak referee and sometimes the coach. A well-meaning dictator is a problem; a dictator who is also a bully is a much more serious problem. Two such players on one team will cause conflict, and other players may take sides to the detriment of the entire team.

There are two starting points from which to deal with a dictator. First, in your team talks and during practical coaching sessions, stress the importance of a good first call. You do not have to explain Welford's single-channel hypothesis (page 236); giving a simple, practical demonstration of the confusion caused when several players shout at the same time will make the point.

Second, players must clearly understand the difference between shouting and talking to colleagues. Emphasize that only two types of calls are helpful to the player with the ball: "Time" (meaning the player has time to look up and play the ball) and "Man-on" (meaning that a challenge is imminent).

Make sure that all of your players, including the dictator, are fully aware of the importance of good communication. Try the following strategies (if all of these solutions fail, then short periods of substitution following an incident may help to get the message across):

- In practice, play Silent Soccer (page 268) to condition the dictator to silence. In this way you will demonstrate that other players can think and act for themselves and emphasize that successful teamwork depends on thinking for oneself. The dictator must realize that excessive shouting can hinder team effectiveness.

- If the dictator is a good player and is well liked, then he may make a good captain. Appointing the dictator captain allows this player to talk to other players during the game. If you use this strategy, you must introduce the dictator to the skills of leadership. Teach the player to use encouragement rather than negative criticism, to recognize good plays, and to lead by example.

- If your dictator does not possess leadership qualities or is too unpopular to appoint as captain, then you need another strategy. In pregame talks, emphasize the need to recognize the difference between shouting and calling. Also, use incremental goals to work toward behavior change (e.g., the player tries to go 20 minutes without shouting at teammates or tries to save calls for moments in the game when they can be really useful).

Poor Tactician

The poor tactician persistently makes the same mistake during a game and as a result either ruins a good play or exposes the defense unnecessarily. Examples include the attacker who continually runs offside, the defender who rushes in and commits herself unnecessarily, and the midfield player who makes too many inaccurate or poorly planned passes.

Such unthinking actions are not done deliberately, but they have to be minimized if a team is to be successful. You can use two methods to improve tactical awareness. The first is described in chapter 3, which establishes the importance of using small-team games to develop tactical appreciation, and in chapter 14, which addresses several ways of coaching better teamwork.

The second method, which is useful if you have a particularly difficult problem to resolve, is based on recent thinking in the field of behavior modification psychology. The method involves a careful analysis of the problems followed by the construction of a checklist to monitor progress.

We will explain the method using the example of a player who continually runs offside, but keep in mind that the method is the same whatever the problem. If a player is continually caught offside, first sit down with her and analyze all the possible reasons for being caught offside. This will inform her as well as provide information for your checklist. The causes can be divided into two groups, those for which the player is personally responsible and those over which she has no control.

The player is not responsible when the referee gives a bad call or when a teammate delays the pass too long. The player is responsible when she falls for a deliberate offside trap played by the opposition, runs too soon out of anxiety to gain the advantage, fails to look both ways along the line of the defense, turns her back on the passer and runs away, or forgets the rules and stands in line with the defenders. Arrange the factors that the player can control into a table, as shown in figure 18.1. Each time the player gets caught offside, record the reason.

Behavior modification theory does the rest, with a little help from you. Now the player is personally involved, is able to analyze and evaluate the reasons for her mistakes, and becomes both more knowledgeable and more coachable.

Figure 18.1 Offside Checklist

Name:	Date:	Date:	Date:	Date:
Caught in an offside trap				
Ran too soon				
Failed to look both ways				
Turned and ran away from passer				
Didn't know the rules				

From Hargreaves and Bate, *Skills and Strategies for Coaching Soccer*, Second Edition (Champaign, IL: Human Kinetics).

Dropping a Player

Every time you select a team, you are in danger of losing a friend. Those you don't select are going to be disappointed, and their self-esteem will take a beating. How can you drop a player and still retain his respect and allegiance to the team?

Be sure that the player being dropped is the first to know; don't let him find out secondhand. Tell the player personally. This is a responsibility that you cannot delegate to others. Give the player an honest reason. If it is a matter of tactics (e.g., you want to play a different system and the decision is only a temporary one) or if it is for reasons such as injury, which are not related to loss of form, then informing players will be easier. The difficulty comes when the player has lost form and is playing badly.

We discourage dropping a player because of one bad game. First, this would be an admission of poor selection on your part. Second, a player can have a poor game for a variety of reasons, such as very superior opposition, poor support from colleagues, or personal reasons. Third, the player will probably realize that he had a bad game and will seek to improve on the next occasion. In all these cases, you can do much between games. When a sequence of poor games occurs, we suggest that you drop the player only if you have a replacement or can implement a change in tactics that is likely to improve performance. Don't drop a player unless you have an alternative strategy. There is no point in dropping a player unless you have a better replacement or a system that is more likely to be successful.

Finally, never drop a player from the team in one move. Instead, use the substitutes' bench as a platform both onto and off the team, unless you have a second or lower team on which an immediate place is available.

The strategies suggested here are all related to one objective: protecting the self-esteem of the player. It is easy to hurt the pride of a young player and, worse, turn him away from soccer. When you discuss the reasons that resulted in the player's being dropped, try to focus on the way the player acted; avoid making a judgment on the player as a person. For example, consider a player who continually avoids going into a tackle. To bluntly tell this person that he is "chicken" would be to attack him as a person. Such an opinion might be true, but it would probably hurt the player's feelings considerably. A better way would be to highlight two or three examples during the game when the player's judgment or decision not to move into the tackle was wrong and exposed the team in a way that cannot be allowed to continue. This puts the focus on the poor judgment of the player, not on his character. From this kind of base it is much easier to rehabilitate the player and eventually restore him to the team. At the very least, the player has something concrete to practice and knows exactly what you expect in the way of improvement.

Fitness and Conditioning for Soccer

• • • • • •

FITNESS AND CONDITIONING are complex subject areas embracing many abilities. Players have to run; sprint; accelerate; jump; change direction; move backward, forward, and sideways; and stop and start—and they must keep on doing these activities for 90 minutes or longer. They also have to pay careful attention to their diet and general lifestyle to ensure that they are gaining every advantage from their fitness training.

This chapter addresses the basic physiological information in a clear, straightforward manner. We have also designed drills for the abilities required in soccer; to conduct these drills, you need only have access to a field, a stopwatch, a tape measure, and marker cones or flags. We do not deal with gym work or weight training. Of course, muscular strength is important, but if your time and facilities are limited, you must give priority to the major fitness elements required in soccer.

We do recognize the very important fact that players have different starting levels of fitness and that some players will always be fitter than their teammates. To accommodate these differences, we have designed a series of tests and activities, for which performance data for youth boys aged 9–16 are listed. You can use these activities to train players of various levels of ability, in a group situation, at the same time. This is both demanding and enjoyable for the players involved and also gives you standards that you can use to measure your players' achievements and compare them to each other in terms of fitness on that particular activity.

Fitness training is, by definition, demanding. It is your duty to check the physical condition of your players; keep records; ensure that training is progressive, especially preseason; give your players time to improve; always provide a thorough warm-up; and cater to individual differences. It is also your responsibility to have a complete first aid kit available and be able to provide initial care for minor injuries and recognize serious injuries. You must also have emergency telephone numbers on hand.

To get players fit, you must understand how the body releases energy and how it responds to exercise. Fortunately, the necessary physiological information can be reduced to a few easily remembered key concepts including, in particular, the difference between aerobic and anaerobic respiration, the build up and absorption of lactic acid, and the difference between fast- and slow-acting muscle fibers. These terms are explained in the chapter, in simple language, together with the appropriate conditioning activities. We begin by identifying five basic strategies which, collectively, explain how we approach fitness training for soccer (see page 345).

Cardiorespiratory Fitness

Like a car, which has a battery for starting and gas for sustained running, the body has two kinds of energy. The body uses the phosphocreatine and glycogen in the muscles to start activity, but it needs a supply of oxygen to continue.

Five Strategies for Fitness Training

Fitness training for soccer can be based on the following objectives:

1. *Study and identify the fitness requirements that are unique to the sport and the various positions within the team.*
   For example, every soccer player needs to develop the kicking muscles, but wingers are more likely to benefit from concentrating on speed and acceleration, whereas midfield players need endurance training.

2. *Train players in one fitness component at a time.*
   Of course, all of the components are related, but each one requires a unique training regimen. There is a difference between anaerobic and aerobic conditioning, as you will see. Always target a specific goal and conduct your program accordingly.

3. *Keep in mind that a soccer team comprises 11 individuals with varying physiques.*
   A training method that works with one player may not work with another. Later in the chapter you will learn how to incorporate individual training programs into your practices. Individual programs are much more effective than generic programs; the activities we have designed enable you to train individuals in a group system.

4. *Keep records so you can analyze the success or failure of your program.*
   Careful records enable you to compare performances over a number of seasons and between teams. Indeed, with select teams you can even set minimum qualifying standards similar to those used in other sports, and you can easily compare the performances of players within your team.

5. *Strive to motivate players so they will want to train hard.*
   Good supervision and extrinsic motivation are important, but far more important is the intrinsic, self-motivating drive of wanting to improve. Training should never be a punishment. Try to add enjoyment to activities through carefully graded handicap situations, which are easily arranged.

An activity that does not use oxygen is called *anaerobic*; an activity that does use oxygen is called *aerobic*. Soccer players need both aerobic and anaerobic fitness. They use short bursts of energy and yet continue to play for up to 90 minutes or longer.

Aerobic Fitness

To improve aerobic fitness, young players have to run continuously for 20 to 30 minutes. They have to run at a pace fast enough to elevate their heart rate to over 130 beats per minute, and they must do this three times a week. This means that you will have to encourage your players to run on days when you do not have team practice, because running uses too much practice time.

The most famous and the best field test of aerobic fitness is Dr. Kenneth Cooper's 12-minute run/walk test. Ask your players to run or walk for 12 minutes, and measure how far they travel. A fit youngster will cover 1 1/4 to 1 1/2 miles (2 to 2.4 km) depending on age and sex. A very fit youngster will cover up to 2 miles (3.2 km). However, aerobic fitness is related to body weight, so make allowances for heavy players (and try to help them slim down). Fortunately, two benefits of playing soccer is that it helps children develop aerobic fitness and lose excess weight.

Anaerobic Fitness

Soccer calls for repeated bursts of strenuous activity, and this kind of fitness is developed through interval training, which varies the ratio of work and rest. It is important to get the ratios right to reduce the impact of a by-product of exercise called lactic acid, which begins to accumulate after 30 seconds of hard exercise. We therefore recommend that you either work players for less than 30 seconds and give them a rest of 60 seconds between runs, or keep them working for 60 seconds or more but then give them a longer rest (e.g., 4 or 5 minutes).

When assigning repetitions for interval training, start small and increase gradually. You should determine the number of repetitions by the age and level of fitness of your players. We believe that three repetitions are enough for children under 14, even those who are very fit. Players should not attempt five repetitions unless they are very fit and are over the age of 16. We never give adults more than six repetitions because the players begin to pace themselves and this detracts from the training effect. We believe it is better to have quality than quantity.

Testing Anaerobic Fitness

The timed shuttle run test is an excellent field test of anaerobic fitness. It reflects very well the soccer pattern of running, stopping, turning, and accelerating. Use this test after a warm-up, and do not follow it with any other tests, because players will need several minutes to recover from lactic acid buildup. To assess where your players rank in comparison, table 19.1 provides the typical times for male youth players who complete 3 shuttles with a 60-second rest between

Table 19.1 Typical Shuttle Run Times for Male Youth Players

Age (years)	9	10	11	12	13	14	15	16
Average (seconds)	120	117	114	111	108	105	102	99

runs. International soccer and hockey players average 30 seconds per run for 6 runs with a 35-second rest period between runs. Very fit players will beat 180 seconds total. Note that it is very important to time the rest period between runs just as carefully as the runs themselves. When engaged in serious testing, we always use two sets of timekeepers with their own watches. The person who times the rest period gives the command to start the next run.

The shuttle run is also an excellent training activity in addition to being a valid anaerobic test. Although the shuttle run is a well-used activity, it can be a rather boring form of training. With a simple modification it has become one of my most successful activities for both testing and training. If you make your grid lines long enough, you can put several players on the run at the same time and they will compete against each other, which helps motivation. You can also use handicap shuttles, in which you give the slower players a 5-yard or even a 10-yard head start. Or, you can pair players for partner work. As one player finishes a run, a partner takes over. The object is to be the first pair to complete a given number of runs. By pairing your fastest and slowest players, you can get a better competition. If you are using the activity for general training, do so at the end of your coaching session.

 ## Shuttle Run Test

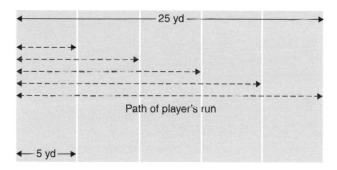

Path of player's run

Equipment   One stopwatch

Organization   Chalk lines are drawn at 5-yard intervals. The players stand at the start line. You can conduct this test with individual players or small groups of three players, for example.

Instructions   On the command "Go," the players sprint to the 5-yard line, touching it with one foot, and return to the starting line, touching that line with one foot. Without stopping, the players follow the same procedure with the other lines: 10-yard, 15-yard, 20-yard, and 25-yard lines. Record the time for each run and calculate the total time.

Training for Anaerobic Fitness

Following is an activity to help your players achieve anaerobic fitness. Remember, however, that you can design your own drills to measure and develop anaerobic fitness by using the same basic processes described here. Simply measure the distance the players have to cover, record the time each player takes to complete the drill, and control the rest period between repetitions as well as the number of repetitions players complete. Review our recommendations earlier in the chapter about the severity of the workload to prescribe for young players. If you have fit adult males, give them six 40-second repetitions with a 40-second rest as a starting activity and see how they respond. Now that you know how to control the variables, the drills are in your hands!

Pass and Run

Introducing a ball will enliven all forms of training. However, because a ball is a variable you cannot always control, it can detract from the serious effort required to stress the system. In the following activities, we provide several suggestions about how to use a ball with a minimum of interference. In every case, you must still set the working period to either 35 or 60 seconds and adjust the rest period appropriately. Please note that although this, and similar activities, appear quite simple, properly conducted, they provide excellent endurance training.

Equipment
Two balls for every three players; a supply of cones or flags

Organization
Players are in teams of three (one runner and two servers) or teams of four (two runners and two servers) for younger players to allow each runner to rest after his turn. Chalk lines are drawn 25 yards apart, and two markers are placed 5 yards from the end lines.

Instructions
In turn, each player makes a set number of runs, as follows:

- As the runner comes to the 5-yard marker, the server passes to the runner, who immediately passes the ball back to the server. The runner then turns and sprints back across the area to the other 5-yard marker, where the passing sequence is repeated with the next server.

- The runner starts with the ball. As the runner approaches a marker, he passes to the waiting server, who returns the ball. The runner then dribbles to the other end and repeats with the other waiting server.

- The runner must head the ball back to the server. The pattern of running remains the same as do the number of repetitions and the rest period given.

- The runner receives a thrown ball, controls it, passes back to the server, turns, and sprints across to the other side. As with all of the variations, the quality of service must be supportive.

Acceleration

The ability to accelerate is priceless in soccer, and you must try to improve this ability in all your players including the goalkeeper. Acceleration is a result of three things: mental alertness, strong, fast reaction of the muscles, and practice. Practice is the most important of all with young players because the body literally must learn how to accelerate. The muscles have to establish movements, and the brain has to lay down cell assemblies, which are little groups of brain cells that control the actions. Players must keep acceleration work to less than 10 seconds in order to reduce the possibility of lactic acid accumulation. Such training, called anaerobic alactic training, conditions the fast-acting muscle fibers.

Testing Acceleration

A good test for speed of acceleration is the Hargreaves 4-second acceleration test, as follows. To assess where your players rank in comparison, table 19.2 provides typical distances for male youth players who accelerate for 4 seconds. The average distance covered by professional players and Olympic hockey players is 30 yards, and the record is 32 yards.

Table 19.2 Typical 4-Second Acceleration Distances for Male Youth Players

Age (years)	9	10	11	12	13	14	15	16
Distance (yards)	19	20	21	22	23	24	25	26

To use the test as a training activity, measure how far your players can run in 4 seconds and then reverse the practice. Start them at their best distance and let them sprint back to the start. By putting two, three, or four players against each other, you make each run into a race and provide competition. Players who can run at different speeds can compete because of the handicap difference. The back runner can see those in front and tries to catch them; the front player runs as fast as possible to avoid being caught. This provides good motivation and good fun.

For an elimination activity, follow the same organization, but this time, eliminate the winner in each heat. Those left try again until only two players are left. Of course, you will also organize winners' races while the main group is resting to ensure that everyone runs the same number of sprints during the session. In this way you will soon identify your fastest and the slowest sprinters and can then train them accordingly.

4-Second Acceleration Test

Equipment   Ten markers, such as flags or cones; one stopwatch

Organization   Players are in groups of 12 or more (one runner, one timekeeper, 10 additional players who act as judges). Markers are placed at the following distances from a start line: 24, 25, 26, 27, 28, 29, 30, 31, and 32 yards.

Instructions   Players must wear soccer boots (cleats), and the test must be done on flat, firm grass. To begin, the runner stands with his back to the direction of the sprint and with both heels on the line. On the command "Go," the runner turns and sprints past as many markers as possible in 4 seconds. The timekeeper starts the watch on the command "Go" and then concentrates on the second hand. When the hand reaches 4, he shouts "Stop."

The timekeeper has to be accurate. An error of 0.1 seconds is allowed either way (e.g., 3.9 or 4.1), but outside this margin the test is invalid. With practice, a good timekeeper can achieve a high degree of accuracy, especially with a digital watch. Have players who have already run or are waiting for their turn count the number of markers the runners pass.

Training for Acceleration

To help your players practice acceleration, select players of equal ability and organize the following activities.

 ## *Through the Legs*

Player A has a ball, and player B faces player A with legs set wide apart. Player A passes the ball through the legs of player B, who must turn, accelerate, and stop the ball as quickly as possible. Next, arrange a marker between 5 and 10 yards away from player A. Player A now has to pass the ball just hard enough to permit player B to stop it before it reaches the marker. This practice depends on how well player A judges the force of the pass. If it is too soft, the challenge will be too easy; if it is too hard, player B will not even try to accelerate because she will see that the task is impossible. Given time to practice, all players will quickly improve because the challenge to both players is infectious.

 ## *Turn and Go*

Two players stand back to back and at an equal distance from the ball. On command, they turn and accelerate. The first to touch the ball wins. No tackling is allowed.

 ## *Turn and Tackle*

Players stand back to back. Player B has the ball. On command, player B dribbles forward, while player A turns and chases.

Backing Off and Turning

Players face each other. Player A runs gently forward causing player B to back off. Player A now accelerates past player B, either to the left or right. Player B has to turn and stop player A from outrunning him and must do so without obstructing him in any way. Have the pair do this several times across the field and then change positions.

 ## *Resistance Running*

Player A and player B hold a towel at player C's waist, providing resistance, while player C tries to sprint forward. This practice is well known to sprinters and is excellent for conditioning the leg muscles that accelerate the body forward. However, make sure the towel is in good condition, and warn players not to let go of the towel.

Speed

Speed and acceleration are closely related. In soccer we are more concerned with acceleration because a player seldom sprints more than 30 yards at a time. However, players must also practice sprinting distances between 30 and 40 yards. In this way they will improve acceleration and be able to sustain speed when they are involved in a race for the ball. To assess where your players rank in comparison, table 19.3 provides typical times for male youth players who complete a 50-yard flying start test, as described next. Professional soccer players and Olympic hockey players average between 5 and 5.5 seconds, very fast players achieve 4.8 seconds, and slow players can take up to 6 seconds.

Table 19.3 Typical 50-Yard Flying Start Test Times for Male Youth Players

Age (years)	9	10	11	12	13	14	15	16
Average (seconds)	9.0	8.6	8.2	7.8	7.4	7.0	6.6	6.2

In track and field sprinting, running style is important. The body leans forward, the head is kept still, the arms pump forward and backward in a straight line, and the knees are raised high to increase stride length and drive the athlete forward in a series of explosive bounds. In soccer the player enjoys few opportunities for prolonged straightaway running, and for this reason running style is less important. Indeed, the arms are usually carried low and moved across the body, the head is moved about to watch the ball and other players, the body remains upright, and the stride length is much shorter because the player must prepare to arrive at the ball or change direction.

For all these reasons, speed training in soccer should always be done on grass, in soccer boots (cleats), and if possible in competition with someone of similar ability. Don't worry about style; simply emphasize the basics—using the arms and driving the legs. As with acceleration, what matters is that you give your players the opportunity to practice the act of sprinting.

Testing Speed

There are many tests of speed. The following speed test enables you to evaluate your entire team very quickly and without any help.

 ### *50-Yard Flying Start Test*

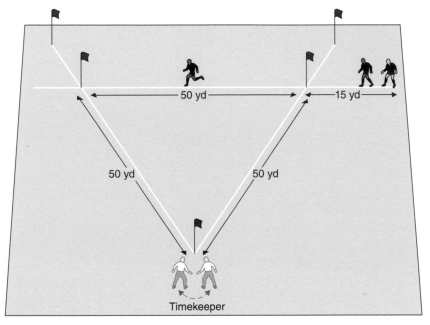

Equipment   Five markers such as flags or cones; one stopwatch

Organization   The players are in a group of unlimited number on a field marked as follows:
Measure 50 yards along the sideline with the halfway line as the midpoint. Then measure 50 yards into the field along the halfway line, and mark all three points with corner flags or cones. The players stand 15 yards behind the start line because they need this distance to reach maximum speed as they cross the start line and begin the timed section. The timekeeper looks along the line of the markers (the two small lines marked with flags at the top of the diagram) that the player must run between so that the timekeeper can see exactly when the player crosses the line.

Instructions   The players must sprint the distance in the fastest time possible, from a flying start. They should be sprinting all out as they cross the starting line. Players are allowed two attempts, and only the fastest time is recorded. Players have at least 5 minutes' rest between trials. This is needed to let the players walk back to the start and recover. Players wear boots (cleats) and soccer clothing. The grass should be flat, level, and firm. Wet or soft conditions will reduce performance times. Players must be properly warmed up and run one at a time when called by the timekeeper.

Training for Speed

The following three training activities are both popular and effective. They make an excellent finale to a training session or can be used before you move into game practices. All are based on team competitions.

 ## *Circular and Continuous Relay*

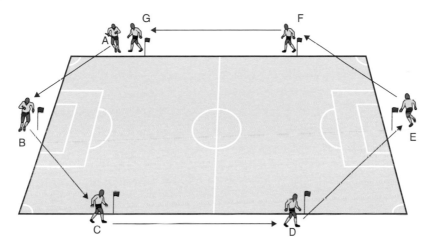

Equipment   Six flags; one relay baton or stick

Organization   Players are in groups of seven; two players are at the starting post and the other five are positioned at the other posts, as shown in the figure.

Instructions   At your starting signal, the players advance one place forward on each run. The relay continues until the last player (player G) has completed his sixth run and everyone else is now back at their starting positions.

Coaching Progressions

1. Two teams race against each other but in the opposite direction. This is highly motivating because the players cannot easily judge who is winning until the final two runners converge on and cross the finish line.

2. Two teams race. Record the difference in time between them and handicap the winning team by that amount for the second race.

 Shuttle Relay 1

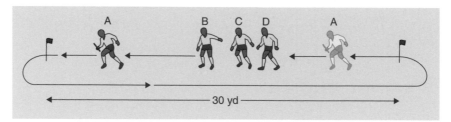

Equipment Two markers for every four players

Organization Players are in teams of four between two markers fixed 30 yards apart; players stand as shown in the figure.

Instructions Players exchange the baton as in a normal track and field relay (i.e., player A passes to player B after her turn). Each player sprints in turn until all four have finished. By timing each team, you can introduce handicap races (e.g., the slowest team starts first).

 Shuttle Relay 2

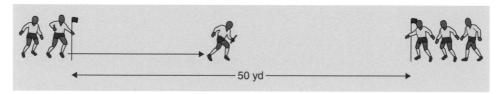

Equipment Two markers for every six players

Organization Players are in teams of six positioned behind two markers placed 50 yards apart (or less if you want to use this practice for acceleration) as shown in the figure.

Instructions The first player sprints to the opposite player. The incoming player runs to the left-hand side of the marker post. The receiving player holds his hand behind the marker to receive the baton. This prevents any cheating by starting too soon.

Pressure Training

Pressure training is fun and is a very effective training method. It involves selecting one player and normally one skill such as heading or collecting the ball. You then serve the player balls in a continuous stream, starting slowly and then increasing the tempo as the player becomes accustomed to the practice. The drill becomes harder and harder for the player, who has to try to maintain a high skill level even when tired—hence the name *pressure training*.

Organizing pressure practices is quite simple. You either provide one server with a plentiful supply of soccer balls and some helpers to replenish the stock, or you provide several players with balls who serve in turn to the player under pressure. For example, to practice heading, have three players stand in a triangle with a ball each. One player stands in the middle. Each server throws the ball in turn, and the header in the middle has to return the ball to each server in sequence. The speed of the throws should depend on the ability of the header.

To practice diving heading, one player kneels down and receives a continuous service from one or two servers. The rate of service should depend on the skill and response of the header, and the ability of the servers to recover any misdirected returns. Provide the servers with an ample supply of soccer balls. With advanced players, the service can be directed to either the left or right of the receiver, who responds with extended diving movements similar to those used in the full-game situation when attacking the goal.

Footwork

This section on footwork concerns fitness and agility training (ball skills and dribbling are covered in chapters 4 and 6). To practice footwork, many soccer teams use manufactured rubber cords and low obstacles similar to those used in American football drills to encourage players to achieve high knee lift and changes in direction at high speed. They often conduct drills in a "follow the leader" succession and time each player. Professional soccer teams have adopted these American football drills, and similar practices are now commonplace in soccer training. Youth and school coaches can easily follow suit and design their own training practices according to the equipment and space they have available.

The following suggestions are offered as a starting point; the first two are tag games (Catcher and Nomination Tag). The last three, Zigzag Test, Zigzag Run, and Zigzag Variation, are agility activities that you can use to test the agility of your players. To assess where your players rank in comparison, table 19.4 on page 357 provides the typical times for male youth players who complete the Zigzag Test. Professional players can complete one run in less than 6 seconds and three runs in 18 to 19 seconds.

 *Catcher*

Organization   Arrange a group of four players in a 10- × 10 yard square or similar; one player is the catcher and stands outside the square.

Instructions   On your command, the catcher enters the square and you time how long it takes for the catcher to touch (not tackle or strike) the four other players, who must stand still when caught. Give each player a turn as catcher.

Coaching Points

- Catchers should watch how a player's feet are placed and try to move in the direction of the foot that is solidly on the ground. Tennis players call this "having your foot in the hole." If they move in that direction, they will catch their opponent off balance.
- Players should practice dodging and changing direction to avoid being caught.
- For safety, players should not swing around the body of a caught player (using their arm to swing around a players' body by holding on to him) or touch stationary caught players, although dodging behind and around them is all part of the game.

Coaching Progression

1. Group the players into categories for variety (e.g., defenders, forwards) perhaps finishing with the fastest catchers in an all-winners group.

 Nomination Tag

Organization   Arrange players in groups of five or six in a 10- × 10-yard square or similar area (e.g., center circle).

Instructions   Give each player a number, or use their names. Start all the players moving freely in the circle, and then call out the name or number of one player, who becomes the catcher. The catcher must then catch as many players as possible in a given time (e.g., 60 seconds). When caught, players stand still.

Coaching Points

- Catchers should watch how a player's feet are placed and try to move in the direction of the foot that is solidly on the ground. Tennis players call this "having your foot in the hole." If they move in that direction, they will catch their opponent off balance.
- When the catcher changes, this is similar to a change of ball possession in the game. Players should react quickly to the new catcher just as they would when the ball changes possession in a game. Rapid reaction is a key skill for all players.

Coaching Progression

1. During play, randomly call out the name or number of a new catcher (or catchers). The game changes immediately, and all players must be alert to the fact that their name may be called out at any moment.

Table 19.4 Typical Zigzag Test Times for Male Youth Players

Age (years)	9	10	11	12	13	14	15	16
Average speed (seconds)	8.1 for 1 run and 27 for 3 runs	8.2 for 1 run and 26.3 for 3 runs	8.0 for 1 run and 25.6 for 3 runs	7.8 for 1 run and 24.9 for 3 runs	7.5 for 1 run and 24.2 for 3 runs	7.3 for 1 run and 23.5 for 3 runs	7.1 for 1 run and 22.8 for 3 runs	6.9 for 1 run and 22.1 for 3 runs

 **Zigzag Test**

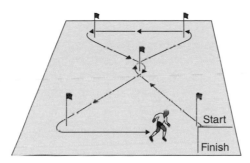

Equipment   Five flags—should be at least 4 feet tall to prevent players from leaning when they turn

Organization   Arrange flags in the shape of an X with the distances between the outer markers measuring 16 feet by 8 feet. Place the center marker where the diagonals intersect. Players must wear boots (cleats), and the ground must be firm and flat.

Instructions   At top speed, players zigzag in a figure-eight pattern through the flags. Set the interval between players with regard to safety and the speed of the players.

Coaching Points
- Players must always face the direction in which they are running.
- Players should be reasonably upright.

 **Zigzag Run**

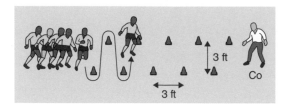

Equipment Ten cones or flags

Organization Arrange a sequence of 10 markers 1 yard apart.

Instructions Players dodge sideways as they move forward through the lines of posts. Players start as soon as the player in front has cleared the first two flags or cones. Start by demonstrating (or having a player demonstrate) the zigzag sequence of moves required to move through the grid. Also, demonstrate how to return safely to the starting point. When returning, players must move backward and, for the safety of players on the grid, keep well to the side.

Coaching Points

- Players should keep eyes and body facing forward at all times, especially when moving backward.
- Footwork must be as rapid as possible using short steps and keeping the arms out sideways for balance.
- Players should concentrate on driving off the outside foot to change direction.

Coaching Progression

1. As the players become familiar with the drill, start them off at shorter intervals to get several players on the drill at the same time; this changes the drill from work to fun.

 **Zigzag Variation**

Equipment Eight cones or flags arranged in a straight line 2 feet apart

Organization Teams of five to six players line up at the start.

Instructions Players zigzag forward through the cones as fast as possible. Set the interval between players with regard to safety and the speed of the players. Players return to the starting position by moving backward down the side of the grid. For safety, ensure that they do this well to the side of the drill.

Coaching Points

- Players should keep eyes and body facing forward at all times, especially when moving backward.
- Players should drive off the outside foot to change direction.
- Players should keep arms out sideways for balance and keep the body low.

Coaching Progression

1. Use the grid layout described earlier, but now the players have to run and jump directly over the obstacles (cones) with alternate feet leading or with the same foot leading.

Skill Circuits

A skill circuit is a great way to increase players' fitness in an interesting and enjoyable way. To do this, you plan a series of soccer skills in a sequence and let the players take turns competing against each other or against the clock (a sample skill circuit is shown in figure 19.1). With imagination and some equipment, you can play any number of skill circuits, even with only a few markers.

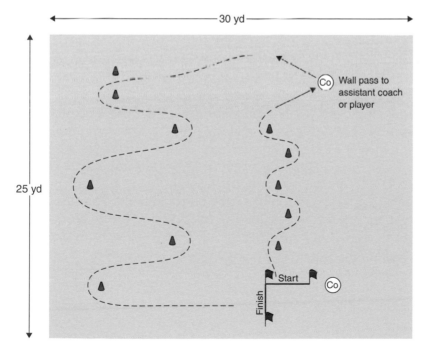

Figure 19.1 Sample skill circuit.

To run a skill circuit, start the stopwatch and the first player simultaneously. Start all the other players at 15-second intervals, letting the watch run. When each player finishes, deduct the starting time from the finishing time to see how long it took to complete the circuit (performance time). With a little practice, and because the starting interval is fixed, is becomes quite easy for the coach to call out the performance time as each player crosses the finishing line. Alternatively, the assistant coach or a player can record the finishing time and the performance time can be calculated later.

For variation, start the players at different points on the circuit and have them try to catch the player in front. In this game the practice would be continuous, but you would set a time limit (e.g., 3 minutes). Or set out two identical circuits with a common starting and finishing point; the player who completes the circuit first is the winner.

Nutrition

As you know, the adult and senior youth game of soccer lasts for about 90 minutes, with the actual playing time being somewhere around 60 minutes. Distances covered can be greater than 7 1/2 miles (12 km) at the highest levels, and of course, this will vary with positional demands and styles of play, and from game to game. Some players will complete over 0.6 miles (1,000 meters) of high-intensity running and as many as 1,100 instances of different activities (e.g., jumping, turning, sprinting) within those 90 minutes. Soccer is a high-intensity, intermittent activity that requires strength, endurance, speed, and agility.

The demands of the game result in fatigue, which sets in as the game progresses. It is induced by the length of the playing time, the high-intensity exercise, accumulation of lactic acid, dehydration, and muscle carbohydrate depletion, and it inevitably results in impairment of physical and technical performance and the decision-making process. Both you and your players must know how to load, preserve, and restore the energy supplies needed to fuel practice and game play and how to hydrate and rehydrate the body.

An effective diet is high in carbohydrate, low in fat, and high in fluid intake; it includes a moderate protein intake and a variety of foods. Youth soccer games generally have shorter playing times and reduced demand compared with adult games, but young players still need to fuel both the demands of playing and the requirements of growth and development. Young and growing players are often obsessed with the game of soccer, practicing and playing whenever they can, be it casual practice and play with friends, training for team performance, or playing against other teams. To sustain this level of involvement, the young player must both prepare for and recover from both practice and play.

Energy is needed to maintain the integrity of the body; promote movement; and sponsor the growth, development, and repair of the body. It is also needed for respiration, digestion, and the absorption and assimilation of nutrients that are vital for the body's functioning. Good food choices that supply this energy are important for daily life and for long-term health and are crucial in providing the high-octane fuel required for involvement in the game of soccer. They enable players to recover between training sessions and to prepare for game play, and they assist in preventing illness and injury as well as being important for general growth and development.

The human body needs energy (fuel) to undertake the demands of life in general and sport in particular. A well-balanced diet should meet the energy demands for play and provide all the essential nutrients needed for health, growth, and competitive performance. When young players train and play regularly, they draw on their bodies' energy supplies more often.

Essential nutrients that the body requires to function are carbohydrate, protein, fat, water, and vitamins and minerals as well as fiber. With all athletes, the two most important nutritional factors are energy provision and fluid replacement. Diminished stores of glycogen (derived from carbohydrate) can result in significantly reduced distances covered in the second half of games. Low levels of glycogen can also result in an impairment in decision-making ability because the brain and nervous system depend on blood glucose for metabolism.

Carbohydrate

Carbohydrate provides the crucial energy needed to practice and play soccer. It is stored as glycogen in the muscles and liver and as glucose in the blood. When exercise intensity is high, carbohydrate is the major source of energy. However, because the body stores only relatively small amounts of carbohydrate, we need to replenish it on a daily basis. Carbohydrate intake fuels both practice and game play, and also helps in the recovery of glycogen stores between training sessions. The more intense the training schedule, the more carbohydrate your players need and the more they should consume. Different levels of training take place from day to day, week to week and month to month. With the onset of high-intensity training, players need increased supplies of carbohydrate for the optimum functioning of their bodies.

Carbohydrate is found in sugars and starches in the diet, such as bread, pasta, rice, potatoes, and breakfast cereals as well as sugar, confectionery, fruits, and juices. Approximately 50 percent of daily food intake should be some form of carbohydrate. It is important before, during, and after training. A high-carbohydrate snack 30 to 60 minutes before training, consisting of a sports drink, fruit, or fruit juice, can add a boost of carbohydrate. A large meal requires around 3 hours to digest and add carbohydrate to the stores already available. Pretraining and pregame carbohydrate intake should consist of pasta, baked potato, bread, rice, or cereals.

The carbohydrate consumed the day before training or competition provides the crucial fuel for exercise in that it is converted into glycogen and stored in the muscles ready for use. The carbohydrate consumed on the day of training and competition supplements these stores. If the carbohydrate store is depleted during exercise, the body will not function as effectively, resulting in mental and physical fatigue, a slowing of reaction time, possibly a lessening of concentration, and a lack of energy for the demands of exercise.

The body needs to replace carbohydrate used during the session. Regular intake of sports drinks replenishes both fluid and carbohydrate, but players should be careful not to drink too much of any liquid before or during exercise. Within 2 hours of exercising, the body should begin to replace the lost carbohydrate and rehydrate. Glycogen replacement occurs three times quicker within 2 hours of exercising than at any other time. The process can be commenced almost immediately after exertion with the consuming of small snacks and sports drinks before the return to larger meals when the player is able. This process enables the body to recover more efficiently before the next training or game.

A depletion of carbohydrate limits a player's ability to maintain high-intensity running and sustain prolonged endurance activities. Given that soccer is a 90-minute game, a high-carbohydrate diet is of utmost importance for players who perform and train on a daily basis.

Protein

Protein does not provide the main source of energy for exercise unless both fat and carbohydrate stores are significantly depleted. It is estimated to provide between 5 to 10 percent of the energy the body needs, especially for moderately intense, prolonged exercise. Protein is mainly responsible for the building of new tissues and the repair of older tissue, and it is broken down during digestion into amino acids, of which there are 20. Some of these acids (known as the essential amino acids) can only be replaced through the diet. Protein is found in such foods as meat, poultry, milk, fish, eggs, baked beans, yogurt, and vegetables. Protein also makes a significant contribution to speedy decision making and general alertness as well as to tissue repair and antibody production to fight infection.

Vegetarians need to consume more protein than those who are nonvegetarian. Players do not need to ingest extra amounts of protein before training and competition, but protein is an important factor in the recovery process alongside carbohydrate, given its role in repairing the tissues damaged in exercise. A failure to replace protein after exercise can result in a noticeable loss in muscle strength. Female players may need less protein during endurance events than men do.

Fat

Fat provides the most concentrated energy supply; players need fat in their diets to provide the essential fatty acids necessary for the body to function efficiently. Fat also helps maintain body temperature, protects vital organs, builds body tissue, acts as a storage site for vitamins, and is a vital source of energy during low-intensity exercise. Although fat is twice as rich in energy content as carbohydrate, the energy it provides is released much more slowly. When glycogen stores are depleted, fat becomes the major supplier of energy.

Fat is found in butter, cheese, milk, fried foods, and meats; these foods should comprise around 30 percent of the daily intake. Essential fatty acids, so important for the body, are found in oily fish, walnuts, sweet potatoes, and sunflower seeds. Of course, an overload of fat will lead to an increase of weight, which is a major concern both to society and to athletes.

Vitamins and Minerals

Vitamins are not a source of energy. Rather, they are required for growth and cell formation and help to regulate our water balance. Because the body cannot produce vitamins, we must take them in through our diets.

Minerals help to control fluid balance in the muscles and, along with vitamins, are found in such foods as fruit, vegetables, fish, eggs, and dairy products. Eating a varied diet usually supplies the body with the necessary vitamins and minerals.

Fluids

As the body's temperature rises with exercise, the body's natural cooling system functions by releasing sweat, which cools the body by evaporating from the skin. Before and during practice and game play, players should consume plenty of fluids to provide for this evaporation and to help blood circulation to the muscular tissues. Prior to exercise, players should be well hydrated if not slightly hyper-hydrated. Both physiological and cerebral functions are impaired if dehydration is allowed to occur. Any fluids lost during the course of play should, if possible, be replaced immediately, even during the event. This replacement strategy should be used in practice sessions so players can become accustomed to the routine.

When dehydration occurs as a result of fluid depletion, the body temperature is elevated and heart rate can increase. In hot and humid climates, fluid replacement should take place at short and regular intervals so that the reduction in work capacity is slowed down as the body loses weight; a 5 percent reduction in body weight can result during heat exhaustion! Severe dehydration can be fatal (and it is not so long ago that players in intensive training sessions were denied drinks!).

The fluid replacement strategy will be influenced by the intensity and duration of the work your players are doing, the climatic conditions, and the unique physiological makeup of individual players. Water is essential for the body's functioning, but players get an added advantage if their drinks include carbohydrate compounds because this increases the rate of carbohydrate delivery to the intestines. Most sports drinks contain electrolytes lost by the body through sweat; electrolytes are needed to regulate the body's fluid balance. Chemicals such as sodium, potassium, and magnesium are necessary to maintain blood volume and to provide carbohydrate for the muscles.

Although water alone will assist in the rehydration process, diluted fruit juice with a touch of salt added will also help replace essential carbohydrate. You can make your own sports drink by mixing 800 milliliters (0.8 qt) of water, 200 milliliters (0.4 pt) of fruit juice, and 1 to 1.5 grams of salt. This will aid the necessary fluid and carbohydrate replacement process.

Good Nutrition at a Glance

You have the major responsibility of giving dietary advice to your young players. Use the following guidelines to help them appreciate the benefits of a healthy diet, which is of paramount importance to any athlete:

- Carbohydrate intake is vital for providing energy for the body's normal and sporting demands. (Know the foods that are carbohydrate rich.)
- Eat five portions of fruits and vegetables daily—they are a rich source of carbohydrate, vitamins, and minerals.
- Take care to include protein in your diet—fish eaten twice a week is beneficial.
- Avoid excessive amounts of fatty foods, but make sure you eat some because fat is important for the body.
- Before exercise, take in a plentiful supply of carbohydrate foodstuffs and hydrate well.
- Before and during exercise, drink on a regular basis, frequently ingesting small amounts of a recognized sports drink if possible, especially in hot and humid conditions. On game and practice days increase the amount of fluid you consume.
- Make sure you refuel, rehydrate, and recover after all training sessions. Each player reacts differently, so you must find an appropriate personal strategy.
- After exercise, as soon as possible, replenish both the carbohydrate and the fluid lost during the activity.
- Effective recovery before the next training or playing event requires rest and the replacement of carbohydrate, fluid, and salt.
- Enjoy a variety of food, and always be aware of excess in any category.

GLOSSARY

aerobic—Type of exercise that uses oxygen.

anaerobic—Type of exercise that does not use oxygen and that produces lactic acid.

angle, narrowing the—Moving toward the player with the ball; especially applied to goalkeepers.

angle of passing—The direction of a pass in relation to either the defending or supporting players.

angle of the run—The direction a player runs in relation to a specific situation.

angle, widening the—Movement of the receiving players into usually safer receiving positions; also describes the movement of the player in possession of the ball who may adjust position to create better passing angles.

back door—See *blind side*.

back four—The conventional defensive line comprising the right back, the two center backs, and the left back.

back line—The rearmost defending players or unit of the team.

ball—An alternative term for a pass (e.g., "good ball").

ball watching—Attending to the position of the ball but failing to see the tactical situation that is developing or the movement of a specific player.

blind side—Any part of the field that is out of the defender's line of vision. Also called the *back door*.

blindside run—A run by an attacker beyond the defender's line of vision.

block tackle—A committed frontal tackle done in an attempt to win the ball.

box—The penalty area.

calling—Verbal help between teammates.

center—See *cross*.

chip—A pass made by a stabbing action of the kicking foot to the bottom part of the ball to achieve a steep trajectory and heavy backspin on the ball.

closing down—Advancing to restrict space in front of an opponent while covering the opponent's path to goal.

coming off your man—Avoiding the player covering you to create space in which to receive the ball.

committing the defender—See *defender, committing the*.

conditioned play—Play to which an artificial restriction has been applied (e.g., all players must pass the ball on the first touch).

covering—When a defending player supports the first defender by adopting a position that enables the covering player to challenge if the first defender is beaten; in team terms, having enough players goalside of the ball to defend adequately.

cross—A pass played into the penalty area from the sides, or flanks, of the field; also called a *center*.

cross, far-post—A cross aimed toward the goalpost farther from the kicker.

cross, near-post—A cross aimed toward the goalpost nearer the kicker.

crossover—When a player running without the ball crosses the path of the player who has the ball; also called *scissors*.

cushion—Control of the ball by withdrawing on impact the surface in contact with the ball (e.g., the thigh).

decoy run—When a player runs into a position to pull defenders away from certain parts of the field so a more effective pass can be made to a teammate filling the resulting space.

defender, committing the—Moving toward or past a defender, with or without the ball, in such a way as to attract the attention of that defender, allowing him no opportunity to observe other attackers or tactical development.

defense, back of the—The area between the rearmost defenders and their goalkeeper.

disguise—See *feint*.

direct soccer—A style of play in which a team adopts tactics that move the ball forward as often as possible as a priority, sometimes resulting in a sacrifice of possession because of the urgency and frequency of the forward play.

dribble—Close, skillful control of the ball, especially when seeking to beat a defender.

dummy, selling the—A successful attempt to trick or unbalance and therefore gain advantage over a defender.

early ball—A pass played at the first opportunity, usually into space for a teammate to move into.

eye contact—A method of nonverbal communication particularly used to initiate rehearsed moves.

feint—An action that attempts to confuse or trick the defenders; also called *disguise*.

first pressing line—The area of the field in which a defending team attempts to apply aggressive and controlled pressure on the ball holder and immediate support players.

flank—An area of the field within, approximately, 15 yards of the touchlines.

flight, line of—The flight path of the ball.

give and go—See *push and run*.

goalside of the ball—The position between the ball and the goal one is defending.

half-volley—A volley in which a player contacts the ball immediately after it hits the ground (i.e., on the fly).

higher position on the field of play—The compact team unit applying pressure on opponents with the ball closer to the opponents' goal, rather than allowing them to carry the ball toward their own goal before applying pressure.

instep—The upper surface of the foot or shoe (i.e., the laces).

inswinging—The action of a ball curling in toward a target.

jockeying—Holding up or delaying the advance of an opponent who has the ball, usually by trying to force him toward or along the touchline.

killer pass—A through pass that splits the defense.

late tackle—A challenge that, whether intentional or accidental, makes unfair contact with the player after she has played the ball.

line of recovery—A path a defender takes when running back toward the goal to get into a position goalside of the ball.

lofted drive—A powerful kick with the instep through the bottom half of the ball.

man-to-man marking—A defensive tactic in which each defender takes responsibility for a specified opponent. The defender marks and follows his opponent's every move before applying the appropriate defending techniques when the opponent moves to or receives possession of the ball. See also *one-on-one marking*.

marking—Positioning close to an opponent to prevent her from receiving the ball.

narrowing the angle—Moving nearer to an opponent to reduce his passing or shooting opportunities.

offside trap—A play in which a defensive player or unit, usually acting on a call or signal, moves forward in such a way as to catch at least one opponent in an offside position.

off the ball—Movement away from the area around the player who has the ball.

one-on-one marking—A system of defense in which each defender marks a particular opponent (e.g., at a throw-in). See also *man-to-man marking*.

one-touch play—Play in which the player passes the ball immediately after receiving it.

one-two pass—A pass involving an immediate return of the ball to the passer. See also *wall pass*.

on the ball—When an individual player is in possession of the ball.

outswinging—The action of a ball curling away toward a target.

overlap run—Movement of an attacking player from a position behind the ball to a position ahead of the ball.

passing on—When one defending player transfers both an opponent and the defensive responsibilities for that opponent to another defending player, while assuming further defensive responsibilities herself.

penetration—A principle of play which is used to assess a team's ability to break through the opposition's defense.

peripheral vision—The outer part of the field of vision.

pitch—The field of play.

platform—Control of the ball with the use of any flat surface of the body.

pressure training—A method of training players in rapid succession for a limited period.

push and run—A play in which a player plays a short ball to a teammate and immediately runs, often for the return pass; also called *give and go*.

push pass—A pass made with the inside of the kicking foot.

running off the ball—Running to support a teammate who has the ball.

running with the ball—Moving with the ball at speed without dribbling past an opponent.

scissors—See *crossover*.

screening the ball—Maintaining control and possession of the ball by keeping one's body between the ball and the challenging opponent; also called *shielding the ball*.

selling oneself—Overcommitting oneself to a challenge for a ball and being beaten.

set piece—A restart after an infringement or when the ball goes out of play (i.e., goal kicks, throw-ins, corner kicks, indirect free kicks, and direct free kicks, including penalties).

set plays—Moves worked out in training and used in games to exploit set pieces.

shadow marking—Assigning one player to mark a dangerous opponent closely for the entire match.

shielding—See *screening the ball*.

showing oneself—Making it obvious to the player with the ball that one is available for the pass.

sliding tackle—A tackle made by sliding one's supporting leg along the ground.

space, creating—Increasing the distance from opponents.

square ball—Any pass made across the field that is approximately parallel to the goal lines (at right angles to the touchline).

square defense—A defense spread in a line across the field. Such a defense is lacking depth and is vulnerable to the killer pass, and is thus said to be caught square.

stretched defense—A defense that is spread out and has no cover.

striker—A forward player whose major responsibility during team play is scoring goals.

support play—Assisting the passer by moving into positions that increase his passing opportunities.

supporting player—When an attacking player is positioned to receive a pass from the player in possession of the ball.

sweeper—A defender who plays behind and covers the rest of the defense.

swerve pass—A pass made by imparting spin to the ball, causing it to swerve. The direction in which the ball swerves depends on whether the player contacts the ball with the outside or the inside of the kicking foot, and on which side he strikes the ball.

switching the play—Changing the point of attack, notably with a cross-field ball.

tackle—A challenge, using the foot, to win the ball.

taking a player on—Trying to beat a defender by dribbling past her.

target player—The front player who presents himself as a target for midfielders' passes.

thirds of the field—Areas roughly 35 yards in length signifying the defending, middle, and attacking thirds of the field.

through pass—A pass played between two or more defenders into the space behind them, into which a teammate runs.

top roll—The forward rotation on the ball, in a straight line, which causes the ball to hug the ground.

turning one's opponent—Causing an opponent to turn, usually by playing the ball past or by moving past her.

turning with the ball—Receiving the ball when facing one's goal and turning, with the ball under control, to face the opponents' goal.

volley—A pass made before the ball touches the ground.

wall—A line of players forming a human barrier against a free kick near the goal.

wall pass—A pass played by two attacking players in which the player acting as the wall plays the ball back, first time, at a similar angle to which the ball was received. The pass is usually made behind an opponent. See *one-two pass*.

wall player—A player acting as part of the wall in a wall pass.

wedge—Control of the ball with the use of a rigid surface (e.g., the sole of the shoe).

weight of the pass—The pace or force of a pass.

wide-angled support—Support at an angle wide enough to give the greatest possibility for passing the ball forward.

wide player—A front runner or attacking midfielder who plays near the touchline (not necessarily a winger).

winger—An attacking player whose main role is to play on the flanks, get to the goal line, and supply crosses to teammates in the central areas.

work rate—A player's overall physical contribution to the team effort, particularly running off the ball and covering.

wrong side—The vulnerable, or "blind," side of a defender that allows the attacker to gain the advantage of being between this defender and his goal. See *blind side*.

zonal back line—The rear defending unit of a team in which all players take responsibility for an area or zone of the pitch while also accepting responsibility for marking, tracking, and defending against an opponent who enters their zone.

zonal defense—A defensive system in which each member has an approximate area or zone and is responsible for covering any opponent who enters that zone.

ABOUT THE AUTHORS

ALAN HARGREAVES, MA, MEd., DLC. Alan played for Lancashire, Loughborough Colleges and English Universities. A fully qualified Football Association coach, he directed national residential coaching courses for players up to 18 years of age and codirected the Soccer Academy for Young Players in California. He was head coach for the British Colleges soccer team and coached professional soccer for five years—two years with Stoke City and three years with Crewe Alexandra. He has conducted numerous coaches' and players' courses in England and California and was a consultant in fitness training for soccer and hockey.

Formerly chairman of the Madeley School of Graduate Physical Education, Alan directed the fitness training program for the 1980 and 1984 British Olympic Men's Field Hockey Team. He has also worked extensively in universities, soccer coaching clinics, and residential camps, many for the American Youth Soccer Organization.

Now actively retired, he enjoys golf, tennis, and traveling with his wife, Janet.

RICHARD BATE, BED (physical education). Dick played for Sheffield Wednesday, York City, and Boston United football clubs and represented the British Colleges while a student. He is a UEFA Professional License Holder, an FA Staff Coach, an AFC Staff Coach, a UEFA "A" License coach, and an England Youth Team Coach.

Dick has coached at Leeds United FC, Notts County FC, Lincoln City FC, and Hereford United FC and has been the Technical Director at Watford FC. He was also the Technical Director for the Malaysian Football Association and the Canadian Soccer Association.

He has directed and conducted several UEFA Professional License courses and over 25 UEFA "A" License courses and, together with S. Subramaniam, devised and instigated the Coach Education Programme throughout Asia on behalf of the Asian Football Confederation. Currently, he is Director of Elite Coaching Courses for the English Football Association.

Dick lives in Ross on Wye, England, with his wife, Maggie, and enjoys traveling, reading and walking in his leisure time.